CW00471283

Contents

Foreword

Born in the North West of England with a passion for both rugby league and football, Gareth had decided that the bright lights, glitz and glamour of the Premier League following his beloved Arsenal were starting to lose their appeal.

The disconnect between the club and the fans was becoming more and more prevalent with the continued increase of season ticket prices, the hype of broadcasters Sky, Amazon Prime and BT Sports, and the gap between the haves and have-nots in what has traditionally been known as the "working man's game". The love for the game was beginning to dwindle, and rather than just give up, Gareth decided to make a stance and a change.

For most fans who attend Premier League games, there seems to be an unwritten rule that they have to have a second club to follow or support, normally from a lower league. Gareth's wife, Kay, may have had an influence on this book as her footballing passion and heritage stemmed from following London's second oldest club, Leyton Orient a team founded in the East End and one that now would not only hold a glancing interest to Gareth but one where he would be emotionally attached and immersed by the family and community spirit that has engulfed the O's faithful since 1881.

As a follower of the O's for over four decades, I can say it's not a team or route any normal person would choose. Most Orient fans are born into the "religion" and have the gift of this fabulous club passed to them through family members. I mean, when you have the likes of Arsenal, West Ham, Spurs et al on your doorstep, why would you support a team that flirts with the lower leagues rather than one that graces the top flight and European football?

Casting an eye over history, the Orient have been "through the mill" with heartbreak and disappointment ahead of success and silverware. The fact that Gareth, Kay and the O's faithful still have a club to support is a miracle in itself.

After missing out on penalty kicks at Wembley for promotion to the Championship at the end of the 2013/14 season, then-chairman Barry Hearn sold the club to an Italian business man (whose name Orient fans are not allowed to mention). The club suffered a rapid decline in fortunes and within a couple of years actually lost its Football League status for the first time in 112 years.

In June 2017, only the intervention of lifelong Orient fan Nigel Travis and his Texan business partner Kent Teague saved the club from the threat of liquidation. The two are now the saviours of the Orient, and to have been able to put a team together and play the first game of the 2017/2018 season away at Sutton was another miracle. It didn't matter about the result, it mattered that the fans and supporters had a team to continue to cheer and support.

All fans that have a "second club" enter a new fanbase which can be tribal and territorial at times. The first perception is, "Are they here for a brief spell?" or would their love of football lead them to cross a line that most fans don't? Every football fan knows "You can change your partner, you can change beliefs and views, but you cannot change your football team", so Gareth's decision to follow "little old Leyton Orient" could have been greeted with scepticism.

I met Gareth when I was first approached by his wife Kay on the train en route back from a long away trip to Carlisle. Both had followed me on social media and seen my passion for the club. To be honest, I think he was scared, so he sent Kay to do a man's job for him!!! My Orient tattoos broke the ice, and we talked about the pain and suffering of supporting a team at the bottom of the professional footballing pyramid and conversely the joy we get from the camaraderie of enduring such long away trips. I remember joking and saying, "If you are serious about following the O's, be careful, it gets you in so many different ways".

Seeing Gareth both home and away, including a number of ludicrous places on cold and wet Tuesday nights, over the coming weeks and months proved to myself and fellow fans that this wasn't a gimmick, it was a show of unity to what would become a friendship going forward. You could witness the "Orient Blood" starting to filter through his veins and the enjoyment that he got from being part of the group. His transition from a casual observing fan to one who started to embrace -- especially -- the matchday mentality was visible for everyone to see.

Over the coming months and with fans actually starting to see the team performing on the pitch, for a change, there was optimism in the air. Gareth's interest began to gather momentum. The grass roots of football, the terrace banter and the interaction with players --dare we say our --"herO's" -- captured his interest more than I think, he could ever have imagined. The transition from supporting a team in the Premier League to Leyton Orient is simply night and day: polar opposites in a matchday experience. But the romance we all feel was happening to Gareth right before our eyes.

Gareth has been one of the new generation of O's fans that has seen success and ironically has witnessed Leyton Orient's best spell in their history, culminating in promotion to League One this past April.

On the 22nd April 2023, Orient completed the "full circle" -- beaten on the exact same day in 2017 by Crewe to condemn us to non-league football, to beating Crewe 2-0 to clinch the

League Two title. Could the turn in fate be down to Gareth himself? Is he our lucky mascot?

When it gets you, it gets you, and this book epitomises the joy and pain of our pilgrimage and captures the emotions of what we call "Our Religion".

Daren Reisman, aka Lord Dazza, Leyton Orient diehard, May 2023.

Acknowledgements

First of all to you the reader for purchasing this book, all proceeds will be donated to the JE3 Foundation (www.je3foundation.com). Your purchase will contribute to helping them carry on their magnificent work in changing outcomes in the face of cardiac arrest by empowering every person to act fast, with the right skills and access to life-saving resources, in memory of the late and still very very sadly missed Justin Edinburgh.

To my darling wife, soul mate, best friend and awayday accomplice, Kay. What were you even thinking in not only encouraging me to take on this madcap adventure, but then deciding to join me on it? It really wouldn't have been possible without your love and support, as well as your encouragement (nagging!?!) to finally get the book finished!

To the one and only Lord Dazza both for welcoming us to the Orient family and for your simply brilliant Foreword. Your support, encouragement and humour has meant so much. Undoubtedly next time we bump into each other on an awayday you will be in my seat!

To Herman (aka Leyton Laureate) for your expert and uber-efficient editing and input into this book. I can't believe your involvement has led to you wanting to join us on one of our awayday adventures, be warned though it is incredibly addictive!

To James Muddiman (jkmuddiman Art (jkmartwork.com)), for allowing me to use your fantastic picture of Brisbane Road for the cover, it really is very much appreciated.

...and finally to everyone at Leyton Orient Supporters Club, The Orientear fanzine, The Orient Hour on Phoenix FM, and the entire Orient Family for not only welcoming and accepting a Premier League interloper (and an Arsenal fan at that!) but making me realise just how very special our club from E10 is.

Up the O's!

Chapter 1: The Motivation

Growing disillusionment with Arsenal, the Premier League and modern football

I don't really know where this idea came from. In many ways I guess it had been forming in the back of my mind for a number of seasons (for that is how us hopeless football obsessives measure our time: in seasons, not calendar years!). However, during the summer of 2021 I came up with the utterly mad idea of putting my ludicrously over-priced Arsenal season ticket on hold and instead spending the money I was wasting at the Emirates on endeavouring to watch as many of Leyton Orient's matches as I possibly could for the season. My very own Premier League / Arsenal gap year if you will.

The football that I fell in love with was that of the late Seventies and the Eighties, prior to the advent of the Premier League, when the game seemed more real, closer to the fans and not the made-for-TV entertainment revenue-generating vehicle that football at the highest level seems to have become.

Back in the beginning of my football-supporting life, Liverpool were unquestionably the most successful team in the land, and probably Europe for that matter. Teams seemed to emerge almost from nowhere to challenge them, based on having a talented crop of players graduating at the same time, excellent managers with new and innovative approaches, or indeed unearthing hidden gems from the lower divisions or the Scottish League.

During the first coronavirus UK lockdown in spring 2020 I passed the time bereft of live football by immersing myself in nostalgia. I wrote a series of blog posts (https://football-nerd.org/) celebrating the achievements of the teams that made a mark during that very different era: Clough and Taylor's Nottingham Forest, Aston Villa winning the league title and European Cup in a brief stint at the top of the game, the rise of Graham Taylor's Watford, Howard Kendall and Everton almost changing the balance of power on Merseyside, first Coventry City and then Wimbledon upsetting the odds and winning the FA Cup in successive years, and of course George Graham leading Arsenal to the title on the final day of the season at Anfield.

Writing those pieces was very much a labour of love. I thoroughly enjoyed reminiscing through the research about the game that completely took over my life in my formative years. However, the process also highlighted how far removed the modern game is from those halcyon days. Sure, most of the best players in the world ply their trade in England, and the quality of the game, in terms of the skills and abilities of the protagonists, has improved almost beyond our imaginations. We are able to watch more English clubs than ever before compete in European competition, and with the right TV subscriptions or Internet streaming knowhow we can watch pretty much any match we want to from around the globe. So why does it feel so false? Why does the game feel like it sold its soul in the never-ending pursuit of commercial wealth?

To put it succinctly: because the game is false, and like the commercialisation of blues music of yesteryear, Premier League football feels beyond saving. The reason that Leicester City winning the Premier League in 2016 felt so special was because it disrupted the usual status quo whereby the teams with the most money fill up the top spots in the table and usually carry off all the major trophies. Despite the marketing and advertising claims, the Premier League isn't really the most competitive league in the world, it just has more teams rich enough to challenge at the top of the league in comparison to Spain, France, Italy and Germany.

Beyond what happens on the pitch however, the true "success" of the Premier League has been all about commercial and financial growth. In their excellent 2019 book, "The Club: How the Premier League became the richest, most disruptive business in sport", Jonathan Clegg and Joshua Robinson highlight that during the first quarter of a century of its existence "the league's twenty clubs have increased their combined value by more than 10,000 per cent, from around £50 million in 1992 to £10 billion" at the time the book was written. That is not only staggering from any perspective, but it also shines a bright light onto how the game has changed from primarily being a sport to something with a much greater focus on the business and commercial side of things.

A few years back, then-Arsenal manager Arsène Wenger suggested at the club's AGM that for the top clubs there were five trophies in a season, with the third in terms of priority after the Premier League and Champions League being qualification for the Champions League the following season, rather than the domestic cups. He was pilloried by both the media and long-suffering Arsenal fans. It may not have been a popular view, but, as so often, he was spot on in the accuracy of his observation. He was merely summarising how the game had at that point changed. The financial gain from participation in UEFA's flagship competition far outstrips any glory from winning a cup final and an actual trophy, at least in the eyes of those who now run our top-level football clubs.

It was way back in 1977 that my dad took me to my first football and Arsenal match, at Goodison Park, as I was born and brought up in my very early formative years on the Wirral. It would take me a few more years, three to be precise, and the loss of two cup finals in the space of less than a week to fully commit to the Arsenal cause very much at my cousin Ian's encouragement, he being seven years my senior and a dedicated Arsenal fan since they beat my uncle's beloved Liverpool in the FA Cup Final in 1971, however. Having spent time growing up in Holland and the United States, it was only when we returned to England living for four years in Hertfordshire that I was able to go to my second Arsenal live game. Even then the cruellest of inventions for any teenage football obsessive -- Saturday School -- severely limited the number of times I could go and watch my team in the flesh.

A return to the Wirral and attendance at **that** match at Anfield in 1989, fired my desire to live in London and to get an Arsenal season ticket as soon as I was able. I spent my student years living in North London and attending games at Highbury and anywhere else close by when money allowed.

After a brief sojourn back up north and then most bizarrely in Kent of all places, I formally and officially moved to London for good at the start of 2002. However, while Arsène's fantastic early achievements had made it probably the best time ever to be an Arsenal fan, it also meant that getting a ticket to watch them play had become somewhat difficult with a significant waiting list to even have the chance of buying a season ticket.

The Emirates Stadium move and the creation of Club Level with its deliberately small waiting list and eye-watering prices opened a small window of opportunity for anyone stupid enough to allocate a sizeable chunk of their annual disposable income for the privilege, and so I took the plunge.

My time as a season ticket holder coincided almost precisely with the beginning of the club's ongoing decline from the pinnacle of the game in this country. The stadium move needed to be financed, Roman Abramovich had rocked up to buy Chelsea in West London and was continuing "to fire £50 notes at us from his Russian tank" as former co-owner and vice-chairman of Arsenal David Dein so vividly put it, and the game was changing beyond all recognition.

Those initial seasons as a regular were tough -- there was the ongoing count of how long it had been since Arsenal had last won a trophy, the best players being poached by those clubs with available cash and a subsequent need to rely on youth. But I kept going, relishing the prospect of my football-watching routine, going on awaydays whenever I could secure a ticket and simply enjoying following my team. There were the FA Cup wins in 2014, '15 and '17, of course, but things were continuing to change within the ownership of the club until eventually in 2018, Stan Kroenke became the outright owner.

In hindsight, it seems apparent that it was Arsène who was the one just about holding everything within the club together, as almost as soon as he departed the true picture emerged of just how apathetic our owner was. The executive team designed to fill the chasm left by Wenger fell apart in dramatically quick time, either forced out, off to pastures new or dismissed for their politicking. The season and a half with Unai Emery in charge started to show the lack of support from those above, and as performances deteriorated on the pitch, it became completely clear that there was no one in the background with sufficient football knowledge, experience, or passion to start to put things right. Equally it seemed completely clear that Mr Kroenke wasn't going to rescue the club by dipping into his own fortune, and the stagnation of the whole club was going to be allowed to fester, at least until it started to impact the financial bottom line.

Despite the frustration of humdrum performances, I kept going, too loyal to jack in my season ticket, or as I liked to tell myself, to ensure that when the good times did return, I would still have my seat. There were some brief flurries of optimism when Mikel Arteta took over, but then in March 2020, Covid-19 changed the world as we knew it and football was put on hold as we adapted to a new normal, forced to watch on TV at home with games played behind closed doors when it did come back. Stripped of its true essence -- the atmosphere created by the fans -- football isn't the same. Being consigned to watching at home simply reinforced that feeling and encouraged many of us to start to re-examine our relationship with our club.

If things weren't bad enough at that point, it soon became clear that the very nature of football fandom in England was about to be challenged like never before. The thankfully short-lived, for now at least, concept of the European Super League for which all of the Big Six of the Premier League (Manchester City, Manchester United, Liverpool, Chelsea, Tottenham and Arsenal) had signed up looked like it might destroy the very concept of the game as a sport. The essential premise of the proposal was that the founder clubs would create their own closed shop "competition" without the threat of relegation and would essentially be creating a cartel if you will. Beyond that, though, it was abundantly clear that the intended target audience for this was the global TV market and not the "legacy supporters" -- the name given to those of us who actually go to games, spend significant amounts of our hard-earned cash for the privilege, and create the atmosphere that provides the backdrop that appeals to the mass television market.

The fact that Arsenal were involved despite crawling to an eighth-place finish in the league and without European competition for the first time in a quarter of a century, was neither surprising nor unexpected, given our owner's track record in being interested in nothing but the cash he can reap. In many ways the complete and utter confirmation that the supporters didn't even feature in the owner of our club's thinking in the slightest is probably the straw that broke the camel's back for me. I am sure the supporters of the other members of the "Shameful Six" felt the same, but it was clearest amongst Arsenal and Manchester United supporters, given festering disillusionment at the way in which the owners were destroying our clubs.

Leyton Orient – new hope provided by the way things used to be

While I was enduring the years of decline at the Emirates, my wife Kay and I discovered a new way of spending our Saturdays. Having lived in Stratford some years before, she had been a fairly regular attendee at Brisbane Road, home of Leyton Orient, and now recognising an opportunity for us to be able to go to football together, she encouraged me to give it a go. Fatefully the game we chose was against Colchester United on the 29th April 2017. For anyone not totally obsessed with the mighty O's, that was the day that with relegation out of the Football League for the first time after 112 years already confirmed, a pitch invasion to protest against much-despised former owner Francesco Becchetti forced the abandonment of the final home game of the season. We certainly know how to pick them!

Despite Orient's plight, or maybe even because of it, we vowed that we would lend our support to the club, and the following season, even if it was in the non-league National League, we would try and get to as many games as we could despite my Arsenal-watching commitments. It was to turn into quite some adventure.

That summer, Orient were rescued by new owners Nigel Travis, the Essex-born, Orient-supporting, US-based Chief Executive of

Dunkin' Donuts, and Kent Teague, a Texan multi-millionaire, former Microsoft executive and founder of a US private equity firm. Somehow, supported by former manager and now Director of Football Martin Ling, they managed to pull a squad together, hire a head coach and get ready for the season ahead in a mere matter of weeks. It was when they replaced coach Steve Davis with the former Tottenham defender and much more experienced lower league manager Justin Edinburgh in the autumn, however, that things really started to roll.

A mid-table finish at the end of that first season was followed by a surge to the National League title in 2018/19 and with it promotion back to the Football League. From the remnants of what was left behind to mission accomplished in the space of just two seasons, optimism was high that the O's could not only stay in the League, but that with the right development and recruitment they could aspire to push for promotion to the third tier, if not immediately then over the course of two or three seasons.

Then the unthinkable happened. Just a matter of weeks after guiding Orient back to the promised land, Justin Edinburgh suffered a cardiac arrest from which he tragically never recovered and was lost to us at the age of just 49.

Undoubtedly the grief strengthened my attachment, but through the summer of 2019 and into the next season, I found Orient taking up more and more of my thinking. I knew deep in my heart that I couldn't give up Arsenal, but somehow, I cared more and more about my adopted team based in London E10. I had already become a regular contributor to the fanzine, The Leyton Orientear, and I also found that more of my blog posts focused on how and what Orient were doing and less about the Premier League and Arsenal, unless it was to criticize the modern game and the ongoing alienation of true football fans.

I realised quite early in the process that Leyton Orient and lower league football was much closer to the game that I fell in love with all those years ago. Money was obviously important to the club's ambitious aspirations but, unlike Kroenke et al from the Premier League, the owners seemed to want the very best for the club and for the fans. They certainly weren't in it to make money, given how much they had to plough in to rescue it and keep it afloat on an ongoing basis.

Through 2019/20, up to the suspension of live matches as a result of the global pandemic, I went to as many Orient games as Arsenal ones, more if you count pre-season friendlies, and I realised I was enjoying it more. Plus, there were several away games within easy enough reach of London to attend, something that the vagaries of Arsenal's away scheme had rendered nigh on impossible after the cap on the pricing of away tickets was introduced and those with the most credits hogged all the available tickets.

However it was more than that. It was the camaraderie amongst the Orient faithful, based in no small part on the gallows humour essential when following this club with a rather turbulent recent history, but also the fact that real fans hadn't been priced out and were treated like fans not customers or members of the paying live stadium audience. Brisbane Road isn't the most salubrious of football grounds, but it feels like a proper version unlike the soulless concrete bowls being created in the upper tier of English football, Emirates Stadium most definitely included.

When the English Football League (EFL), comprising tiers 2-4 of the league structure in this country, returned in September 2020, I used the money that Arsenal owed me from the games I had been locked out of to buy myself an Orient season ticket. Even though we anticipated it would be a while before we were able to return, the missus was happy enough to do the same which is probably the moment that the adventure we were just about to embark on began to grow in our hearts. While we were only permitted into a pre-season friendly at Bishops Stortford (I told you we were serious about this!) an EFL trophy game and a solitary league game until lockdown, watching every game Orient played on the somewhat quirky Orient TV, the club's own live stream, had us even more hooked. As far removed as it was from the super slick productions of Sky and BT, it felt more real.

As we toured the country with the O's from the comfort of our own living room, you could tell that both of us were champing at the bit to do it for real. Then came the offer of a season ticket holiday from Arsenal, a realisation from the club that through the impact of Covid, many existing fans might not have the money, the inclination, or the ability to renew for the 2021/22 campaign, they were offering us a year off, the chance to not have to fork out the usual cash to watch a team and a club very much going backwards, without having to give up our season tickets for good -- although as I was reliably informed by the box office, if there turned out to be a huge demand for tickets ahead of 2022/23, I might have to go back on the waiting list if there were no seats available. I think I know football well enough to have suspected at the time that this might not be an issue given the club's recent track record!

Around that time, I had just finished reading the excellent book "Orientation" by Adam Michie, a Spurs fan disillusioned with the Premier League, who adopted Leyton Orient so that he could enjoy going to football with his mates again, as well as part of a search for his lost love of football. While it was a little bit before my time as an Orient supporter, I have no doubt whatsoever that the suggestion that this might actually be an option, and that it might be better than I even hoped, probably pushed me towards the edge. Adam, if for some strange reason you are reading this, thank you for showing me the way, and if our paths ever cross at Brisbane Road I probably owe you a pint or two.

I was one of the ones "lucky" enough to get a ticket for Arsenal's last match of the 2020/21 season at home to Brighton, and as I handed over my £19.90 (almost enough for a full price ticket at Brisbane Road!) for a mediocre cheeseburger, lukewarm chips and a pint, my mind was fully made up right then and there. I could definitely live without this for a season, and having spent a year deprived of live football save for four matches, I needed and wanted to get back to basics, to feel what I felt all those years ago. So I renewed my Orient season ticket, as did the missus, and we committed to trying to go to as many Orient matches home and away as we possibly could during the 2021/22 campaign.

As I embarked on this journey, I had a few suspicions of how I might feel at the end of it, and indeed a number of friends, both Orient supporters and those who follow other non-Premier League clubs, suggested that it was unlikely that I would ever go back to Arsenal. From my own perspective I simply decided to focus on enjoying the ride and seeing where it took me.

Chapter 2: Introducing the 2021/22 O's

Dismantling the old and bringing in the new

The summer of 2021 saw a significant amount of upheaval and change for Leyton Orient. At the close of the 2020/21 campaign there were a total of just seven players still under contract and a further seven who had been offered new deals. Of the latter group, three decided they were off to pastures new in early June, leaving just the very bare bones of a squad on which to build.

However, the sacking of Ross Embleton, who had been the assistant to Justin Edinburgh in the National League title win and who had been asked to step up on two occasions in lieu of a more experienced manager, and the decision not to retain interim player-manager and club legend Jobi McAnuff meant that the first item on a very busy summer agenda for Director of Football Martin Ling and the Board was the recruitment of a new man in the dugout.

The chosen man was the very experienced 59-year-old Kenny Jackett, whose managerial career had covered six clubs prior to arriving at Brisbane Road, including promotion to the Championship (tier 2 of English football) with both Millwall and Wolves as his standout achievements. The new manager and the significant churn within the playing squad meant that even for relatively regular Orient watchers it felt like something of a journey into the unknown. To help set the scene, let's introduce the Orient squad that entered the 2021/22 season.

⇨ **Lawrence Vigouroux:** Signed in January 2020, despite having represented Chile at youth international level, he was actually born in Camden (a fact instantly discernible if you ever hear him speak!). Vigs was Orient's stand out performer through the 2020/21 campaign and deserved player of the season. Other than one or two mad moments (keepers eh?) "Chile's Number One" is generally solid and reliable and undoubtedly saves more points than he costs the team.

⇨ **Sam Sargeant:** Dependable enough young reserve keeper, was initially trusted with the number one spot in the first season back in the League until being usurped by Vigouroux. Went on loan to Barnet for an initial two-month spell from late August, then after a brief return went out on loan again, this time to Wealdstone, at the back end of the campaign.

⇨ **Rhys Byrne:** May not have expected to feature too much but emerged as the go-to back-up/ cup keeper in the early part of the season when Sargeant was loaned out.

⇨ **Tom James:** Recruited on a one-year deal from Hibernian once pre-season had already started. The Welshman quickly emerged as a fan favourite, thanks both to his steady defending and his ability to get forward effectively with good delivery from crosses, an eye for a goal and a dangerous long throw. Was unquestionably one of the O's standout performers until injury brought his season to an abrupt end in December.

⇨ **Dan Happe:** Came through the youth ranks to establish himself as a stalwart at centre back through the promotion-winning season and beyond. A tough but decent ball-playing defender, he seems to always attract potential suitors from higher divisions but signed a two-year contract extension in June 2021. Another whose season was ended early due to injury.

⇨ **Jayden Sweeney:** A promising young left-back who after the departures of the more experienced Joe Widdowson and James Brophy went into the season looking to add to his one League appearance at the end of 2020/21.

⇨ **Shadrach Ogie:** Young central defender who can also fill in at left back. Shad, who has represented the Republic of Ireland at Under-18 level, firmly established himself as not only a member of the first team squad but one of the first choice eleven over the course of the season.

⇨ **Adam Thompson:** Arrived in January 2021 to add much-needed experience to the backline at the time. Thommo was just starting to establish himself in the side and with the Orient faithful until a horrific clash of heads at Grimsby in March 2021 ended his season with a cut to the head and a broken ankle. Infamously brushed off the pain to enjoy fish and chips with the rest of the squad on the coach on the way home.

⇨ **Omar Beckles:** Newly signed ahead of the 2021/22 season, the Grenada international centre back boasted four years' experience in League One. Quickly became one of the most popular members of the side and emerged as the stand-in skipper when needed. Also contributed some important goals during the season.

⇨ **Connor Wood:** Another new signing geared towards adding experience, Wood joined from Bradford where he made over 100 appearances. Started as first choice but was left on the sidelines after an alleged falling out with Kenny Jackett. He later returned to the fold when Jackett was eventually dismissed in February.

⇨ **Alex Mitchell:** signed on Transfer Deadline Day on a season long loan from Millwall, the 19-year-old is a tall, tough and imposing central defender who impressed on loan at National League Bromley at the end of the previous season.

⇨ **Craig Clay:** One of the squad hastily assembled when Nigel Travis and Kent Teague took over and was a key member of the National League winning side. It looked like his days might be numbered at the start of the season as he was used initially as a back-up right back. However, the tenacious midfielder forced his way into Jackett's thinking and emerged as one of the first names on the team sheet. Another player whose season came to an early end due to the need for an operation.

⇨ **Dan Kemp:** Another January 2021 signing, it took Kemp a while to establish himself in the team after his arrival but seemed to carve out a niche for himself as a creative wide midfielder/ number 10. Featured regularly in the first half of the season thanks mainly to injury to Paul Smyth but moved to MK Dons in January.

⇨ **Hector Kyprianou:** Popular amongst the fanbase as "one of our own" when he emerged during 2019/20, he would no doubt have been hopeful of pushing on and really establishing himself this time out, but his form seemed to plateau as it often does with young players.

⇨ **Darren Pratley:** Kenny Jackett's first signing, the midfielder has significant experience at higher levels including a season in the Premier League with Bolton in 2011/12. The 36-year-old had played for Jackett in the past and was clearly trusted by the new gaffer. His acquisition seemed to be motivated to fill the Jobi McAnuff-sized hole as the senior player in the squad. He was immediately appointed skipper.

⇨ **Callum Reilly:** The second Transfer Deadline Day signing announced, Reilly signed for the O's after reaching the end of his contract with AFC Wimbledon. He barely featured throughout the season due to ongoing injury issues leading to him being referred to as "the lesser spotted Callum Reilly" amongst the Orient faithful.

⇨ **Theo Archibald:** An old school winger when operating from the left but also effective as an inverted option from the right, signed on a season-long loan from Lincoln City. Orient fans took to the former Celtic academy player almost instantly. His contribution of 8 goals and 9 assists meant that the vast majority of fans were hopeful of being able to retain him should he be deemed surplus to requirements at Sincil Bank.

⇨ **Ruel Sotiriou:** Young striker who has already represented Cyprus Under-21's, made his breakthrough in late 2019 but struggled for playing time in 2021/22 until Jackett's dismissal. Enjoyed a rich vein of goal-scoring form once reintroduced to the team by interim boss Matt Harrold and then under new manager Richie Wellens.

⇨ **Paul Smyth:** Signed after reaching the end of his contract with Queens Park Rangers, the tricky forward carried a lot of potential when he was brought from Loftus Road. Was incredibly unlucky with injuries throughout the first part of the season, but once he was able to stay fit towards the end, he gave us a key glimpse of what he is all about and scored some spectacular goals.

⇨ **Aaron Drinan:** Signed from Ipswich Town for an undisclosed fee, the Irish forward made 22 first team appearances, albeit 16 of which came from the bench, for the Tractor Boys the previous season. Finished the season as Orient's leading goal-scorer with 16 goals, 13 of which were in the League.

⇨ **Harry Smith:** A 6-foot-5 striker who was promoted to League One with Northampton Town during 2020/21. "H" scored in his second appearance away at Carlisle and was relatively prolific in the first half of the season before the goals seemed to dry up. He was largely confined to the bench later in the season as Drinan was preferred as the focal point of the attack.

⇨ **Tyrese Omotoye:** Signed on a season-long loan from Norwich City after impressing and scoring on trial against Gillingham, although he struggled to make an impact and eventually left for Carlisle in January.

⇨ **Dan Nkrumah:** A young forward who impressed against a strong West Ham XI in a pre-season friendly. Made only sporadic appearances during the season but is definitely one for the future.

Chapter 3: Planning the Campaign

At this juncture it would be completely remiss of me if I didn't introduce you to my accomplice and travelling partner on this mad adventure, my wife Kay. Kay has put together some of her thoughts on the absolute folly that saw her agreeing to join me on this mission to completely submerse ourselves in following Orient for the whole campaign and in trying to watch as many games, home and away, as we possibly could.

Kay's Thoughts

The first thing that you have to understand about my husband is that his utter and all-consuming obsession with football knows no bounds whatsoever. This a man who spends most of his waking time thinking about football and all sorts of useless pieces of information and trivia, who worries about what people might think of him if he turns down the opportunity to go to a (any?) football match, who meticulously maintains spreadsheet records of every match he attends and who got up at 3 am to undertake a 36-hour "daytrip" to Azerbaijan to watch his team, Arsenal, lose the Europa League final a few years ago.

When he was offered the chance of a season ticket holiday by Arsenal, while of course retaining his Orient season ticket, he then started suggesting that as he was free of Arsenal-watching commitments for the next nine months or so, this might be the perfect opportunity to try to go to every single Orient game in a season. To my utter amazement during a conversation over a few beers one evening, it dawned on me that he was actually serious, and even worse, not only did I find myself encouraging him, but at the same time suggesting that I would even accompany him on the away trips on top of going to Brisbane Road every other week. What on earth was I thinking?

I clearly hadn't thought this through properly. By agreeing to join him, I had in one move sacrificed every other weekend and a selection of midweek evenings which would no doubt require two days off work, to traipse around the country to a variety of far-flung destinations with no guarantee that Orient would even have a good season.

One look at the League Two table and the other clubs in the division revealed that we were in for trips to Barrow, Exeter, Forest Green (where is that even near anyway?), and various other off-the-beaten-track towns, perhaps most daunting of all Carlisle. I just knew deep down in my heart that the furthest away trips would inevitably take place on Tuesday evenings deep in the depths of winter and that at some point, somewhere, I was going to see my arse and lose it completely -- most likely halfway to some obscure northern town in midweek when we find out that the game has been called off due to adverse weather conditions. I also couldn't help but wonder/dread in which one of these far-from-exotic locations I might be forced to spend Christmas and/or New Year.

However, the more I thought about it the more I started to realise that the Covid pandemic has changed the world as we know it, that it would be highly unlikely that we would be able to travel abroad without restriction, testing or quarantining for at least the duration of the football season, and with Arsenal having had their worst season in decades we might never have another opportunity to do something like this ever again --to break from the routine of our life and to embark on perhaps the most insane and exciting adventure imaginable, well at least for two hopeless football obsessives, that is.

With some trepidation, we waited for the fixtures to be announced. Surprisingly when they were released, we worked out that this did in fact look doable, and I decided I was going to commit to this adventure and enjoy every single minute of it.

Thursday 25th June 2021- EFL Fixtures Released

It was with nervous anticipation and a healthy dollop of apprehension and excitement that we waited for the 2021/22 fixtures to be released. When they were finally announced, we pored over them in minute detail, looking at the connotations and where we would need to be and when over the course of the season.

First came the good news: the much dreaded (at least by Kay anyway!) Carlisle away was to be the second away match, and not only would it be in August, but it also fell immediately after Kay's birthday when we had already booked the time off work. Kay briefly wrestled with the idea of stopping off in the Lake District to do some hill-walking, but in the end her fear of heights and my fear of train delays stopping us from getting to Carlisle in time for the match meant that we "agreed" to go straight up to Cumbria on the day itself. Probably the right decision in the end, but also the realisation that our mission was going to take precedence over the rest of our life for the next nine months or so.

The fixture gods, or indeed the man with a spreadsheet planner, had also deigned to give us Tranmere away on the 18th December. As those of you who were paying attention in the opening chapter will have realised, I spent a significant part of my younger life growing up on the Wirral and have several friends and family members who follow Rovers. The game at Prenton Park fell three days after my birthday and a day before my father's, and I could think of no better way to "celebrate" than with a trip to Merseyside.

With the early away trips looking fairly doable, the next worrying date was 29th September when my Dad was scheduled to get married, and it came as a massive relief to discover that there was no midweek fixture scheduled for the night before, and the week was bookended by a home game against Mansfield Town and a trip to Port Vale, less than two hours away from London.

To Kay's utter relief, the Boxing Day fixture was to be Colchester away, although assuming we would still be allowed out of our houses at that point and not in yet another national lockdown, that would likely require a very early start, hangover or no hangover. New Year's Eve could thankfully be spent in London as all we needed to do was to get ourselves to Brisbane Road by 3pm for the game against Bristol Rovers.

The much-dreaded Tuesday evening away in the depths of winter turned out to be Exeter City, which would no doubt require an overnight stay. After hours of careful study, any doubts or thoughts of backing out we might have had were pushed to the back of our minds as we started to think about the logistics of each trip. While the point of our challenge was more about throwing ourselves into even more Orient watching than we had previously managed, deep down we were probably both completely committed to walking into Brisbane Road on 7th May for the final match of the season (at least before the play-offs) in a position to be attending match number 46.

Leyton Orient League Two Fixtures 2021/22

Date	Day	Opponent	Venue
7/08/2021	Saturday	Salford City	Moor Lane (Peninsula Stadium)

14/08/2021	Saturday	Exeter City	Brisbane Road (Breyer Group Stadium)
21/08/2021	Saturday	Carlisle United	Brunton Park
17/08/2021	Tuesday	Harrogate Town	Brisbane Road (Breyer Group Stadium)
28/08/2021	Saturday	Bradford City	Brisbane Road (Breyer Group Stadium)
4/09/2021	Saturday	Newport County	Rodney Parade
11/09/2021	Saturday	Oldham Athletic	Brisbane Road (Breyer Group Stadium)
18/09/2021	Saturday	Bristol Rovers	Memorial Stadium
25/09/2021	Saturday	Mansfield Town	Brisbane Road (Breyer Group Stadium)
2/10/2021	Saturday	Port Vale	Vale Park
9/10/2021	Saturday	Barrow	Holker Street (The Dunes Hotel Stadium)
16/10/2021	Saturday	Walsall	Brisbane Road (Breyer Group

			Stadium)
19/10/2021	**Tuesday**	**Forest Green Rovers**	**Brisbane Road (Breyer Group Stadium)**
23/10/2021	Saturday	Stevenage	Broadhall Way (Lamex Stadium)
30/10/2021	**Saturday**	**Hartlepool**	**Brisbane Road (Breyer Group Stadium)**
13/11/2021	Saturday	Rochdale	Spotland (Crown Oil Arena)
20/11/2021	**Saturday**	**Sutton United**	**Brisbane Road (Breyer Group Stadium)**
23/11/2021	Tuesday	Scunthorpe	Glanford Park (The Sands Venue Stadium)
27/11/2021	Saturday	Northampton Town	Sixfields Stadium
7/12/2021	**Tuesday**	**Swindon Town**	**Brisbane Road (Breyer Group Stadium)**
11/12/2021	**Saturday**	**Crawley Town**	**Brisbane Road (Breyer Group Stadium)**
18/12/2021	Saturday	Tranmere Rovers	Prenton Park
26/12/2021	Sunday	Colchester	Colchester

		United	Community Stadium (JobServe Community Stadium)
29/12/2021	**Wednesday**	**Newport County**	**Brisbane Road (Breyer Group Stadium)**
1/1/2022	**Saturday**	**Bristol Rovers**	**Brisbane Road (Breyer Group Stadium)**
8/1/2022	Saturday	Bradford City	Valley Parade (Utilita Energy Stadium)
15/1/2022	Saturday	Oldham Athletic	Boundary Park
22/1/2022	**Saturday**	**Port Vale**	**Brisbane Road (Breyer Group Stadium)**
29/1/2022	Saturday	Mansfield Town	Field Mill (One Call Stadium)
5/2/2022	**Saturday**	**Colchester United**	**Brisbane Road (Breyer Group Stadium)**
8/2/2022	Tuesday	Exeter City	St James Park
12/2/2022	**Saturday**	**Salford City**	**Brisbane Road (Breyer Group Stadium)**
19/2/2022	Saturday	Harrogate Town	Wetherby Road

			(The EnviroVent Stadium)
26/2/2022	**Saturday**	**Carlisle United**	**Brisbane Road (Breyer Group Stadium)**
5/3/2022	**Saturday**	**Stevenage**	**Brisbane Road (Breyer Group Stadium)**
12/3/2022	Saturday	Hartlepool	Victoria Park
15/3/2022	Tuesday	Forest Green Rovers	The New Lawn Stadium (The Fully Charged *New Lawn)*
19/3/2021	**Saturday**	**Rochdale**	**Brisbane Road (Breyer Group Stadium)**
26/3/2022	**Saturday**	**Barrow**	**Brisbane Road (Breyer Group Stadium)**
2/4/2022	Saturday	Walsall	Bescot Stadium (Banks Stadium)
9/4/2021	Saturday	Sutton United	Gander Green Lane (VBS Community Stadium)
15/4/2022	**Friday**	**Scunthorpe**	**Brisbane Road**

			(Breyer Group Stadium)
18/4/2022	Monday	Swindon Town	The County Ground (The Energy Check County Ground)

23/4/2022	**Saturday**	**Northampton Town**	**Brisbane Road (Breyer Group Stadium)**
30/4/2022	Saturday	Crawley Town	The Broadfield Stadium (The People's Pension Stadium)
7/5/2022	**Saturday**	**Tranmere Rovers**	**Brisbane Road (Breyer Group Stadium)**

Pre-Season

Pre-season in football is very much like a phoney war: it provides an opportunity to have a look at any new signings, and sometimes as was the case for Orient this season, it offers supporters the opportunity to run the rule over a new manager and his staff to try to gauge our prospects for the season ahead. At the higher levels of the game, it is about money-making tours around distant but lucrative television markets. But ultimately it serves a purpose in getting the players ready for the upcoming campaign.

For Leyton Orient, the 2021 pre-season was about new manager Kenny Jackett gathering together what was for the most part a squad made up of lots of new players, shaping the system and style that he wanted the team to play, and giving us fans a look at the new signings and whether the team looked better prepared for a promotion push and improvement on the 11th-placed finish in 2020/21. For the most part it did just that.

The pre-season programme actually started up in Scotland with a training camp and a friendly against Dundee which we lost 3-0. However first up at home for the new look Orient was the visit of a West Ham squad that was splitting itself between two matches, the other one at Northampton, on the same evening, just two days after England's defeat at Wembley in the Euro 2020 Final. As an aside, and maybe it is a sign of getting older, but is it just me or is the gap between the end of one season and the start of the next getting shorter? The fact that the West Ham starting line-up featured the likes of Mark Noble, Aaron Creswell, Angelo Ogbonna, Michail Antonio, as well as David Moyes overseeing things from the dugout, meant that we could view this as a proper friendly, if such a thing exists these days of course.

As newly renewed season card holders, Kay and I were lucky enough to secure tickets in the ballot for this one, given that some of the Covid restrictions were still in place ahead of the full relaxation of the rules the following week. In truth, I think we would have been desperately unlucky not to get tickets. However having not been to Brisbane Road since December, we counted it as a triumph of sorts, even if the reduced capacity for the game meant we were still going to be exiled in the West Stand away from our usual seats on the other side of the ground. Orient put in a creditable display and held the Europa League-qualified Hammers to a goalless draw.

The following week Orient hosted Tottenham in the second playing of the Justin Edinburgh Foundation (JE3) Trophy, our still hugely missed former manager having represented Spurs creditably during his playing days. In a classic case of annoying timing, my rugby league team St Helens were taking on Castleford Tigers in the Challenge Cup Final, so given that we were just about to dedicate every week for the next nine plus months to Orient, we decided a day out at Wembley was the order of the day. Once again, the O's held their own and drew 1-1 with their more illustrious opponents.

Next it was a trip to Maidenhead, whom we had encountered before in the National League days. A visit there was actually Kay's and my first Orient awayday, and that we enjoyed it so much probably played an initial role in sparking the idea of this season-long adventure that we now found ourselves on. Any Orient fan who was there that day will surely remember: beers from a shed, the fact that we filled their ground for them, or indeed one of only 3 goals that James Alabi ever scored for us in a grand total of 45 appearances. This time we opted to watch and listen in the company of Dulcet Dave on the Orient TV stream for one last time.

In a game that Orient made more of a test than it needed to be, we scored early through new skipper Darren Pratley, only to be pegged back midway through the second half and then go on to win it again with a late penalty converted by Cyprus Under-21 international Ruel Sotiriou.

The final pre-season engagement was the visit of League One Gillingham to Brisbane Road. Even though we had some friends visiting from Nottingham, Kay and I had made it abundantly clear that while they could choose to come with us or do whatever else they felt like, our attendance was non-negotiable, this being the final warm-up match before things started properly.

As we made our way down the High Road in Leyton we were chuffed to find a new bar had opened up on the corner with Adelaide Road, apparently called Wine Bar & More. They served draft beer and had some nice seats outside in the sunshine, so we felt obligated to pause, have a pint or two and judge whether it was worthy to join our portfolio of pre- and post-match drinking spots. Suffice it to say that it did and became quite a popular venue with us over the course of the season.

It was another comfortable and organised display by the O's -- an early goal from new signing Omar Beckles after his return from representing Grenada in the CONCACAF Gold Cup and a second later in the first half from a trialist who had been drafted in due to the unavailability through injury of most of our attacking options were enough to see off our higher ranked opponents. After the game we of course regrouped in the wine bar and got talking to some Gillingham fans who seemed far from enthused about their prospects for the season ahead.

With the main pre-season programme now completed and Kenny Jackett suggesting in an online Q&A the following Monday that there wasn't going to be anyone new coming in until the end of August if we felt we needed it, that was the preparations out of the way, and it was now just a week to get through before the adventure proper could get underway.

Chapter 4: August 2021
The long-awaited season kicks off, as we embark on our first awaydays up north, establish our Awayday Rules and watch the O's grow into #Jacketball

National League champions...you'll never sing that!

Game 1: Saturday 7th August 2021, Salford City v Leyton Orient

If you are not completely familiar with Leyton Orient's recent history -- and let's be honest unless you are an O's fan it is perfectly understandable that you might not be -- you may not know that our exile in non-league coincided with the continuing rise of Salford City, a club featured in the BBC documentary series "Class of '92: Out of Their League" and under the ownership of former Manchester United stars who came up through the youth ranks: Nicky Butt, Ryan Giggs, Gary and Phil Neville and Paul Scholes, in conjunction with Singaporean businessman Peter Lim.

The former United players and Lim first took over the club in 2014, at roughly the same time as Orient had just blown one of their best chances of promotion to the Championship (or Second Division as us stubborn traditionalists will always call it!), by letting a two-goal lead slip at Wembley before finally being beaten by Rotherham on penalties in the League One Play-Off Final. From that fateful moment the trajectory of the two clubs was completely opposite. Powered by Lim's cash and in particular Gary Neville's drive and contacts within the game, Salford rose spectacularly from the Northern Premier League Division One North (Tier 8 of the English football pyramid) right the way up to the National League (Tier 5) in just four years.

Salford's first season in the National League in 2018/19 coincided with Orient's second at that level, the O's having fallen spectacularly from the brink of promotion to the Championship all the way to non-league football in the space of just three seasons. In the end, both teams were promoted to the Football League in 2019, Orient as champions and Salford as play-off winners; however, anyone who followed the media at that time would be forgiven for thinking it was Salford who had actually won the league, such was the hype around them.

Orient sees itself as a traditional club steeped in history, whereas the Ammies, as Salford are still known based on their previous status as amateurs, are seen as one of those nouveau-riche clubs without any real tradition or history – a fact reinforced by the knowledge that upon taking over, the new owners changed the club colours from the traditional tangerine and black they had worn since their establishment in 1940 to red and white, of course a choice not too dissimilar to those utilised by a certain Manchester United.

With the fixture list offering up a trip to our old friends from the North West for the first match of the campaign, one which would see fans being allowed back into grounds as normal for the first time in almost a year and half, it was fair to say that there was a fair bit of excitement amongst the Orient faithful and especially within the Platt household about this being the first stop on our season-long travels. So much so, that as soon as it was announced that tickets were on sale, yours truly was sitting refreshing the Orient ticketing page until the very moment that they were available for purchase -- oh the joys of working from home! I may not have got the very first pair of tickets purchased, but of course I did feel some sort of deluded pride that I was in the medal hunt, to borrow an Olympics pun with the rescheduled 2020 Tokyo games being on at the time.

We had already decided that as the first away trip was going to be Salford, we would treat ourselves to a weekend "staycation" in Manchester as a kind of reward for our commitment to the cause. In truth our excitement had been building for this ever since the end of June when the fixtures were released, so by the time the clock ticked round to lunchtime on the Friday before the match, both of us having secured early release from work without even having to lie about the reasons, we were both absolutely champing at the bit to get underway.

Of course, being the organised and experienced awaydayers that we are, we knew the script and arrived in good time to enjoy a couple of pints at The Signal Box bar at Euston Station and to stock up on supplies for the train: sandwiches, crisps and plenty of M&S's finest Belgian lager being the prerequisites for trips of this ilk.

On arriving at Manchester Piccadilly station, we were chuffed to find that Kay's choice of apart-hotel was in the first road after the station approach, a walk of less than five minutes and an ideal location right in the heart of Manchester. Once we had checked in, we decided there was only one thing for it, and we headed off to Canal Street for a few drinks. If you have never had the pleasure of hanging out in Manchester's Gay Village then you don't know what you are missing. It is very good fun even for those of us who should really be old enough to know better. Be warned, however, drag queens patrol outside many of the bars attempting to entice passing drinkers to come into the establishments they represent with the promise of free/cheap shots of fluorescent undefined alcohol.

During the course of one such negotiation, one of these "hostesses" accused me of staring at her "breasts". Emboldened by party spirit, I reassured the damsel that the only pair of tits that I was looking at was the two inebriated chaps walking towards us dressed in full rugby league kits! With a potential cultural incident successfully avoided, we got on with enjoying the rest of our evening before retiring back to the apartment. It probably says something about our age and stamina (or lack thereof!) that just as we were leaving, Canal Street was truly starting to come to life.

Saturday morning, matchday, we decided that given the usual Manchester climate of drizzle, rain, heavier rain, slight respite, drizzle, rain, heavier rain and so on, and given that Moor Lane was in the middle of nowhere (god bless footballgroundguide.com), our best option to get to the identified pre-match hostelry, The Star Inn, was to secure a cab. When we told our cab driver, a former Manchester United season ticket holder, we were headed towards Salford City not Old Trafford where 50,000 were allowed into a pre-season friendly against Everton, he was actually relieved, as apparently the traffic going the other way was horrendous, although of slight concern was his assertion that he had never heard of the Star Inn.

Thankfully sat nav was on our side, and we got there in good time. Assuming you are not one of the very few people that know about the Star Inn, it is a gem of a pub bought by its regulars in October 2009 to become Britain's first urban co-operatively owned pub. It is friendly and welcoming, and in the unlikely event that you ever find yourself in that corner of the world we would highly recommend it.

After a little while as the only Orient fans in the pub, unusually not an issue at all, we were joined by fellow travelling O's Dan and Rob, who had apparently started out from Southend at 7 am that morning. Oh, how we chuckled, until it dawned on us that in two short weeks we would be doing similar to get to Carlisle, and no doubt for other lengthy trips later in the season. I was quick to reassure Kay that the earlier the start and the longer trip, the more dedicated to the cause it meant we were. I think she bought it...just about!

After a couple of pints and a chat about how the O's were shaping up ahead of the new season (quick synopsis: happy to have an experienced manager, the team was looking much better organised and robust, but we were all a bit concerned about where the goals might come from) we decided that as it was raining again we might as well treat ourselves to another taxi instead of the 20-minute walk to the ground. We did offer to give Dan and Rob a lift, but they declined, preferring the walk. I guess if they had spent that long travelling up, a bit of fresh air and a stretch of the legs were probably welcome. As it happened, our politeness very nearly stood us in good stead after the match.

Such has been Salford's quick rise through the tiers that while they have developed the ground itself nicely, the facilities have yet to catch up. The bar, food stall and toilets, in the away end at least, are all converted portacabins or cargo containers and there is very little cover outside of the stands. Still, we managed to enjoy a beer and some chips, although Kay was most perturbed that the tray of chips she had ordered for £2 was barely enough to constitute a small portion in McDonald's or any other fast food outlet. She felt they would be overpriced at £1 although thankfully they apparently tasted nice and did the trick.

Starved of away trips for so long, this one had caught the imagination of the Orient travelling faithful, with just under 500 fans making the trip. That may not seem a lot, but given the total attendance was just 1,968, it is just over a quarter of the total crowd. We were all in an almost demob happy mood and had actually significantly added to our previously miniscule selection of chants, some of them deliberately aimed at our rivals -- "National League Champions...you'll never sing that" being most notable, although the logic of assuming that Salford being relegated just so they could win the league to be promoted again seems somewhat far-fetched!

Just before kick-off, we saw Dan and Rob looking slightly bedraggled but having made it on time. The match itself was fairly evenly balanced. If anything, Orient started the better of the two teams, but the worrying lack of firepower meant we didn't create too much. Just as it had been in the final friendly against Gillingham it was centre back Omar Beckles who found the net for Orient, this time following up after skipper Darren Pratley's shot from a corner had been blocked with just over half an hour played.

Going a goal behind seemed to wake the hosts up, and just nine minutes later they pulled level thanks to a strike from distance from new signing Matty Willock, brother of Arsenal's Joe and QPR's Chris. 1-1 at the break.

While it remained fairly even throughout the second half, the hosts looked the more menacing from a goal threat perspective, and we had to be thankful for a number of decent saves by Lawrence Vigouroux in our net. Neither side could find the decisive breakthrough, and we finished with a point a piece -- not a bad point at all, given we were bedding in a new side, still missing Harry Smith who is meant to be our main goal threat, and away from home at one of the favourites for promotion.

As we exited the ground, confident in the knowledge that we had already organised our cab back into town, we were brought crashing down to earth as five minutes passed, then 10, and then 15, then it dawned on us that our order hadn't gone through properly and our best bet was to walk back to the Star Inn. Just as we started off on our way, we spotted Dan and Rob on the other side of the road waiting for their taxi, and they very kindly offered to let us jump in as we were all heading back to the centre of Manchester. Alas, due to Covid restrictions, the capacity was reduced to three people, and as the others had a train to make, we bid them farewell and headed back to the pub to watch the Lions lose to South Africa before getting back into town for a meal at the excellent Ducie Street Tavern, immediately across the road from our hotel.

We headed back to London on the Sunday, the journey taking three hours longer than it had on the way up, thanks to detours due to engineering works and a signal failure at Stafford. Annoying as it was, we hoped that had bought us some travel karma and we wouldn't experience too many delays and issues with our travel on our remaining trips, especially as next on the travelling itinerary was the daytrip to Carlisle.

Final Score

Salford City	**1**	**1**	**Leyton Orient**
M. Willock 41			Beckles 33

Up for the Cup

League Cup (aka EFL Cup) 1st Round: Wednesday 11th August 2021, Leyton Orient v Queens Park Rangers,

Our return from Manchester/Salford was greeted with the news on Monday that Orient's game against Harrogate Town scheduled for the following Tuesday had been postponed thanks to an outbreak of Covid within the Sulphurites' squad. Annoying news from a football obsessive point of view, as I hate it when games are postponed, as I feel like I am being denied my regular fix. It also made me start to fret incessantly about the midweek QPR cup game and the Exeter game scheduled for Saturday suffering a similar fate. Thankfully neither did, despite rumours of a couple of senior Exeter players testing positive for Covid. However, at the time it would prove incredibly naïve to believe that the ongoing pandemic wouldn't impact the season further.

My fears of postponement, ridiculous though they are, did have some substance to them. The previous season an outbreak of Covid-19 within the Orient squad had forced us to forfeit a League Cup second round tie at home to Tottenham. While that game would of course have been played behind closed doors due to the government restrictions at the time, it still felt as if we had been deprived in quite a cruel way. When the draw was made for the first round of this season's League Cup a few weeks before the start of the season, it felt deserved that in QPR we had drawn a London club from a higher division at home, especially when we received the news that it had been selected by Sky Sports for screening, the club having reportedly missed out on £250,000 from Sky when the tie didn't go ahead the previous season.

The TV selection meant that the game would be played on a Wednesday night, which was slightly disconcerting in terms of our usual routine, as the vast majority of Orient's midweek games, like many/most EFL clubs', are usually played on Tuesdays. As we set off for Brisbane Road, it was one of those pleasant late summer evenings that are ideal for watching football, and Kay commented it was going to be one of those games that start in the light and then finish when it has gone dark, which just seem special for some reason for regular football match attendees.

With the ticket allocations for cup matches requiring a greater proportion of tickets to be given to visiting sides, we had been displaced from our usual seats in the East Stand and instead were once again required to decamp to the other side of the pitch. Often in the past for cup games when we have had to do this, it is because the club know they only need to open one or possibly two stands. Seeing other people, away supporters no less, in our usual stand was going to be very strange indeed.

The first sign of the size of support QPR were bringing with them came as we passed the wine bar which was filled with the famous blue and white hooped jerseys. It was reinforcement that our best option was to head into the ground and have a bite to eat and a beer in there. I picked up my compulsory programme but couldn't spot anyone selling the Pandemonium fanzine, which I knew was out that day and usually raises a smile or two. I made a mental note to keep an eye out at half-time or on the Saturday to see if I could pick up a copy.

In a classic moment of not paying attention properly, or as I explained it to Kay because I was in the midst of an in-depth bit of analytical thinking about the potential line-up and tactics for the evening, I walked straight past the new burger stall just inside the gate without realising that it was actually operational and headed straight to the bar, where I dispensed with a hot dog in record time. It was only while we were sipping our pre-match pints that it dawned on me/Kay gleefully informed me that the burgers smell ok and why hadn't I had one. I promised myself that if they were doing them in the East Stand on Saturday, I was going to have to try one, being something of a self-proclaimed burger aficionado.

In many ways, with the opposition coming from two divisions above, this was something of a free hit for Orient. No one was expecting us to win, but if we somehow managed to pull it off, then it would make a decent statement of where we were in our early development under Kenny Jackett.

As we took up our seats, it soon became apparent that not only had QPR brought a significant number of fans with them, they were also going to be as noisy and boisterous as they could be, although their doing so had Kay worrying whether she would find her actual seat still there and undamaged when we went back on Saturday. In fact, the noise from the travelling support served to wake up the home supporters and create an atmosphere like a proper football match, something none of us had been able to enjoy at Brisbane Road since the previous December.

Orient seemed to set out to try and contain QPR in the opening period, and the defensive shape and organisation highlighted again the influence that the new manager was beginning to have on the team. However, when you try to contain a team right from the kick-off, there is always the fear that they will nick an early goal and force you to come out and open up. So, it was to prove when one of their centre backs, Rob Dickie, lost his marker Dan Happe in the area from a corner and nodded home.

Orient's response to going a goal down was encouraging, as rather than simply throwing men forward, there was a feeling of stepping up a gear and taking the game to QPR. This seemed to specifically focus on getting the ball to traditional style winger Theo Archibald on the left and allowing him to deliver enticing balls into the area. It took a while for the forward players to start getting on the end of these, but just before half-time a corner from the left glanced off Beckles' forehead and just evaded Happe following in at the far post. Still, it gave us encouragement for the second half.

Whatever Kenny said to the lads in the dressing room at the break, it certainly did the trick as they carried on in the ascendancy, quietening down our friends from Loftus Road in the stand opposite, a true indication of which team looked the most likely to score next.

As time wore on, the home crowd, reinvigorated by our improved display, were willing the lads on to nick an equalizer. On a number of occasions we looked to be through only to be denied by the linesman's flag. Even from our position at the other end of the ground I was convinced at least one of them should have been allowed to play on!

Then with just over 15 minutes remaining, right back Tom James fizzed in one of his rapidly becoming trademark long throws, and Aaron Drinan held off a defender well and poked home his first Orient goal. The celebration on three sides of the ground were as much in relief that our enterprising play hadn't gone in vain. Right at the death, we forced two good saves in succession, but the final whistle signalled penalties.

The cliché still exists in football that penalty shootouts are a lottery and that anything can happen. While this isn't strictly true -- it is about which team can hold their nerve combined with how the keepers perform -- it does however always feel harsh when you lose one. Sadly, so it was to prove for the O's. After each team had successfully converted their first three (Drinan, James and Dan Kemp for Orient), up stepped Cyprus Under-21 international Ruel Sotiriou, who crashed his effort off the cross bar. QPR converted their final two penalties, and it was all over. Even though we exited the competition at the first hurdle, we did so with our heads held high, having matched a team from the second tier.

Sadly, after the match, some of the QPR fans somehow seeing this win as a major victory of some kind decided to treat the local area to some childish wannabe aggro, nothing too menacing but equally not something that is needed or wanted.

Final Score

Leyton Orient	**1**	**1**	**Queens Park Rangers**
Drinan 74			Dickie 16

*QPR progress on penalties

First home league game

Game 2: Saturday 14th August 2021, Leyton Orient v Exeter City

As fun as awaydays and cup ties are, there is always something very special about the first home league game of a season for your stereotypical football obsessive. Its arrival, even after a summer where there has been an international tournament to break up the lull in football action, signals the chance for us all to get back into our usual matchday routine, to go to our usual pre- and post-match hangouts and to catch up with people we haven't seen for a while. This season it felt even more special after the pandemic had kept us out of our football grounds, save for the odd limited-capacity test events, for approaching 17 months.

As seems to happen fairly regularly for these occasions, the sun decided it was going to make an appearance, so Kay and I decided that a few pints outside the wine bar were definitely the way to get ourselves ready for Orient's official home opener.

Unusually for Orient fans there was a very tangible feel-good factor ahead of the first match of the campaign at Brisbane Road. The well-received appointment of Kenny Jackett as manager, the seemingly positive new signings, and a decent point at promotion-favoured Salford followed by a creditable performance against QPR had meant that a waft of optimism had replaced the usual feeling of pessimism that most of us use to guard against future disappointment. Of course, though, a vital part of following the O's is to never get too carried and pretty much to always expect it to go spectacularly wrong at some point. As we would see as the season progressed, this was a wise perspective to take.

Breaking with tradition for us, we decided to head to the ground just after 2 pm rather than our previous approach of staying for a last pint and then trying to hurriedly get in and neck another before "Tijuana Taxi" blares out of the loudspeakers signalling Orient's arrival onto the pitch. For those of you currently scratching your heads and wondering whether I have been on the tequila myself while writing this, allow me to provide a little context.

There seems to be some debate over the actual first time the song was played, or indeed the reason for it being chosen in the first place, but Herb Alpert's tune was adopted as the team's run-on music at the end of the Sixties and has proven popular with supporters ever since. So much so that none other than famous Orient fan (and something or other to do with the West End musical scene apparently!) Julian Lloyd Webber is a massive fan of the song and once reportedly protested over a move to change it: "Tijuana Taxi is good because the away side must think, 'They're really a bunch of nutters here'... You can't change it."

Arriving at the ground earlier than usual gave us the extra time to get something to eat. However rather disappointingly, for yours truly at least, the burger stall that I hoped would now be open just outside the East Stand concourse after my disappointment of the previous Wednesday was showing no signs of doing so. Maybe it was all a mirage? A steak and kidney pie did the trick to stave off the hunger for a bit.

Rather bizarrely, despite having been season ticket holders for the whole of last season, Kay and I had never actually sat in our selected seats since we bought the tickets. The previous trip for a home league match against Newport back in December 2020 had seen us rather disconcertingly having to take up seats in what is normally the away section, the far left-hand side of the East Stand. It was really great to be able to sit where we know we belong and to catch up with a few familiar faces.

For readers not familiar with what was at the time officially called the Breyer Group Stadium for sponsorship reasons but known to every Orient fan and any traditionalist football fan as Brisbane Road, it is probably fair to say it is slightly quirky. Leyton Orient first moved into the ground in 1937; prior to that they had played in a different area of London, Clapton, and were known as Clapton Orient. Orient replaced amateur side

Leyton FC who moved elsewhere. Probably the most striking feature of the ground are the blocks of flats in each corner that were constructed in the mid-2000s when portions of the land were sold to a property developer in order to fund the modernisation of the two stands behind the goal (the North Stand and the South Stand aka The Tommy Johnson stand), and the new grandstand on the western side of the ground. The apartments in the corner blocks have balconies that provide a view of the pitch, and although Kay is fully aware that one of these would be my ideal dream home, she has yet to agree to move there!

The East Stand is the most readily identifiable part of Brisbane Road. Anyone who has seen pictures of it may well have noticed the gable in the roof proudly emblazoned across in big red letters, "Leyton Orient". Kay and I sit immediately underneath this feature. Other than the replacement of the roof (including the refurbishment of and new lettering for the gable) and a quick lick of fresh paint over the summer, the old main stand seems to have remained largely untouched since it was bought from Mitcham Stadium in 1955 and then expanded in 1962. It is probably to do with the charm, character and throwback feel that Kay and I choose to sit here rather than in any of the other more modern areas. That and the fact that you can be at the bar in the Coach & Horses less than five minutes after the match finishes!

Orient fielded an unchanged line-up from the cup game three days previously, although the relatively small squad at this stage of the early season may also have influenced the manager's selection. The O's carried on from where they had left off against QPR, very much on the front foot. After just seven minutes, Aaron Drinan scored his first league goal for the club and his second in all competitions, calmly slotting the ball home after chasing on to a flick on by winger Theo Archibald from a long ball forward.

Just before the half-hour mark, it was 2-0, when big Omar Beckles repeated his efforts from the previous week at Salford, this time bundling home a free kick after skipper Darren Pratley had waved a boot at it.

Orient started the second half with a similar impetus rather than sitting on what they already had, until that is Exeter's Jevani Brown raced into our area colliding with Lawrence Vigouroux the goalkeeper as they both looked to take control of a loose ball. The referee pointed to the spot, though to me it looked 50/50 and fell into the "seen them given both ways" category.

Vigouroux was our undisputed player of the season in the previous campaign, and he simply exudes confidence in everything he does. No one in the ground save for the travelling fans would have been massively surprised when he not only saved Matt Jay's weak effort but was then alert and up on his feet to turn away a follow-up from the rebound.

With quarter of an hour left to play, Exeter had a man sent off thanks to a second yellow for a clumsy and late challenge on Pratley, and Orient wasted little time in exploiting the extra space. The third goal came from a sweeping move which started all the way back with Vigouroux, progressed up the right flank through Drinan, moved wide to accommodate 6-foot 5 striker Harry Smith making his first appearance since signing due to injury, and ended up with Lincoln loanee Archibald nodding home. 3-0 in the home opener, or "Exeter's big day out" (in London) as the Tommy Johnston stand, home of our most fervent supporters, took great joy in reminding the visitors.

Beyond the result, it was the style of the football that was most encouraging, the type of football that Jackett reportedly wanted the team to play: slick, crisp and full of attacking intent. So impressive was it that the club's social media pages tagged it #Jacketball. Early days and way too soon to get carried away, but the signs were very good.

As we headed out of the ground to the strains of Status Quo's "Rockin' All Over The World", another of Orient's traditions after home victories, we felt it was about time we renewed our acquaintance with the Coach & Horses, a hostelry we hadn't graced since the days when you had to have a substantial meal to be allowed to order a pint. There was a wedding on, which took up the backroom of the pub, confining Orient fans to the beer garden or front bar, leading us all to question, why anyone would think of getting married on a Saturday in the football season? Maybe there really are people in this world who don't revolve their entire existence around going to football matches. Philistines!

Final Score
Leyton Orient	**3**	**0**	**Exeter City**

Drinan 7
Beckles 25
Archibald 76

The first big away daytrip

Game 3: Saturday 21st August 2021, Carlisle United v Leyton Orient

As alluded to in the introduction section, one of the most daunting prospects of this madcap adventure upon which we had embarked was the need to drag ourselves to the far-flung corners of the country -- and beyond in the case of Newport -- probably in the depths of winter, and no doubt with a significant proportion of matches in midweek. Thankfully the first of these was scheduled for a Saturday in August in "sunny"

Carlisle. As it was Kay's birthday in the week preceding the trip to Cumbria we had thought about combining it with a holiday, possibly in the Lake District, Penrith ("Penrith?!?!" for fans of Withnail and I!) or even in Scotland given its close to proximity to the border. Instead, to save holiday allowance and because we were imbued with a new sense of adventure having survived Manchester/ Salford, we decided a 600-mile, 8-hours-plus round trip was the only genuine way to do it.

When my alarm went off at 6 am on the Saturday morning, it has to be said it was something of a shock to the system, but we scraped ourselves together, helped by more cups of tea than is usual in an hour, and got out the door in plenty of time for our 8:37 am train. It was a good job that we did as Transport for London had decided to stop the Northern Line at Moorgate due to planned engineering works. As we made our way on the Hammersmith & City Line to Kings Cross and walked down to Euston, I made a mental note to not only set off in plenty of time in future but also to check for any engineering works.

Once on board we congratulated ourselves on a job well done so far and enjoyed the coffee that had taken too long to make and give to us at Euston. Being the sensible(sic!) types that we are, we had vowed not to drink until we had at least reached the North West of England. In truth we lasted until about 11 am and somewhere in the Midlands before finally crumbling and ordering a couple of bacon rolls and four beers; mind you that may have had as much to do with the card machine in the buffet car being broken, the crap Wi-Fi and the difficulty of getting the Avanti At-Seat app to work, as much as any great discipline from the pair of us!

As we headed through the Lake District the scenery was lovely and it was almost easy to forget that we were headed to Carlisle on serious Orient business, not for a relaxing break in the countryside. When we arrived in Carlisle, only about 10 minutes or so behind schedule, we were pleasantly surprised to find that the town, including the 900-year-old castle was much more picturesque than we had imagined/feared. Still, as we said previously, this wasn't a day out, and there was serious business to take care of, so we set off on the 20 minute or so stroll up to Brunton Park, in the customary North Western drizzle, of course.

Given the choice of Carlisle Rugby Club or the Beehive pub as close to the ground pre-match hostelries, we opted for the Beehive on the simple principle that it was on the same side of the road as we had been walking on. It was busy inside, so much so that we were lucky to get in before they made people queue and wait for others to leave. Finally securing a couple of pints after a long wait but at a very reasonable £7.65, we even managed to find a table with a view of several screens to watch what remained of Liverpool v Burnley in the early kick-off.

Not wanting to spend more time waiting at the bar and out of the goodness of our hearts to let others into the pub (honest!), we decided to go into the ground, reckoning as experienced football fans that given how far away we were from home it would be much easier to get served in the away end than by staying where we were.

In something of a shock for those of us used to the "treatment" of away fans in London and at higher levels of the game, the stewards were very friendly. The one we asked the way to the away end pointed us in the right direction but also suggested that if we changed our minds and wanted to support Carlisle he would show us the way to that end, whereas the one searching bags, upon discovering a packet of cigarettes, pointed out where we could go for a smoke if we fancied it.

Once inside we discovered the beer was even cheaper than in the pub, although being the never-pay-attention-to-anything-other-than-the-football type I didn't realise there were pie and pint deals, much to Kay's annoyance when she returned from the toilet. That was soon rectified with a sausage roll and a Scotch Pie (well you could almost see the border from where we were!) as solid accompaniment to our liquid refreshment.

Brunton Park is one of those traditional and slightly quirky grounds that looks like different bits have been added as time has progressed and the club's finances have permitted. The main stand is a partially covered grandstand with a paddock terrace in front and two new similar structures on either side that were definitely added a good few years later. The home terrace behind one of the goals has a roof made up of three triangular sections, while behind the other goal is a small, uncovered terrace which seemed to only be used for away fans to put up their flags.

The newest stand is the Pioneer Stand opposite the old main stand, a portion of which, like Brisbane Road's East Stand, is given to the away fans. As decent as the stand and facilities are and even though the view is a lot better, it still doesn't feel right to my traditionalist sensibilities to be sitting/standing alongside the pitch when we are away from home.

As promising as Orient had looked up to this point through pre-season and the initial league matches, the first half in this one was poor. Where previously, especially against Exeter the week before, we had combined defensive organisation and robustness with some slick attacking football, for the opening 45 minutes we were the complete opposite. Our passing was sloppy and seemed to find a Carlisle player as many times as its intended target, and when we did play it to feet, we were weak in holding off the opposition.

From a defensive perspective, it was all too easy for Carlisle to get in behind us. Jayden Sweeney filling in at left back for the injured/dropped (depending on which rumours you believed) Connor Wood was looking particularly exposed. Things were made worse by Orient conceding a penalty after just seven minutes for a handball by big Omar Beckles. In fairness, or at least to my very biased eyes, it looked very much a case of ball to hand and generous in the least. Up stepped Tristan Abrahams, who had been on loan with Orient between January and May and had contributed the square root of naff all, so of course, when he converted no one in the away section was in the slightest bit surprised. That is just how football irony works.

With the lads struggling on the pitch, the away fans contented ourselves with singing vaguely insulting songs to the Carlisle fans; anyone who has ever been to a football match in England will of course recognise the usual standards utilised by visiting fans: "Carlisle's a shithole, I wanna go home!", "Is this a library?", "Your support is fuckin' shit" etc. But the most bizarre one was "You're just a shit town in Scotland" which led Kay to wonder if they actually thought we were north of the border?

In the previous two seasons under rookie manager Ross Embleton, we had always seemed to struggle when things needed to be changed on the pitch. I guess the intention behind bringing in a vastly experienced manager in the form of Kenny Jackett was that he would be able to draw on a tremendous knowledge and knowhow to change the team. At half-time Harry Smith replaced the struggling Ruel Sotiriou, with Aaron Drinan moving out to the right wing, just as he had in the second half against Exeter the previous week, while Shad Ogie, capable of playing centre back or left back, replaced the struggling Sweeney.

The impact of the changes was clear almost from the start of the second half, as Carlisle's defence struggled to deal with Smith's height and downright awkwardness, and we were able to push higher up the pitch as a result. There were a few sights at goal from Orient including a header from Smith that went wide from a promising position, but we had to wait all the way up until the 73rd minute before we could nick the equalizer. Drinan seized on a loose clearance just outside the penalty area and slid it through for Smith who cutely dinked it over the keeper to cheers of relief from the travelling O's faithful. We were able to see out the rest of the game, and on the long journey back to London we could reflect on a point salvaged and a job done well enough.

Final Score

Carlisle United	1	1	Leyton Orient
Abrahams (Pen) 8			Smith 74

Awayday Rules

⇨ Most trips will involve getting up at stupid o'clock on Saturday morning, which as hard as it sounds is way easier than getting up for work during the week.

⇨ Always check TfL (or similar local transport website) to make sure you arrive at the station in plenty of time.

⇨ It is perfectly acceptable (nay almost compulsory!) to drink beer at 8 am on a Saturday morning or on a commuter train at 5 pm on a Tuesday night.

⇨ Just like special forces soldiers, travelling football supporters are trained to eat whenever they can, as you never know when the next opportunity might present itself.

⇨ Any trips that involve changing trains en route will inevitably stir up a sense of worry at even the slightest delay, so usually the best tactic is to set off

---

with a contingency train that would still get you there on time even if you miss your planned connection.

⇨ Always check Football Ground Guide for the following:

- How to get from the station to the ground and vice versa. While in most cases it is preferable to walk (and stop at the pub, please see below), on rare occasions this requires a bus or a taxi, which you then need to factor in how to get back to the station after the match.

- Where's the best pub between the station and the ground? And especially for trips that require an overnight stay, where's the nearest 'Spoons for breakfast in the morning?

- Does the ground sell beer?

- What's the food like?

⇨ Always ensure that you know what time the train home is and whether you can get any train or have to stick to your booked one.

⇨ Always identify a handy off-licence to stock up on supplies for the way home.

⇨ Check whether you have to take your allocated seats or whether you can sit anywhere. On the rare occasions that you do have to sit (well, stand!) in your allocated seat, there is invariably a fellow travelling O's fan in it.

⇨ Please refer to the Awayday Songsheet later on for

the full catalogue of derogatory songs for everywhere we go.

Kay jinxes Orient by inviting some friends along

Game 4: Tuesday 24th August 2021, Leyton Orient V Harrogate Town

The rearranged game against Harrogate ended up being rescheduled for the Tuesday after it had originally been planned. The two full days of recovery after Carlisle were just about sufficient to get ourselves ready for the next match. Awaydays take it out of you when you are of a certain vintage!

Heading into the game, Orient and Harrogate were two of just five unbeaten teams even at this very early stage; the others were Carlisle whom we had just played, Bradford whom we would face in four days' time and Forest Green Rovers, another one of the favourites for promotion.

For some not completely understandable reason, a couple of Kay's colleagues from work, both Romanian, one of whom has a football daft Brazilian boyfriend, decided that they wanted to take in a football match in England, having never done so before. Quite why they agreed when she mooted the chance to come to Brisbane Road on a Tuesday evening is anyone's guess! Still, once they had remembered to bring the tickets with them at the second time of asking, we finally met up at the wine bar.

Obviously new recruits to Orient-watching aren't as up-to-speed as those of us who spend our entire lives fretting over our team, but even so I think they were genuinely surprised when I drained my pint and set off for the ground with 20 minutes to go before kick-off. For your genuine football obsessive, missing kick-off because of your own actions is anathema. It was a good job that I had set off in good time as the scanning of the new season cards at the turnstile was taking much longer than needed and I only just made it in in time to pick up my customary programme and to get to my seat before the first few bars of Tijuana Taxi sparked into life and the teams walked onto the pitch.

The way Orient started the game made even yours truly wonder if I had made the right decision in getting in in time. After the slick attacking play witnessed in the previous home game against Exeter, this was the complete antithesis. With Aaron Drinan ruled out through an injury sustained at Carlisle, it meant that Harry Smith started as the lone striker. Whether it was by specific instruction or the players themselves assuming that the best way to play with a 6-foot-5 striker was to lump the ball forward to him whenever they found themselves in possession, we ended up playing a long ball game that didn't really work. Despite his size, Smith struggled to win any of the balls pumped in his general direction, and when he did, the rest of the team was too far away to support him effectively. The rest of the party joined me about 15 minutes into the half where all I had to report was that they really hadn't missed anything.

Harrogate for their part were structured, organised, and had a good team shape, which Orient just couldn't seem to break. Their lone striker, Luke Armstrong, was a live wire throughout, popping up all along the front line, as his incessant pressing and chasing gave Orient's defenders no time at all on the ball. The fact that he scored two goals before the O's even realised they were in a game came as no surprise to anyone watching.

With Orient 2-0 down at the break, the work colleagues amongst our party decided that they would be better off having an extra drink or two, leaving Henrique the Brazilian and yours truly to brave the start of the second half alone.

In the opening few minutes of the second stanza, Orient were given a fantastic opportunity to get themselves back into the game when we were awarded a penalty for handball. However, as Harry Smith stepped up to take it, the ref took umbrage to something said by one of the visitors' coaching staff, but instead of letting us take the penalty and deal with it afterwards, he decided in his infinite wisdom to call time off and march over to brandish a card to someone on the Harrogate bench. Talk about effective distraction tactics! Smith's penalty was too close to the keeper and made for an easy enough save.

Orient carried on trying to open up Harrogate's well-marshalled rear-guard, but without changing tactics, they got little return at all and the game drifted to an inevitable defeat. Back in the wine bar after the match, we reflected on a poor performance that we hoped would just be a blip, a very bad night at the office. Strangely all three of our guests suggested that they would be up for coming again, although from our point of view, we might not invite them back given how their attendance had clearly jinxed the O's!

Final Score
Leyton Orient   **0   2   Harrogate Town**
                                              Armstrong 8, 31

#Jacketball makes a welcome return

Game 5: Saturday 28th August 2021, Leyton Orient V Bradford City

After the reality-check provided by Harrogate Town and the poor football that Orient had played in midweek, it is usually good to have a match coming up quickly, especially a big game against another promotion hopeful as an opportunity to try to bounce back.

Bradford City were relegated to the fourth tier in 2019, just under 20 years after they had briefly been a Premier League side. Whether completely true or not, Bradford fans are quick to assert that they are the biggest club in the division, and the fact their home match against Oldham a couple of weeks previously had attracted a crowd of just over 17,000 of course supported their case.

Before heading to Brisbane Road for this one, I faced the first dilemma of this Orient adventure, with Arsenal due to face champions Manchester City live on TV in the 12:30 pm kick-off. All through the week I had convinced myself that as Arsenal were bound to get thumped, I could, in theory at least, just head to Orient as usual and see how Arsenal were getting on for whatever remained of the second half. However as Saturday drew closer, the debate with myself grew more intense, until when I woke up on Saturday morning I realised as bad as it was going to be, I simply couldn't not watch it-- football obsession of the highest order!

So it was that Kay and I found ourselves walking into one of our old pre-match haunts, the Leyton Star, at precisely 12:10 pm. Probably as a result of the pandemic and the various associated lockdowns and draconian regulations around social mixing that we all had endured for far too long, there seemed to have been a change in the way people use the pub. It was always a popular venue amongst locals and football fans (both West Ham and Orient, if both are at home, as well as many Premier League barstool fans who go to watch whichever game is on) alike, but every single table had been reserved. For those of us who still remembered the days of walking into a pub without even thinking about booking, it seemed very strange. Thankfully we were able to find our usual spot, which was free until the evening, so we plonked ourselves down and settled in. A bit later we were even able to offer "our spare seats" to some other Orient fans who didn't realise that booking a table in a pub is clearly part of the new normal either.

This book is about following Orient, so I of course won't go into any detail about the Premier League (spoiler alert: read on to the end of the chapter if you are really that desperate to know!). However, being 2-0 and a man down after 35 minutes against a team managed by Pep Guardiola isn't exactly thrilling entertainment, even for those of us who feel alienated by the club.

In an effort to abate the Arsenal-based gloom, we decided to head down to the ground a little bit earlier than we would have previously, as thankfully the East Stand refurbishment had seen the removal of the TV in the concourse, so I could pretend it hadn't happened at all. Plus, Kay and I seemed to have developed an unhealthy addiction to the pies on sale at Brisbane Road in a mere matter of weeks.

As downbeat as I felt after the humbling by Harrogate Town, not just in terms of the scoreline but also in the way that Orient were stifled, outfought, and outplayed by the visitors, I did have a sneaky feeling deep down in the very back of my mind that an experienced manager such as Kenny Jackett would know what to do to put things right on the pitch again. In his programme notes ahead of this match, Jackett highlighted the poor performance the previous Tuesday suggesting: "Harrogate were more manly than us, more streetwise to League Two in regards to how to get the result and genuinely defended better than us". He wasn't wrong. However, the key test of any manager must be not just identifying what didn't go well, but actively changing things to make them better.

Encouragingly, after the pre-match formalities, as the players took their positions ready for kick-off, the change in formation was clear. The previous 4-2-3-1/4-3-3 had gone to be replaced with a lopsided 4-4-2, with the tenacious Craig Clay providing greater bite in midfield and winger Theo Archibald pushing forward to be closer to the front pair, who were an old school big man-little man pairing of big Harry Smith and the more diminutive Ruel Sotiriou.

The first half felt like two decent and well-matched sides testing each other out, and there really wasn't much in terms of goalmouth action to stick in the mind except for a good double save from Lawrence Vigouruox in the Orient goal. Having said that, the new formation seemed to be making Orient look both more solid out of possession and more threatening when they did have the ball.

After some quick half-time refreshments (a pint and an incinerated sausage roll) and a catch-up with a couple of our East Stand associates, we headed back to our seats hopeful for a bit more in the way of action. If the first half was uneventful, the second period was much more entertaining, as it started very much with Orient on the front foot and taking the game to their at-the-time unbeaten opponents. Archibald was the first to test the Bradford keeper with a stinging drive after cutting in from the right onto his favoured left foot. Then Smith rattled the crossbar with a header from a Connor Wood cross from the left, but the ball bounced straight down and stayed in front of the goalline. Still, this was more than the O's had offered from an attacking point of view since the second half up in Carlisle.

The first Orient goal came out of nowhere, very much a case of blink and you've missed it -- Ruel Sotiriou let Tom James' long throw bounce over his head as he turned and darted into the penalty area, getting to the ball almost on the goal-line before somehow firing a shot over the goalkeeper and into the top left-hand corner from a ridiculously tight angle.

As the Orient players celebrated in front of the travelling support, words were exchanged between Smith and some Bradford fans in the front rows. After the match, it was suggested that Smith had mimicked smoking a cigar, which could have been construed as an awful reference to the Valley Parade Fire tragedy back in 1985, which would have been despicable if true. In his apology, Smith suggested that the Orient players had had lighters thrown at them by the Bradford fans and he was merely responding to that.

Such was the furore that the police and stewards had to go into the crowd to eject the Bradford offenders, which also included the shouldn't-be-funny-but-really-is (especially to puerile football fans!) sight of one of the policemen being knocked off his feet. Thankfully he seemed ok, and it was more "It's a Knockout" than any real aggro. Given that no further action was taken against the O's player afterwards, we had to believe Smith's version of events, as stupid as it was to get involved in the first place.

The all-important second goal came with 8 minutes left to play, as James played the ball forward for Archibald charging through the middle from deep in his own half. Archibald manged to flick the ball onto Smith in the inside left channel before being clattered, and the striker calmly stepped back inside and fired low into the bottom left-hand corner beyond the grasp of Richard O'Donnell, the Bradford keeper. As Kay said at the time, if the first goal caught everyone by surprise, you just knew Harry Smith was going to shoot as soon as he got control of the ball.

After the frustration of Tuesday evening, it was another solid and promising performance from the O's, especially in the second half, against another of the fancied teams, definite grounds for some more cautious optimism about our prospects at the end of the first month.

Once we had stayed to applaud the players, we headed round to the other side of the ground to get our tickets for Newport away the following Saturday and to officially join the Supporters Club. Given that we were intending to go to every match this season, it felt like the right thing to do; plus we know that some of our destinations over the course of the season may be better reached on the coaches that the Supporters Club organise. It wasn't just for the cheaper beer, honest!

Final Score

Leyton Orient	**2**	**0**	**Bradford City**

Sotiriou 66
Smith 82

Meanwhile back in the Premier League...

Arsenal started the season with three straight defeats: going down 2-0 away at Brentford on the opening Friday night, being bullied by Chelsea in the first home game and then getting utterly destroyed and completely outclassed 5-0 by a Manchester City team who were all over them, even in the half an hour or so that Granit Xhaka was still on the field. As a result, the Gunners sat bottom of the table with no goals scored and nine conceded. Rumours were circulating that the number of empty seats for the game against Chelsea was much higher than anyone at the club was letting on, and it was being suggested that Mikel Arteta's chances of remaining manager even until Christmas were dangling by a very thin thread.

Despite the potential impact of the pandemic on their finances, Premier League clubs spent a total of £1.1 billion over the course of the summer transfer window, with two of the biggest deals being the purchase of Jack Grealish by Manchester City from Aston Villa for a cool £100 million and the return of a certain Cristiano Ronaldo to Manchester United for a relatively small fee but with a rumoured wage of £385,000 per week. So much for prudent financial management. Was I missing it...not in the slightest!

League Two table after close of play on 31st August 2021

Pos	Team	Pld	W	D	L	GF	GA	GD	Pts
1	Forest Green Rovers	5	4	0	1	13	8	5	12
2	Harrogate Town	4	3	1	0	8	4	4	10
3	Bradford City	5	3	1	1	9	6	3	10
4	Swindon Town	5	3	1	1	6	3	3	10
5	Hartlepool United	4	3	0	1	7	4	3	9
6	**Leyton Orient**	**5**	**2**	**2**	**1**	**7**	**4**	**3**	**8**
7	Mansfield Town	5	2	1	2	7	7	0	7
8	Northampton Town	4	2	1	1	3	3	0	7
9	Stevenage	5	2	1	2	5	6	-1	7
10	Port Vale	5	1	3	1	3	2	1	6
11	Exeter City	5	1	3	1	5	5	0	6
12	Carlisle United	5	1	3	1	4	4	0	6
13	Colchester United	5	1	3	1	4	4	0	6
14	Scunthorpe United	5	1	3	1	4	5	-1	6
15	Newport	4	2	0	2	3	5	-2	6

Pos	Team	Pld	W	D	L	GF	GA	GD	Pts
	County								
16	Salford City	5	1	2	2	5	4	1	5
17	Rochdale	5	1	2	2	7	7	0	5
18	Barrow	5	1	2	2	5	6	-1	5
19	Tranmere Rovers	5	1	2	2	1	2	-1	5
20	Crawley Town	4	1	1	2	5	8	-3	4
21	Walsall	5	1	1	3	3	7	-4	4
22	Bristol Rovers	5	1	1	3	4	9	-5	4
23	Oldham Athletic	5	1	0	4	4	7	-3	3
24	Sutton United	4	0	2	2	3	5	-2	2

Chapter 5: September 2021

Orient rise up the table, and we commiserate with Oldham supporters, hit the road west and grow our circle of supporter friends. Plus, an awayday songsheet!

Sunburnt in South Wales!

Game 6: Saturday 4th September 2021, Newport County v Leyton Orient

Awayday number three and another early-ish start. This time, even though we had been at a friend's 70th birthday party the previous evening, the alarm call was easier to handle, as firstly we had been sensible and got home at a decent hour, and secondly despite having to trail across London to Paddington to catch the train, the trip to Newport is a much more comfortable hour and a half or so rather than the mammoth trip to Carlisle.

We, of course, got to the station in plenty of time to get our supplies for the train, not wanting to risk another broken card machine/app-based ordering trial. No sooner had we exited the shop than my phone buzzed with a notification on Twitter from Lord Dazza (aka Daren Reisman, a complete and utter Orient diehard whom you heard from in his brilliant foreword to this book!). We had met Lord Dazza on the Tube on the way back from Euston after the Carlisle trip. His Tweet was a simple picture of his group's selection of cans of cider and match tickets. What else could we as self-respecting travelling football supporters do but respond with a picture of ours?

The journey slipped by easily enough, aided by our beer and crisp-based brunch, and just before we were about to arrive, we got talking to some lads in the adjacent seats who were on their way through to Cardiff after a music festival in London. As we bid them farewell, they jokingly said we might need to pick up some sunscreen. As we exited the station, we realised that they may not have been joking at all, as it was a glorious sunny day, just a little different from the rain and drizzle in Salford and Carlisle.

If you haven't been to Newport, it is perfectly set up for an awayday. Rodney Parade is an easy 10–15 minute stroll from the station, but the route there takes you right through the centre of town where there are some cracking pubs. Having completed extensive research on where to drink -- well, looking up Newport on Football Ground Guide and then noting the pubs down on one of my (in)famous index cards which I painstakingly prepare for every away game -- we of course ignored all of the ones on the card and went straight to the first one that Kay spotted, Le Pub.

After Kay had tried and failed to impress the barman with a cockney-sounding "yaki da" (which is allegedly a translation of the Welsh phrase "iechyd da" and is used to say cheers), we decided we might be better off drinking our pints outside in the sunshine. On a serious note, we did notice that the pub was equipped with a defibrillator on the front wall, a reminder of the bond that we share with Newport County as Justin Edinburgh had also led them from non-league back to the Football League six years before he had done the same with Leyton Orient.

Having been listening to the music coming from the pub across the road, we couldn't resist nipping over to Slipping Jimmy's Bar & Grill – a very quirky but very friendly bar where the landlady told us that they had bands on that evening if we were at a loose end. Knowing what the pair of us are like and the fact that we had spotted a Travelodge just near the station, we made her promise that if we came back after the match and were still there at 6 pm she was to throw us out so we wouldn't miss our train home.

After a pint listening to more excellent music, we decided to make our way to the ground. While we had been enjoying our drinks, a couple of policemen stopped to ask if we were ok in knowing where the ground was and pointed out a quicker route than the one I had jotted down on my index card. Being the cynical London residents that we are, we weren't sure we could trust them and checked with the bar staff that they weren't sending us in completely the wrong direction. They of course weren't, and it was just another sign of how friendly the place is.

Even the walk down to the ground is pleasant. You simply stroll down the High Street and then cross over the River Usk, and the ground is right in front of you. Once inside the away end, as the ground is shared with Gwent Dragons rugby team, the bar is actually a rugby clubhouse and very enjoyable, although sadly, of course, football regulations mean that you can't take your pint out and drink it in the sunshine, which seems a bit overkill and restrictive in this day and age.

When we headed out to the seats, we realised that our part of the stand -- again the away fans are given a section along the sideline -- was directly in the sun, maybe our new mates from the train were right all along about us needing our sunscreen.

With two new players having come in on transfer deadline day -- the first announced being Alex Mitchell, a 19-year-old central defender on a season-long loan from Millwall, and the second, Callum Reilly, an experienced central midfielder -- this gave Jackett a few more options, especially with regard to the defence, and he opted to change the system again, going with a 3-4-3. The change to the system led me to suspect that the boss had been wanting to do this from the start of the season but was simply waiting to have enough fit and available centre backs. With Aaron Drinan recovered from his injury, we also deployed what was beginning to emerge as the first-choice front line of Drinan, Harry Smith and Theo Archibald.

The match started in a fairly cagey fashion. Newport had been beaten in the play-off final the previous season and were therefore amongst the fancied teams this time around, even if they had won two and lost two of their four matches to start the season, although their form probably wasn't helped by having to play all four away from home as a result of having the pitch relaid, the perils of sharing with a rugby club one presumes.

After that slow start, things sparked into life fairly nicely after about 10 minutes, as Drinan brought a double save out of their keeper and then Lawrence Vigouroux had to be alert to parry an effort from the edge of the area. Then just past the half-hour mark Smith rose highest to nod home Archibald's corner from the right and give us the lead. I am not sure if it was the celebrations or just the heat, but I, like most of the Orient fans, was sweating like mad. "Costa-del-Cymru", as no one said at the time.

Moments later Archibald tested Joe Day in their goal with a curling free kick from outside the area. Then in added time, just when we thought we would be heading into the break a goal to the good, Newport were awarded a penalty. It was at the far end of the pitch from where we were, but after watching it back on the replay the following day, even my biased perspective couldn't make a case for Craig Clay, who had simply gone through the back of the Newport player. Matthew Dolan calmly sent Vigouroux the wrong way and rolled it into the bottom left-hand corner. It is always a bit of a downer to concede so late in the half, but we were playing well enough.

Having disappeared off to secure herself a portion of chips and to get the half-time drinks in, Kay was most perturbed to find that: i) not only was she not allowed to take her chips into the clubhouse, but ii) I of course couldn't bring a drink out for her, well, unless of course it was a soft drink, which knowing my darling wife oh so well was tantamount to poking a stick in a hornet's nest. So, I went to the bar while Kay finished her snack. Once she was back inside and I had secured us a couple of pints, we spotted Lord Dazza and Co. at the far end of the room and went up to say hi. The guys invited us to stand with them for the second half, an awayday opportunity we weren't going to miss. As it turned out, they had basically secured the back few rows at the far end of the stand and most of the staircase, as well, and it was as close to standing on a terrace as we could get in an all-seater stadium.

As we reached the 49th minute, both sets of fans joined together in a minute of applause for Justin Edinburgh in a pre-arranged tribute (he was 49 when he was so tragically taken). We of course all gave a rousing rendition of our song: "Here's to you Justin Edinburgh, Orient loves you more than you will know", and there can't have been many dry eyes amongst the Orient faithful. I was glad I was wearing my sunglasses; the loss of our former manager still feels so incredibly raw.

If Orient had been deflated by the very late first-half equalizer, they weren't showing it. Just eight minutes into the second half, Connor Wood fed Darren Pratley driving into the area, and the captain clipped a left-footed cross over to Smith, who rose to head home once again. That was four goals in five appearances for Smith with him, even at this very early stage, looking very much like the source of goals we had been lacking through the latter part of the previous season.

Alas, with 10 minutes remaining, the O's defence failed to deal with a flick on from a long throw and it somehow seemed to trickle into the net almost in slow motion. Another tough one to take, but the performance had been solid and, if anything, we had edged the match and perhaps should have won. Still three points from three tough away games is nothing to be sniffed at.

Kay and I, of course, made our way back to Slipping Jimmy's via a cheeky cheeseburger stop at McDonald's and reflected on another highly enjoyable awayday. Despite the distance, the travel and the cost, there really is nothing like an awayday, and Newport is an exceptional city to head to.

On the way home (no we didn't end up staying to watch the bands in the bar!) we got talking to a Newport season ticket holder who lived in Leytonstone and had been coming to pretty much every home game for 35 years. We spent the rest of the journey chatting away with our new friend, and we were even joined for a spell by a Scotsman who lived in Swindon but who went to watch Forest Green Rovers, as he was on his way back from Exeter. It was something akin to an impromptu lower league travelling supporter version of the Sunday Supplement that used to feature on Sky Sports. It did, however, along with the cans of lager we shared with our colleagues, pass on the return journey very nicely indeed. The one thing that football obsessives can do is to talk endlessly about football and their teams.

Final Score

Newport County	**2**	**2**	**Leyton Orient**
Dolan (Pen) 45+2			Smith 34,53
Telford 80			

Lord Dazza's Guide to being an Orient Fan

⇨ Welcome to the family. Once you are in, you will become hooked.

⇨ There is such a thing as 'the Orient way'.

⇨ Be prepared for heartbreak.

⇨ Making new friends and enjoying their company is sometimes (Ed's Note: often?) better than the 90 minutes of football.

⇨ Expect the unexpected.

⇨ We don't win every week so manage your expectations and appreciate the success when we achieve it.

⇨ Make you own memories and cherish them.

> ⇨ Stay off social media!
>
> ⇨ We have our own identity, players, staff, managers come and go but we, the loyal few remain for the love of the badge.
>
> ⇨ Never fall in love with a loan player, they will inevitably break your heart.
>
> ⇨ Orient is a safe place to watch football and ultimately a place of release.

The LODown Podcast

Having got to know us over the course of the trips to Carlisle and Newport, Daren/Lord Dazza very kindly offered Kay and I the chance to appear on the LODown podcast to tell the listeners about our madcap plan for the season, how the first month had been and how we thought the O's were shaping up at this early stage. As well as regular guests of the show, they had also invited Oldham Athletic fan Matt from the Boundary Park Alert podcast to talk about the troubles they were experiencing, thanks to an at-best incompetent owner – a plight that all Orient supporters would feel a massive level of empathy with given our own experience with our previous owner.

Oldham were a founding member of the Premier League back in 1992 and were in League One when Abdallah Lemsagam bought the club in January 2018. Since then, his three-and-a-half-year tenure had been a catalogue of poor decision-making in terms of recruitment both on and off the field (eight managers in that three-and-a-half-year reign!), accusations of interference in squad matters, the controversial appointment of his brother as sporting director, players and staff being paid late on numerous occasions and a transfer embargo, to name just a few. Such is the anger that Oldham fans were feeling that there had been pitch invasions at their last five home games and threats from the EFL that unless it stopped, games may have to be played behind closed doors.

In response to the latest pitch invasion, Lemsagam banned supporters from buying tickets to Oldham's next two fixtures away at Leyton Orient and at home to Hartlepool and suspended season ticket sales. Thankfully Orient stepped in and made It clear that visiting fans would be able to pay on the day. Their story as told by Matt was both eerily familiar and highly emotional for any true football fan. As supporters of a club that was so nearly destroyed by an owner, but which has survived and is emerging on the other side under the right kind of owners, all Orient fans could do is display our solidarity and support and offer an example of how things really can get better again.

Orient show empathy and support but no sympathy

Game 7: Saturday 11th September 2021, Leyton Orient v Oldham Athletic

A lot of the social media discussion in the build up to this one centred on Leyton Orient fans discussing how best to show solidarity and empathy for the Oldham fans who were planning a protest four minutes into the match. One commenter got himself in a slightly sticky situation when he suggested that even though it was a personal decision for each fan, he felt he should urge Orient fans not to get involved and to concentrate 100% on our own club. Suffice it to say that the vast majority of responses made it abundantly clear what the general feeling to that idea was! Most of the O's faithful were determined to show the Oldham fans that we understood what they were going through and to let them know that we were with them.

It was another nice and sunny day as Kay and I made our way over to E10 filled with a feeling of anticipation and excitement that despite Oldham's plight, which saw them languishing second bottom of the table, having only managed one win against newly promoted Sutton United, this was a perfect opportunity for our boys to stick a few goals in and continue to build on the momentum that was starting to bubble throughout the early weeks of the season, the humbling by Harrogate most definitely aside.

After the podcast on Thursday evening, Dazza had said he would be in the Coach & Horses before the game, so that made our decision easy on where we were going for our pre-match pint. Because of the nice and sunny weather, it was just about standing room only when we arrived in the Coach's beer garden; we did, however, find ourselves a nice perch at one of the barrel tables that even had a seat for Kay. After eventually catching up with Dazza once he had traversed the crowd of fans, we decided to head in as both of us were craving our now routine pre-match sustenance of a pie and a pint.

After the highly encouraging performance at Newport using the 3-4-3 system, our manager saw no reason not to carry on, the only change being the return of Dan Happe in place of Shad Ogie, the former now being fit again while the latter had tested positive for Covid-19 in the days leading up to the match. The new normal strikes again.

When faced with a struggling opposition it is sometimes all too easy for a team with aspirations higher up the table to metaphorically take their foot of the gas, to assume it is going to be an easy victory and to not put the requisite effort and focus in to ensure that the game is won. Thankfully there was no sign of complacency from the O's, who looked dialled in and ready from the moment they walked onto the pitch. Having seen the response that Jackett had got out of the players since their off night against Harrogate, it seemed that our new manager was not a man who tolerated complacency or slacking off in the slightest.

The Oldham fans, rightly angry with their owner, made a hell of a racket right from before the kick-off, aided and abetted by a drummer. Being something of a traditionalist in fan culture, I have to say that in the past I have normally been against drums, trumpets and whatever else modern-day fans bring along with them, but his constant pounding seemed to energise their supporters to even greater efforts. Such had been the racket that they were creating up to the fourth minute, it was actually quite difficult to determine when the protest actually started, the only discernible hint being the clapping in solidarity from O's fans in each of the four stands. It was the right thing to do, there but for the grace of the football gods (well malevolent owners anyway!) go we.

It took Orient just over a quarter of an hour to open up their struggling opponents, as winger/number 10 hybrid Theo Archibald went racing through the inside left channel, and from our perch in the East Stand we could easily see Aaron Drinan charging up in support on the right flank. As Archie entered the penalty area, he selflessly pulled the ball back for Drinan to slot home.

Just over 10 minutes later, we were to notch another goal from a lighting break, as this time right back Tom James latched onto a looping loose ball out on the right, raced forward and, showing incredible composure as he approached the advancing keeper, stepped inside and fired the ball home with his left foot. Both goals were the kind of incisive counterattacks that are thrilling to watch, the way yours truly thinks football should be played.

Orient had the ball in the net again just moments later but Craig Clay's volley from the edge of the area was flagged for offside. With half an hour on the clock, Oldham were rocking and seemed to be there for the taking, but somehow settled things down and even forced a decent stop from Lawrence Vigouroux in our goal and kept the deficit to two goals at the break.

With their ears presumably ringing with some choice words from manager Keith Curle, Oldham started the second half with more intent than Orient had allowed them to muster in the first 45 minutes. Hallam Hope curled an effort just wide of the upright then Raphael Diarra tested Vigs with a drive from fully 25-yards out.

After that brief flurry, though, it was back to Orient being in control, although we had to wait right the way up to 15 minutes to go for the third goal. Archibald did well to win the ball on the goal-line on the left; he beat two defenders with clever footwork and drove into the area parallel to the goal-line before firing low past the keeper and into the net.

In stoppage time, Dan Kemp forced a save from their keeper with a header from point blank range, but Harry Smith was following in to nod the ball home from virtually on the goal-line. The old adage in sport is that you can only beat what is in front of you, and with Oldham very much in the doldrums it was easy enough for Orient, but the victory lifted us up into the third and final automatic promotion place. There was still a very, very long way to go in the season, of course, but there was definitely a good feeling about the club and the way they had started.

Final Score

Leyton Orient	**4**	**0**	**Oldham Athletic**

Drinan 16

James 27
Archibald 75
Smith 90+1

Papa John's EFL Trophy: Tuesday 14th September 2021, Leyton Orient v Southampton U-21's

In their infinite wisdom (sic), the Football League (EFL) in 2016 decided to admit 16 Premier League Under-21 squads, essentially their B-Teams, to the EFL Trophy. In one foul swoop the decision both diluted what was an interesting cup competition for clubs in the lower two divisions of the Football League, and at the same time alienated the majority of fans of those clubs with attendances declining at an alarming rate. Another excellent bit of thinking by the powers that be at the EFL!

Personally, I totally get the whole #BTeamBoyoctt that has seen most fans stay away from the competition as a result of the decision, but for those of us too stupid or too hopelessly addicted to watching football, it still provides further opportunities to watch our team in action and to run the rule over some fringe, reserve and younger players.

Back in the days of being locked out of football grounds, Orient had made the decision along with most of the other clubs in their division, that midweek games would kick-off at 7 pm to aid with travelling for visiting teams, but also as there was no need to allow extra time for us to get to the ground after work. For some not-completely-explained reason, Orient had kept that kick-off time for this year's competition despite fans being allowed into the ground. Maybe the logic was that anyone daft enough to come along to watch these games would properly find a way of getting there. For those of us still working from home, it does mean we have to get out the door fairly sharpish, but it also means that the game finishes just before 9 pm, giving us plenty of time for a pint or two before catching the Tube home.

With the low attendances for these games, the club only need to open the Justin Edinburgh Stand, on the opposite side of the ground from where we usually sit, and even though we have sat there on a number of occasions previously, it still feels a little bit disconcerting. At least there were no visiting fans in our stand to worry about this time.

In an intriguing team selection, Jackett had gone for the 3-4-3 system for the third match in succession but had changed every player apart from the back three of: Alex Mitchell, Omar Beckles and Dan Happe, presumably to start to build the trio's understanding of each other's play, if that was definitely going to be the system employed going forward.

The changes meant that there were to be competitive debuts for goalkeeper Rhys Byrne and midfielder Antony Papadopoulos, although the latter was to be deployed, initially at least, at right wing-back. Callum Reilly, the deadline day signing from AFC Wimbledon, had recovered sufficiently from a knock that had ruled him out the previous Saturday to get his first run out for the club, and there was a second start for Norwich loanee Tyrese Omotoye.

As the game got underway it was very evident that assistant manager Joe Gallen was the one in the technical area shouting instructions. I concluded, wrongly as it would turn out, that Kenny Jackett might have been taking something of a backseat to allow his assistant to gain some experience of taking the team.

After a relatively slow start to proceedings, things started to warm up in terms of action as the Southampton youngsters suddenly seemed to spark into life. There was an effort that whistled over Byrne's crossbar and then Mitchell had to be alert to make a challenge after centre back partner Happe had given the ball away in a very dangerous area. There were a couple of efforts on goal by Southampton and a couple of half chances for Orient, but the game became one of those midfield stalemates that happen from time to time.

At halftime we headed downstairs to treat ourselves to our "dinner" of a pie and a pint, and as we scanned the concourse for somewhere to perch ourselves, we ended up sharing an ice cream cart with a couple of other guys, both of whom were having both a pie and a fully loaded hot dog. As we got chatting away, we soon realised that one of them was American, and it turned out he was one of the new investors Orient had attracted at the start of the season on his first visit to Brisbane Road. We thanked him and welcomed him to the ground, but neither for the life of us could remember what he said his name was, our apologies.

We finished our drinks, bade farewell to our new friends, and made our way back outside for the start of the second half. Just as we approached the front of the stand Theo Archibald and Lawrence Vigouroux were sheepishly hiding behind the wall of the stand, out of view of the dugout and munching away on snacks from the concourse. I jokingly enquired as to whether they should really be eating that sort of thing, to which Archie replied, "Why do you think we are standing here?". It was a refreshing reminder that football players at this level are still human and not completely out of touch with the fans, or indeed reality.

Maybe it was fatigue from facing a fully-fledged Football League side, but the Southampton youngsters' energy levels seemed to drop off in the second half. From an Orient point of view, it felt like a game that was very much there for the taking as long as we could carve out a clear-cut opening. With 20 minutes to play it was really starting to look as if we were headed for penalties.

By means of explanation of the competition rules: while the first stage is a group phase divided into groups from the north and south of the country, if a match ends in a draw at full time, then there is a penalty shootout. The team that wins the shootout is awarded an additional point in an endeavour to try to encourage attacking football.

With just 20 minutes to go, Reilly was taken off to be replaced by young right back Jephte Tanga from the O's academy. It wasn't the change in personnel as such that was important though, it was the fact that Papadopoulos was pushed forward into his more natural midfield role and better able to support the attack that was to prove decisive.

With time ticking down towards the final five minutes, Dan Kemp, a creative number 10 having to adapt to playing out wide in the new system, picked up the ball on the right-hand edge of the Southampton penalty box and pulled it back across the face of goal where Papadopoulos was charging in to slam home. A game-deciding goal on your competitive debut – not a bad evening at all for the young prospect. It will certainly not be the most important game that Orient will play for the season, but a good run out for the reserves and youngsters and a win over a Premier League Academy side is nothing to be sniffed at. The announced crowd was sadly just 634, a reflection of the unpopularity of the competition rather than the Orient support, I would venture to say.

After the match, as were on the other side of the ground, Kay and I decided that this would be the perfect time to visit the Supporters Club for the first time as signed-up members. As we went in, I jokingly asked Keren, who had sorted our memberships for us the other week, whether she needed to see our membership cards. She suggested that as there was hardly anyone in due to the low crowd and the fact that she knew who we were, we probably didn't need to bother.

After a few pints and a catch-up with Adam Parkes, aka Parkesy, from the LODown podcast and a few other people, we decided to head for home. As we were waiting on the platform at Leyton, I caught sight of someone in a grey Orient tracksuit with a rucksack initialled "JG" a bit further down. As we got on the train, I said to Kay that assistant manager Joe Gallen was further up the carriage, and she suggested we should go and have a chat with him. Once I had pointed out the right person -- Kay's observational skills are such that she walked straight past Joe and was headed towards a guy in civvies who was probably on his way home from work -- we had a quick chat with him before we had to get off at Stratford. He told us that Kenny Jackett had picked the team and very much decided on keeping the back three in place, but the reason that he was the one in the technical area was that Kenny hadn't been feeling well so felt he should stay at home. He did assure us that the manager had done a Covid test, and it had been negative, and he hoped he would be back in full health at Bristol at the weekend.

Final Score
Leyton Orient   **1   0   Southampton U-21**
Papadopoulos 82

Awayday déjà vu

Game 8: Saturday 18th September 2021, Bristol Rovers v Leyton Orient

There was a definite feeling of déjà vu for our fourth awayday of the season given that we were leaving from Paddington just after 10:30 in the morning and heading west on a Great Western Railway train. Honestly it could have been Newport all over again. Having got ourselves better organised and not having to be at a 70th birthday on the Friday evening meant that we were at Paddington even earlier than we had been a fortnight previously. With time to kill, what were we going to do?

For an all-too-brief moment we contemplated doing what sophisticated people do when they have spare time before they travel and grabbing ourselves a cup of coffee and perhaps a croissant, to help while away the time. Just as we were about to take the plunge and behave like normal people and head for Costa Coffee or Upper Crust, Kay spotted out of the corner of her eye an establishment much more suited to the way we tend to do things: The Mad Bishop & Bear pub. That sounded like the very place for us!

Once we got to the top of the escalator, we spotted Keren from the Supporters Club and her friends and family who make up the @LOFCPicnicCrew enjoying a swift half and some toast, and that was all the encouragement we needed. Although Keren did jokingly tell us that we would have to order food in order to get beer, this turned out not to be true, but that didn't stop yours truly ordering a bacon bap and a pint of Guinness – a traditional Irish breakfast if ever there was one (Gaz you're not even Irish!). Being more restrained, Kay settled for a pint of lager.

After our pit-stop and stocking up on supplies for the journey, as we were waiting for the train to be prepared, we heard that unmistakable rumble of a crowd of football fans arriving and singing en masse as they descended from the train. It got louder and louder as they approached the barriers, with many of the non-football-au-fait passengers looking somewhat apprehensive about what might be coming their way. It turned out to be Plymouth fans arriving for their game at AFC Wimbledon. Kay remarked that they must have set off and started on the beer early given that it wasn't yet half ten, a definite hint of the pot calling the kettle black, but then football awaydays are very much like holidays where it is perfectly acceptable to start drinking at the airport or station no matter how early it is.

With "lightning reactions", we were the first to notice the platform for our train being announced and being amongst the very the first people to get on the train, we thought we would treat ourselves to an available table. Alas our ultra-speedy response hadn't been matched by the person responsible for updating the seat bookings, and they were still set for the journey into London. When they were updated, to our dismay it turned out our entire table had been booked. Just as we were debating whether to give up our newly acquired spot or not, Keren & Co. arrived letting us know that this was in fact one of their tables. Thankfully our seats were only three rows away, so we were happy to comply.

As we made our way westward, more and more younger people were getting on at each stop, and it turned out there was a music festival on in Bristol as well. The festival goers combined with Orient fans made for a party-like atmosphere on the train. We just felt sorry for anyone who wasn't going to the festival or the match, their quiet daytrip having been spoilt by an outbreak of good-natured boisterousness.

Once we arrived and having planned ahead in infinite detail (yes, I looked it up on Football Ground Guide!) we had just under half an hour to wait for our connecting train. Whereas some of the Orient fans got a cab up to the ground or got a train through to Filton Abbey Wood, we had followed the advice on the website to go via Montpelier, a studenty feeling suburb with a decent array of pubs as soon as you hit the main Gloucester Road. With the sun shining, we headed straight for the Prince of Wales, which had a lovely beer garden out the back.

After a couple of pints, we decided to head up towards the ground. In fairness it is a bit of a schlepp of about a mile and a half up Gloucester Road, but with a good selection of restaurants, bars and charity shops, the latter being very much to Kay's delight. That was until I cruelly informed her that we didn't have time to stop in all of them, and even if we did, what was she going to do with anything that she bought when we got to the ground as I doubted there was a facility to leave your shopping to collect after the match?

She made me promise faithfully that next season we would come back for the weekend and stay over so she could have a good old scout round them all. Given Bristol Rovers' at-the-time plight hovering just above the relegation places, I suggested that we would be more likely to be playing City next season, and their ground was on the other side of town. Even though I had made that last bit up, it turned out to be not inaccurate, but still it seemed a nice enough city to want to come back again.

The Memorial Stadium itself is a kind of strange ground, tucked in behind rows of houses. It was actually a rugby ground and home to Bristol Rugby Club; however after initially allowing Rovers to share it with them from 1996, the rugby club moved to Ashton Gate in 2014 to groundshare with Bristol City. Its peculiar history is reflected in the way it looks. On one side of the pitch is the West Stand which actually looks like it belongs at a racecourse or cricket ground with its row of corporate boxes with balconies in front. On the other side is a grandstand that looks much more like it belongs at a football ground with a paddock terrace in front and open terraces to either side, one side of this being where the away fans are housed (another away view from the side of the pitch -- d'oh!). Behind one goal is a covered terrace, and then dotted around at various points are those small temporary stands that are more suited to rugby union grounds or golf tournaments.

Even though we had had advance warning, it still came as something of a blow, especially as it was sunburn weather again, that due to the away terrace being open and with a view of the pitch from wherever you stood, they couldn't sell us any beer -- a clear infringement of our human rights, if you ask me!

The news got worse when queueing up for something to eat and a cola (yes cola that's how desperate things were getting!), we were told they only had a choice of Ginsters pasties rather than the locally made pies and sausage rolls that they advertise. If it were indeed possible for looks to kill, then the face that Kay pulled upon receiving the news that not only was there no beer, but she would have to settle for a plastic-tasting pastie, would have been a contender to do just that.

Just before the game got underway, Dazza squeezed into the space behind us. We had seen him briefly on the train as we left Paddington, but he had been one of the ones to get a cab up to the ground and was now worried about how he might get back.

With Rovers languishing in 22nd place having made a poor start to life in League Two after being relegated from the third tier at the end of the previous season, it felt going into this match that given Orient's decent form, this could provide an ideal opportunity for the O's to get their first win on the road and to really build on the momentum that had been generated thus far. With the infamous Joey Barton (convicted twice of violent crimes, at the centre of a string of on and off-field incidents including stubbing out a cigar in a teammate's eye, and most recently, just that summer, charged with beating up his wife at a party) in charge of the home side, we could only hope that Orient would do their job and heap more misery on the controversial manager.

Once again it was the 3-4-3 for Orient but with the slight tactical tweak of moving Aaron Drinan to play off Harry Smith up front, with Theo Archibald playing behind the pair as what has been termed, much to Kay's ongoing annoyance as she thinks all tactical speak is largely nonsense, a false number 10/central winger. Whether it was the system or the poor quality of the opposition, the O's got off to an absolute flyer. First up from a corner after just quarter of an hour, Tom James curled in a low in-swinging cross, and Harry Smith was the first to react and found himself all alone to stoop and nod home his 6th goal of the season. As it happened right in front of the travelling support, there was carnage on our terrace with bodies flying everywhere, so maybe it was a good idea that beer wasn't available after all!

As things settled down however it became apparent that one of our fellow supporters had taken a fall and had a nasty cut to his head. He ended up being taken to hospital, but later that afternoon we found out via Twitter that he had been released and was on his way home. At halftime there were reports of another supporter collapsing with a suspected stroke. It can only be hoped that if it were true that he got the help and support he needed as well. Even for us hopeless football obsessives, incidents like these really put the game into perspective.

Back to the action on the pitch, and Orient were all over Rovers, the travelling supporters enjoying telling Joey Barton exactly what we thought of him. For legal reasons and as this is intended to be a family publication, I am prevented from repeating what was sung; however if you aware of Barton's reputation, you can no doubt work it out for yourself.

Just after the half hour mark, Archibald made it 2-0. Another James corner, this one a looping one, was cleared only as far as skipper Darren Pratley on the edge of the penalty area. His effort was blocked but fell to Archie who rifled home from fully 25 yards, a stunning strike and more ammunition for the Orient faithful who, even at this early stage of the season, were clamouring for the club to make his loan move permanent. Maybe his ground-breaking diet of pies and pasties from the concessions stand was the secret!

A mere matter of minutes later, we had the ball in the net again through Drinan nodding home another cross from James, only for us all to halt our celebrations just as they were getting going with the sight of the linesman on the far side waving his flag. Thankfully referee David Rock had a different view of it and overruled his assistant and awarded the goal. No need for VAR in League Two! 3-0 at halftime away from home, it is difficult to make a better statement of intent than that.

As a result of Orient's control of the game, the second half felt like something of a formality, a case of staying solid, seeing out the game and getting the three points in the bag. A little bit of niggle crept into the game, presumably as the Rovers players were angry at being thumped at home and no doubt inspired by their manager. It did give us an excuse to go through our repertoire of anti-Barton songs on a continuous cycle though.

In the final minute, as seemed to be happening a little bit too often in recent matches, Bristol were awarded a penalty after a coming together between Shad Ogie, on as a substitute for the once-again injured Dan Happe, and Harvey Saunders. It was another that seemed harsh to my biased eyes. Brett Pitman smashed it home, and Rovers had their consolation goal. The win pushed Orient up to second in the table and very much carried on the momentum.

As we left the ground and headed down Gloucester Road again, I casually suggested to Kay that we probably wanted to get all the way down to the Prince of Wales again as it was near to the station. Deprived of a beer for the best part of three hours, Kay's reaction was akin to that of a toddler who has had their favourite toy stolen -- she made it abundantly clear that we were stopping in the first one we came to, and as a dutiful husband I could do nothing but comply. While we were in there, we got talking to Chris, a fellow Orient supporter, who we would bump into on several occasions as the season progressed.

Final Score

Bristol Rovers	1	3	**Leyton Orient**
Pitman (Pen)90			Smith 18
			Archibald 34
			Drinan 40

An Awayday Song-sheet

It is the absolute duty of all travelling football fans to take the mickey out of anywhere that we visit, so here are some of the compulsory songs alongside some of the travelling O's "wittier" efforts from the 2021/22 season:

1) "Your support is f**ckin' sh*t!" (whether this is in any way true or not is completely irrelevant!).

2) "(Insert name of wherever you are!) is a sh*thole, I wanna go home!", although immense credit goes to the Bradford City fans at Brisbane Road who opted for: "Bradford's a sh*thole, we're glad to be here!".

3) "Is this a library?" (to point out the lack of atmosphere coming from the home support), usually swiftly followed by: "Doo doo doo, football in a library!".

4) Specific reference to the local area, such as: "You're just a bus stop in Scotland!" (in Carlisle given its proximity to the border), and "Stansted, Stansted, Stansted, Stansted, Stansted, Stansted airport!" (given that Crawley is so close to Gatwick airport and for some bizarre reason we decided to champion the "merits" of the one in Essex!).

5) "Is there a fire drill?" (usually reserved for when your team

is comfortably in control and the home fans decide they have had enough and start heading for home).

6) "What the f**kin' hell is that?" (applicable to any team with a mascot that dares to pass in front of the away end. Both of Orient's Wyvern couple, Theo and Cleo, are of course exempt!).

7) "We filled your ground for you!" (appropriate to any team with a rather small home support).

8) "You're sh*t.......aaaarghhhhhh!" (as the home goalkeeper takes a goal kick).

9) "My garden shed is bigger than this, my garden shed is bigger than this, it's got a door and a window, my garden shed is bigger than this!" (used at Barrow but easily applicable to any of the smaller grounds).

10) "The wheels on your house go round and round, round and round!" (I am sure you can reach your own conclusions on where this might be applicable!).

...and as an extra bonus, aired solely at Bristol Rovers given their manager's rather chequered reputation: "Mrs. Barton's terrified...Rovers are losing!"

Frustrated at home.

Game 9: Saturday 25th September 2021, Leyton Orient v Mansfield Town

Just when you think your team is flying, football has a nasty habit of biting you on the backside. With the O's up to second in the league and on a run of three wins and a draw since the Harrogate reversal, it is fair to say that there was a feeling of optimism amongst the normally guarded Orient support. With the opposition for this one languishing in 20th place, having managed just a solitary point from their previous six matches, perhaps this was a game that we should have been wary of rather than assuming it was pretty much a foregone conclusion. Such is the fickle fate of footballing fortune!

After a quick stop in the wine bar where the barman, David, told us that such had been the O's fine form that he was finishing work early to take the short walk down to Brisbane Road to see what all the fuss was about (ah-hah, that explains where it all went wrong!), we headed down the ground to collect our tickets for Port Vale away the following week, the online ticketing system having once again experienced some kind of meltdown as it seems to do on a fairly regular basis.

Once inside the East Stand and queueing for our obligatory pre-match pies, we carried on the debate we had started the previous evening where we wondered if trying anything other than the steak and kidney pies might constitute some kind of jinx. In the end we decided it was a lot safer if we didn't take the risk, although given what was to follow later, perhaps we should have changed things up.

A lot of the discussion in the build-up to this game focused on the return of former Orient striker Danny Johnson, who had scored at a regular rate for us at least in the first half of the previous season, and how he would compare to our new attacking trio of Aaron Drinan, Harry Smith and Theo Archibald, all of whom had been finding the back of the net with a welcome frequency.

As the game got underway it soon became glaringly apparent that Mansfield's main preparation work had centred on

95

stopping our big number 9 Smith from providing the focal point to the attack by fair means or foul. For a team managed by the son of the legendary Brian Clough, Nigel, it came as something of a surprise to the those of us old enough to remember "Old Big 'Ead's" footballing philosophy and principles that their approach consisted mainly of pulling Smith's shirt every time he went up for a header. It certainly wasn't pretty, but it did prove to be effective, although the referee and his assistants could have been firmer in stamping it out early on and allowing a game of football to break out.

As the game wore on, the O's did seem to get more and more of a grip of it, and by the time we got to the last half hour were largely in control, although just couldn't find the all-important opening goal. Even a late red card shown to a Mansfield player for a kick at Theo Archibald and seven minutes added time didn't help, and in the end we trooped out of the ground frustrated.

As Kay and I reviewed the other scores back in the beer garden of the Coach & Horses, we discovered that out of the top seven-placed teams, only Port Vale, whom we were to face the following week, had won, so we had retained our early position in the automatic promotion places, for now at least.

Final Score
| **Leyton Orient** | **0** | **0** | **Mansfield Town** |

League Two table after close of play on 30th September 2021

Pos	Team	Pld	W	D	L	GF	GA	GD	Pts
1	Forest Green Rovers	9	6	2	1	18	8	10	20
2	**Leyton Orient**	**9**	**4**	**4**	**1**	**16**	**7**	**9**	**16**
3	Harrogate Town	9	4	4	1	15	11	4	16
4	Port Vale	9	4	3	2	10	6	4	15
5	Northampton Town	9	4	3	2	9	7	2	15
6	Exeter City	9	3	5	1	12	6	6	14
7	Hartlepool United	9	4	2	3	9	7	2	14
8	Crawley Town	9	4	2	3	12	13	-1	14
9	Swindon Town	9	3	4	2	9	7	2	13
10	Barrow	9	3	3	3	13	11	2	12
11	Bradford City	9	3	3	3	12	11	1	12
12	Rochdale	9	3	3	3	12	11	1	12
13	Tranmere Rovers	9	3	3	3	4	3	1	12
14	Sutton United	8	3	2	3	10	8	2	11
15	Newport	9	3	2	4	10	13	-3	11

Pos	Team	Pld	W	D	L	GF	GA	GD	Pts
	County								
16	Colchester United	8	2	4	2	7	7	0	10
17	Carlisle United	9	2	4	3	9	13	-4	10
18	Bristol Rovers	9	3	1	5	8	14	-6	10
19	Salford City	9	2	3	4	9	10	-1	9
20	Mansfield Town	9	2	3	4	10	14	-4	9
21	Stevenage	9	2	3	4	7	13	-6	9
22	Walsall	9	2	2	5	9	13	-4	8
23	Scunthorpe United	9	1	4	4	6	14	-8	7
24	Oldham Athletic	9	2	1	6	5	14	-9	7

Chapter 6: October 2021

The O's form starts to dip, as the goals dry up, but we merrily travel on...and also witness a bizarre ending to a first half and start of a second half as a referee seems to forget about time!

Heartbreak in the Potteries

Game 10: Saturday 2nd October 2021, Port Vale v Leyton Orient

With the O's unbeaten on their travels thus far and having faced teams in Salford, Carlisle, Newport and Bristol Rovers, who would have all been amongst those favoured for promotion, the trip to Vale Park was to pose the biggest challenge so far in these early stages of the season. The hosts were sitting in 4th place but just a point behind us, so there was a general feeling amongst the travelling Orient support that even just a point from this trip would be a very good result indeed. For Kay and me, this trip, in a roundabout way, provided reinforcement of our decision to try to follow the O's home and away as much as possible for the entire league campaign.

Back in the days when it was possible for those not on the away season ticket scheme to get tickets for some of the less popular away matches, I had been to Stoke (or Mordor as we "wittily" used to refer to it given the unfriendliness of the local crowd, not helped in the slightest by some of the snobbish put-downs issued by Arsène Wenger towards Tony Pulis and his charges!) with Arsenal on a number of occasions.

Out of a total of six visits I had seen the Gunners avoid defeat just three times, all of those draws, and it got to the point where Kay consistently wondered if there was in fact something wrong with me (apart from the obvious of course!) as she simply couldn't get her head around why I kept going. As

Einstein famously said: "The definition of insanity is doing the same thing over and over again and expecting different results." Clearly he wasn't a football fan because that is precisely the mindset of anyone who is truly obsessed with going to matches, the absolute certain belief that it will be better next time...until it isn't.

Even though I couldn't promise her the full aggravation-fuelled experience of Stoke City v Arsenal, a trip to Port Vale, the other league club in the federation of six towns, definitely appealed, if nothing else so she could see if the place was really as bad as I had consistently described it.

With a much more leisurely departure time of 11:20 we, of course, had got our preparations so finely tuned now that we made sure we arrived at Euston more than an hour before we were scheduled to depart. If you have ever been to an English mainline train station on Saturday mornings between around 9 am and midday, you will most likely have noticed the groups of mainly men either drinking in the pub at such uncouth hours or milling round the concourse with a compulsory carrier bag bulging with cans of lager. This is how you spot a travelling football fan, should you ever require it for anthropological or social studies reasons.

Having planned ahead by adding a buttie (you can take the lad out of the north...) to my M&S provisions before we got on the train, I just checked again that Kay didn't want anything else by means of solid sustenance other than the packet of crisps that she had opted for. It was at this point that my previously super health-conscious wife made a pronouncement that shouldn't have been music to my ears, but it really was. Like some modern-day follower of the Church of Morgan Spurlock (yes, he of "Super Size Me" infamy!) she said that she was as of right now giving up any attempt to try to eat healthily on our awaydays. She was just going to see what was available wherever we were going. After 18 years together, all it took was four and a half awaydays to convert her into a junk food aficionado, worse still, a lower league football ground junk food one at that.

The hour and a half or so journey slipped by easily enough, and we arrived at Stoke with plenty of time to get up to the ground. With Stoke essentially being a grouping of six individual towns, it is actually quite spread out. Port Vale is rather confusingly in Burslem, and the recommended route is to either get a bus and change at Hanley (wherever that is!) to another bus or to jump into a taxi outside the station. Being uber-organised as I am, I had noted down the details of the buses we needed, but when we asked one of the people working at the station, he recommended as we had some spare time we might as well go for a drink at the new (well it certainly wasn't there when I have been before!) Titanic Brewery Bod bar which is part of the station. Who were we to disagree?

After sampling some of Titanic Brewery's finest offerings, it took less than 10 minutes up to Vale Park in a cab, although we did suspect that it might not be so straightforward getting back. Upon arrival it was time for stage one of Kay's new football ground diet, as she treated herself to a cheeseburger from a van outside the away end. It was one of those burgers that would have been sent back in any self-respecting restaurant, but that strangely seem almost appealing at a football ground. So much is her dedication to her new diet that when I asked her for a taste I was greeted with a look of disdain and offered a begrudging bite.

The ground itself is a traditional-looking football ground, and with a capacity of 20,500-plus it is bigger than most of the ones around the lower leagues. It is another one of those grounds that looks like different bits have been added as time and finances have permitted. Upon taking up our seats, I was pleased to reconfirm that our section was not only behind the goal but also that it had a roof, as the weather was rather more wet than it had been in Newport and Bristol. With space potentially available for up to 4,500 visiting fans, the 356 of us who had made the journey did feel as if we were rattling round the place a bit. Mind you, the other three stands accommodating the home support were struggling to be half full at best.

The biggest shock in terms of team news was that Tom James was down to start at right wing-back, with it having been reported in the week that he was suspended after his fifth yellow card of the season against Mansfield. Allegedly he had escaped due to an administrative error upon the submission of the match report.

Early goals have a nasty habit of knocking the stuffing out of a team, and so it was for us in this one when James Wilson nodded the Valiants in front after just six minutes. After that, Orient struggled to really get into the game for the rest of the first half. The home side were largely in control, and we struggled for creativity or to forge out any real chances. So stagnant was it that Kay treated herself to a brief power nap in her seat, which she assured me was nothing to do with the beer and food she had consumed, while the rest of us tried our best to raise the spirits of the boys on the pitch.

Presumably there were some choice words said at halftime (striker Harry Smith suggested as much when being interviewed at half-time in the Crawley game the following Tuesday), but Orient looked much more on their game in the second period.

On the hour mark we pulled ourselves back onto level terms. Paul Smyth, on as a sub for his first appearance since Salford away back in August, slid Aaron Drinan through the inside right channel, and Drinan pulled the ball back across goal where it was turned home for an own goal by Port Vale's Dan Jones. If things had been subdued in the away end in the first half, now it was going mental. Kay was definitely no longer asleep, and she was in fact standing on her seat cheering like mad.

From there the game was very much in the balance until with just four of the 90 minutes remaining James won the ball about 25 yards out from Vale's goal, dribbled forward and let fly, his effort beating the keeper's reach and skidding low into the bottom left-hand corner. Cue pandemonium in the away end mixed with a real sense of relief.

Unfortunately, what happened next felt very much like a kick in the teeth. As we entered added time, Orient managed to concede two sloppy goals and chuck all three points away. There is no disgrace in being beaten by a team who before kick-off were only a point behind us in the league and who were likely to be in the promotion mix come the end of the season, but to throw it away after seemingly having a hard-fought away win in the bag was very hard to take.

As we suspected, we had no joy in calling a cab from the ground but had enough time to retire to the Old Post Office, complete with upside down clock to really confuse drinkers, and give it half an hour or so before trying again. The pub was filled with a mix of home and away fans without a hint of trouble, although we did hear about the despicable racial insults directed towards Orient goalkeeper Lawrence Vigouroux on social media, something that personally I can't get my head around. Yes, support your team and have banter with the opposing fans and players, but this shouldn't even be part of football support.

After some friendly locals advised us we were better off getting the bus, we decided that was our best option, even though the missus had a taxi on order. Even having to change buses was easy enough once we realised that "bus stop B" actually meant "bus stop V" in the local dialect, and we were back in plenty of time for another pint or two in the station pub.

As we boarded the train back to London, we got talking to some fellow travelling O's -- Paul, Harry Kane (not that one, although he did look a bit like him, at least to Kay!) and Phil Bailey (no, not that one, although that really is his name, even if the Kay took some convincing that the artist who collaborated with Phil Collins on the famous record wasn't in fact a white gentleman with grey hair from Essex!) -- and decided that the best way to pass the time on the way back to London was to have a few beers and treat the carriage to a collection of Orient songs and, of course, "Easy Lover". We are sure our drunken warbling was very much appreciated by our fellow passengers, especially the day-tripper Manchester United "fans" on their way home to Surrey. Of course, the only way to round off another cracking awayday, despite the result, was for the five of us to have a pint in the Signal Box pub back at Euston.

Final Score

Port Vale	**3**	**2**	**Leyton Orient**
Wilson 6			Jones (OG) 60
Politic 90+1			James 86
Proctor 90+3			

An evening with Dulcet Dave and Matt

Papa John's EFL Trophy: Tuesday 5th of October 2021, Crawley Town v Leyton Orient

Given our commitment to trying to go to as many league games home and away as possible, alongside the earlier kick-off time of 7 pm, Kay and I decided that we didn't need to go to this one and instead settled for watching it on the Orient Live stream in the company of Dulcet Dave Victor and Matt Hiscock, with whom we had spent all (bar the two matches we were allowed to attend) of the 2020/21 campaign. For those of you who haven't had the pleasure of listening to Dulcet in action, you don't know what you have been missing. There is no doubting his enthusiasm and his extensive knowledge of both Orient and lower league football, but he does have a tendency to drift off on various tangents, whether they are relevant or not, and relatively frequently drops the odd clanger (my humble apologies Dave, if you are reading this, your commentaries really are fantastic entertainment!).

His co-commentator/summariser Matt's role seems as much about pulling Dave back on track and correcting his factual errors, as well as analysing what's happening on the pitch. In keeping with the spirit of real football, it is miles away from the ultra-slick presentation of Sky or BT, as the picture quality is somewhat iffy, mostly being filmed from a single camera, but its magic is its quirky but genuine style. See below for some of Dulcet's highlights from the previous season:

Dulcet Dave Victor's Most Memorable Orient TV Moments 2020/21

1) While commentating on the O's trip to Carlisle in March, he referenced the 1-1 draw in the corresponding fixture at Brisbane Road much to everyone's surprise, as that game actually hadn't taken place at that point, prompting Matt to enquire whether it had been a good game and who had scored for Orient?

2) Referring to Orient's opposition on a number of occasions as Tranmere Rovers when in fact we were actually playing Forest Green Rovers.

3) After a couple of early season airings, steadfastly and

skilfully avoiding referring to any throw-in by former right back Sam Ling as "A Ling Long Throw".

4) Consistently confusing left back Joe Widdowson with forward Conor Wilkinson to give us two new players: Joe Wilkinson and Conor Widdowson. If you have a look at the squad picture from the season, you will see how difficult that is.

5) Due to technical issues, having to phone in his regular updates to BBC Radio London for one match on his mobile at the back of the commentary box while Matt took over the lead commentary role.

6) Giving us the ins and outs of how much gaffer tape he had to use to ensure that his microphone cable stayed plugged in and then invariably having it drop out periodically at Stevenage.

7) Responding to a Tweet received of someone's dog watching the game by suggesting it could be tagged #Orientdogs, only to then be inundated with pictures of dogs watching the game.

8) Being forced to wear a facemask at Morecambe even while doing the commentary, so not only did he sound a bit muffled but his glasses kept steaming up so he couldn't see what was going on for periods of the game.

9) In the same evening at Morecambe letting us all know that his glasses steaming up hadn't been his only issue with his spectacles that day, as apparently he had gone to brush his teeth that morning without them on only to mistake a tube of some form of medicinal cream for the toothpaste.

10) Keeping us constantly updated with Len from Leyton's difficulties with his water supply meaning he couldn't make a

cup of tea; we were all mightily relieved when Dave informed us that Len had given up and was having a beer instead.

As for the match itself, with a much-changed team, the O's made swift work of a similarly altered Crawley Town line-up helped in no small way by an early goal from Ruel Sotiriou. Orient then went on to make it four in total and put themselves second in the group but level on points with leaders Charlton from League One ahead of the final group game against the men from south of the river. That fixture was to be played at Brisbane Road, but of course Dulcet had us all believing it was at the Valley, Charlton's home, before Matt could put him right.

Final Score

Crawley Town	**0**	**4**	**Leyton Orient**
			Sotiriou 7, 59
			Happe 30
			Kemp 77

No beer 'til Barrow

Game 11: Saturday 9th October 2021, Barrow AFC v Leyton Orient

So we were off on our travels for the second week in succession, this time all the way back to Cumbria for our second visit of the season. Once again, we ummed and aahed about whether to stay over, but in the end we decided on another full day adventure. Given it was another early start, we decided that we were going to be good and not have any beer until our arrival in Barrow scheduled for 12 noon. So it was that anyone lurking around Euston at 8 am that morning would have seen the highly unusual sight of Kay and I holding coffees rather than the usual carrier bags of beer and crisps.

As Barrow-in-Furness, to give it its full title, is located in the southwestern corner of Cumbria, you have to change trains at Lancaster when coming from the south and then catch a local train through to Barrow. The second stage of the journey in particular is very picturesque, as it takes you through some of the Lake District itself, with one village in particular, Arnside, on the estuary of the River Kent which forms part of Morecambe Bay, looking like an ideal spot for a couple of days staycation (the new normal eh?) with an intriguing looking fish and chip shop and a local pub.

It takes around an hour to get from Lancaster to Barrow, and upon our arrival we set about finding our bearings, which didn't take long. Holker Street is a 15-minute stroll up the road after which it is named, but more importantly, given our restraint on the journey up, the rather excellent Duke of Edinburgh hotel is a mere two pedestrian crossings away from the station and has an award-winning pub attached to it. A mere matter of minutes after arriving in the town, we were installed at a table with two pints of the highly quaffable local Lancaster Brewery's blonde ale in front of us. We had a perusal of the food options, which we ruled out based on the fact that every plate we saw come out the kitchen was absolutely massive-- they certainly feed 'em in Cumbria. Kay was also of course sticking steadfastly to her newly affirmed dedication to football ground food, meaning that she was saving herself for a pie at the stadium.

By now the pub had filled up with quite a few more Orient fans who had taken the later train or driven, as well as some locals, but the atmosphere was friendly. As it was harder to get served at the bar with more people in, we decided this was the opportune time to make our way up to the ground. It had been drizzly ever since we arrived (what did we expect, this was the very definition of North Western England?), but the stroll wasn't unpleasant, and we arrived in plenty of time for the pie and pint deal that Kay had been craving ever since we set off. At £6 each, it was certainly a bargain.

Barrow were promoted back to the Football League in March 2020 for the first time since 1972 on a points per game basis after being top of the National League when the pandemic brought football to a halt. As a result of being in non-league for all that time, their ground in its current set-up offers a throwback memory to when the O's were in the fifth tier. With relatively recent refurbishment and improvement having been undertaken, it combines the old traditional feel of a non-league ground with a slightly modern finish.

One of the key "improvements" was the installation of a roof above the Holker Street end which is shared by both home and away fans due to a prefab block containing the club's offices and a bar behind the other goal. Despite it being a recent addition, the roof has several annoyingly positioned supporting pillars and the view from the away terrace (tucked next to the weirdest and narrowest stand I have ever seen) is further obstructed by a Perspex screen presumably to protect us from the local youth wannabe hoodlums who seemed to be out in force on the home side. On one touchline is a partially covered terrace and the other a small main stand. The most striking feature of the ground is that every available surface has been painted blue and white, leaving visitors in no doubt whatsoever of the home team's colours.

After two games without a win and especially the tough-to-take defeat at Port Vale, the feeling amongst the travelling support still seemed positive and hopeful that this would be an opportunity to get back on track and to start to rebuild the momentum. With the Bluebirds having won their previous two and sitting just a point behind us going into the game, there were no guarantees, of course.

The only changes to the line-up from Port Vale were the return of Alex Mitchell, the 19-year-old Millwall loanee, who had in quick time established himself as a first choice at the back, to replace Dan Happe and tenacious midfielder Craig Clay being asked to fill in at right wing-back for the now-definitely-suspended Tom James.

The early pressure came from Barrow, which with us being so close to the goal they were attacking made me feel even more jumpy every time the ball came into the box. Seeing live football very close up always tends to make it seem more intense and frantic than if you are further away.

The O's survived the early skirmishes in our goalmouth, but a couple of blocked shots was all we could muster in response. As the half wore on, Barrow forward Josh Gordon seemed to conclude that the best way of fashioning an opening was to throw himself to the ground every time an Orient player came near; whether there was any contact on him seemed to be an unimportant consideration. You can imagine the response it drew from the Orient fans, yours truly most definitely included. Gamesmanship is inescapably part of the modern game, even in League Two, and while we have to live with it, it doesn't mean we have to tolerate it without protest when it happens. Right at the end of the half Theo Archibald's stinging drive from a Harry Smith flick on forced an excellent save from Paul Farman in their goal, but it finished goalless at the break.

Just three minutes into the second half Robbie Gotts broke through their inside right channel, latching onto a cute through-ball and rifled it past Lawrence Vigouroux to give the home side the lead. Conceding a goal away from home is always tough to take, especially as you watch the other three sides of the ground celebrate, but the fact that it was so early in the second period at least gave us hope that we might get back into it.

Manager Kenny Jackett's response was immediate, as he sent on Ruel Sotiriou, fresh from his two goals on Tuesday evening, in place of Aaron Drinan to try to offer something different going forward. Whether it was a case of Barrow easing off or Orient seizing the impetus, all the action was at our end, the goal Orient were attacking. Archibald couldn't get onto a pass from Sotiriou and was then denied by another save from Farman. By means of a warning and a chilling reminder of the previous week, Patrick Brough rattled our crossbar after a swift counterattack.

Then with just over 20 minutes to go, we won a corner out on the left, Archibald flighted it in, and Sotiriou nodded it goalward where defender Omar Beckles was there to stretch out a long leg to poke it home. The celebrations were as much in relief as joy. Both teams had a chance to win it late on, but in the end another away draw felt like a fair result.

With a good hour until our train home, Kay and I had plenty of time for another pint of the excellent blonde beer back at the Duke of Edinburgh and then to stock up on supplies for the train from the handily placed Tesco Express across the road from the pub. Honestly it was almost as if the local council had planned the place perfectly for travelling football fans.

On the train back to Lancaster, we got talking to a Manchester City fan, Paul, one of the genuine ones who has supported them through thick and thin and the Third Division, who, at a loose end due to the international break, decided that an hour and a half trip to watch Barrow take on Orient in the fourth tier was the perfect way to fill an empty Saturday afternoon. We football obsessives are a strange bunch!

We briefly flirted with the idea of going to the pub at Lancaster to kill time in our 30-minute changeover and even got as far as the door, but common sense (not something we often display!)

prevailed and we headed back to the station. Once on the train to London, I caught up with events at Old Trafford in the Super League Grand Final where St Helens (my hometown rugby league team) beat Catalans Dragons (Kay's adopted team) which made the journey more tolerable (for one of us at least!) despite the horrible smell emanating from the loos and the overly long route taken on a Saturday evening. It really is hard to imagine how any train company could be worse than Virgin were, but Avanti seem to have cracked it by simply taking over where Virgin left off but actually making the facilities worse, quite an achievement!

Final Score

| **Barrow AFC** | 1 | 1 | **Leyton Orient** |
| Gotts 48 | | | Beckles 69 |

Back to home comforts

Game 12: Saturday 16th October 2021, Leyton Orient v Walsall

After not having played at home since the end of the previous month against Mansfield, it was good to know that we only had to travel to Leyton for this one, although Kay was slightly upset that we weren't heading off on one of our far-flung adventures, as she had now, by her own admission, become completely addicted to awaydays. We had a couple of beers at home before setting off in a vain attempt to let the rain showers ease, but it did mean that when we arrived, all three of the wine bar, Coach & Horses and Supporters Club were busier than when we usually arrive, so after popping into all of them we decided our best option was to head into the ground for our usual pie and pint.

With Orient having not won in their last three league games we decided that drastic action was called for and that we would try to snap the skid, as they say across the pond, by opting for chicken balti pies instead of our usual steak and kidney. Quite how we felt our choice of pre-match cuisine would have any impact whatsoever on the result is beyond me, but this is how the minds of football obsessives work. Sadly, our new option was quite sweet, and we concluded that whatever the result, it was back to our go-to-choice for the visit of Forest Green on Tuesday evening.

As we went up the stairs to our seats, we were slightly taken aback by the sight of two of our mates, Mark and Kevin, who we have known ever since our Orient journey started at the end of the 2016/2017 season when Orient were relegated out of the Football League, with a toddler sitting between them. They had decided that this was the right time for Kevin's lad to take in his first O's game. It did, however, mean that Grandad Mark, usually one to vehemently offer the linesman in front of us the benefit of his advice through the match, was going to be on his best behaviour for this one.

Tom James returned from his suspension in place of Craig Clay at right wing-back, while Ruel Sotiriou replaced Aaron Drinan in the front line, presumably to spark our attack back into some kind of life after all three of Drinan, Harry Smith and Theo Archibald had drawn blanks since Bristol Rovers away. Meanwhile former Orient forward Conor Wilkinson was on the bench for the visitors, giving me a very nervy feeling that he would inevitably come on and score.

After the success of Mansfield in stopping us playing in the last home game, it was always likely that a team sitting in 19th place in the table going into the game were going to try to follow suit and attempt to blunt our threat. As such, right from the off it looked set to be another scruffy stop-start game. If three weeks

113

previously the referee had arguably been too weak in stamping out Mansfield's shirt-pulling and niggling tactics, Mr Yates in this one seemed only too pleased to award free kicks to Walsall for minimal infringements, but not overly keen to award even the most obvious ones to Orient. It made for a scrappy game, one more to be endured than enjoyed.

The only real points to note in the first half from an Orient perspective were a relatively tame shot from James, a spectacular overhead kick from Smith that dipped just over the bar and an effort from Archibald from range that swerved wide. Other than that, our forwards were feeding off scraps as we seemed to want to lump it forward towards Smith and hope for the best.

In an effort to change things, Jackett made two changes at the break: Paul Smyth, back from international duty with Northern Ireland, replaced the bullied-out-of-it Sotiriou, and Clay replaced left back Connor Wood but was given the remit of adding bite in the midfield as we altered the system. There was a bit more life about our play, but once again we struggled creatively. After a promising start to the season the goals seemed to have dried up lately from our forwards.

For Walsall, Wilkinson came on just past the hour mark and had a couple of sights of goal, but thankfully Lawrence Vigouroux saved the first, and the second was a header he couldn't turn goalward, prompting the East Stand cognoscenti to concur that he had always been shit!

The game drifted towards an inevitable seeming 0-0 for the second home game in a row and a fourth game without a win. With the leaders Forest Green in town in three days' time we could only hope that we would be able to find some attacking flair again, and very soon.

After the match, Kay and I had our usual post-match briefing in the beer garden of the Coach & Horses, as well as a gang of unruly kids whose fathers seemed to think the best approach to parenting was to let them annoy everyone else in the garden while they enjoyed their pints. We met up with some of the guys we had been standing with at Port Vale, and it wasn't long before the awayday songs were given an airing which scattered the dads and lads group and lifted our spirits once again.

Final Score
Leyton Orient   0   0   **Walsall**

That's a bit more like it!

Game 13: Tuesday 19th October 2021, Leyton Orient v Forest Green Rovers

Football is a strange game. On the back of four games without a win in which the early momentum that Orient had built up had been largely stifled, probably the last thing you want to happen is for the league leaders to come to town just three days after you have been held goalless by a team lower down the table. However, such is the nature of the game that we all love, that a positive result can restart a team's form and in actual fact could be just the sort of fixture required to snap the malaise.

Despite both working from home still, we decided to have a few pre-match beers indoors, (as we say in the East End guv!) in order to let the increasingly almost as busy as they used to be rush hour crowds die down on the Tube. Even though most of the offices are still empty at Canary Wharf the footfall of people passing though from 5 pm on a weekday was approaching the way that it used to be before the pandemic. This was a decision that we nearly came to regret.

Leaving our house at 6:30 pm, a whole hour and 15 minutes before kick-off, you would think would normally be ample time to make the relatively short trip to Leyton, a journey that normally takes about 35 minutes. However, we hadn't reckoned on Transport for London having one of its highly inefficient days. The initial alarm bells started to go off when we arrived on the platform at our local Docklands Light Railway station to find that the next train was due in seven (yes seven! For any fellow Londoners!) minutes. This may seem like a perfectly reasonable waiting time for anyone who lives outside of the capital, but for those of us with bitter experience, the fact that it wasn't the usual two or three minutes and the train after was due just a minute later suggested there were delays. Already the football obsessive in me was flapping about missing kick-off, even if we did still have an hour to play with.

As we were finally underway to Canary Wharf, we weighed up whether we were better off changing to the Stratford branch of the DLR or heading for the Jubilee Line instead. In the end we plumped for the Underground option as it is usually quicker. Sure enough, we didn't have long to wait for the train, but it was terminating at West Ham where we would have to change trains again. By now, yours truly was a nervous (and highly irritable!) wreck, fretting that we wouldn't make it for kick-off and somehow I would be outed as some kind of fraud: a self-avowed football obsessive who showed his "true colours" by missing the start of a match.

When we arrived at Leyton, with 25 minutes to spare I hasten to add, I didn't so much ask as declare that next time I would be deciding what time we would be leaving, even if we ended up with two hours to kill when we arrived. Kay, used to my neurotic tendencies especially with regard to football, gave me the kind of nod and sarcastic smile that suggested, I might like to think that, but we all know who is really in charge in our household.

Once safely inside our East Stand home, we even had time for a pie each and to share a pint. After the jinx effect of Saturday, it was of course back to the faithful steak and kidney option, which freshly out of the oven were mouth-burning hot. Like McDonald's apple pies, it is amazing how football grounds can serve up food that is just about warmish on the outside but like molten lava on the inside.

Just as we were taking up our seats after saying a quick hello to Mark and Kevin, who were without-toddler this time so free to "guide" the officials once again, someone asked us if we wouldn't mind moving along the row so he could sit next to his mates, none of whom we had ever seen in our four years of sitting in the same place. Perhaps we could have obliged him, but the very fact of being a season ticket holder invokes a certain kind of hierarchical etiquette. The unwritten but understood by football spectators rule is that as season ticket holders, we choose to sit in the same place often for a number of reasons like tradition, wanting to be near our mates or because we like the view. It is therefore a complete and utter faux pas to either sit in a season ticket holder's seat or to ask them to move. In any case, our seats have our names on in rather large letters.

The fact that during the course of the match our new mate and his associates spent most of it on their phones checking the Champions League scores or going up and down to get snacks gave us even more of the moral one upmanship. Before you judge us, remember this is what football obsessives are like. Can you imagine if we had jinxed it and the O's had lost. We couldn't have lived with the shame!

Back to matters on the field though, and as well as not having won in the league since Bristol Rovers away and with the goals having seemingly dried up from our attacking players, Kenny Jackett decided that our attacking formation needed tweaking. With the use of Theo Archibald behind a front two not really having worked against Walsall, this time it was Dan Kemp, a much more traditional number 10, who started behind the front pair of Harry Smith and the returning from injury Paul Smyth. Such is the difference in height between the two strikers that there really should have been a joke about Big-Smith and Diddy-Smyth.

Whether it was the adjusted line-up, which did seem to offer more creativity going forward thanks to Smyth's pace pushing the defensive line back and Kemp's skills better suited to linking the midfield and attack, or the fact that Forest Green as an in-form team were looking to take us on and beat us rather than stifling our play, this was a much more enjoyable match than those served up in the preceding weeks.

As improved as the performance was, it came as something of a sucker-punch when Forest Green opened the scoring just past the hour mark. The goal came from a corner which the whole of the North Stand behind that goal suggested had quite clearly come off a Forest Green player and should have been a goal-kick. It was impossible to tell conclusively from where we were sitting but given the standard of refereeing we had seen so far this season, we had to take our fellow fans on trust here.

However just as we were starting to fear the worst and a third defeat of the season, the O's suddenly seemed to remember the slick flowing football that they seemed more than capable of producing just a few weeks previously. A swift counterattack from a cleared corner saw Kemp slide Ruel Sotiriou, on as a sub for the fatigued Smyth, through the inside right channel, and he rifled the ball across goal and in for 1-1.

The relief around the ground was tangible, both at having restored parity and that one of our forwards had actually scored again; even the Johnny-come-latelys along the row took time out from Liverpool v Atletico Madrid on their phones. They may have even raised a cheer.

In the end though, neither side could find a further breakthrough, and in fairness a share of the spoils was a more than fair outcome between two decently matched sides. As down as we all felt after the previous Saturday's draw, this felt better, a step in the right direction if you like.

Final Score

Leyton Orient	1	1	**Forest Green Rovers**
Sotiriou 76			Stevens 68

More frustration for the O's

Game 14: Saturday 23rd October 2021, Stevenage v Leyton Orient

This was a little bit of a strange one for Kay and me, as we had actually been to Stevenage to watch Orient before, back at the beginning of February 2020, before the pandemic hit and changed life as we knew it, and also because it is just over 30 miles away from London, or 21 minutes if you get the most direct train. Back in those days, we used to enjoy the odd awayday with Orient when we could but had a strict only an hour away from London rule. Clearly our full Orient addiction hadn't completely taken us over in those days.

Nowadays, having enjoyed some of the longer trips and already looking forward to the others, we were actually disappointed that the journey was so short, as it didn't feel like a proper trip. Arriving in Stevenage just before 1 pm there was only one thing to do, and we headed over to the Old Post Office just across the dual carriageway, which is a pub that isn't a Wetherspoons but has prices of roughly the same range and also shows live football on TV. There did, in fact, used to be a Wetherspoons next door but that has now closed, another victim of the pandemic, one assumes, or possibly in the battle of the bargain boozers, the one that shows the football was always going to win.

As we queued up at the very busy Halloween-decorated bar, Kay spotted an old friend/awayday associate of ours, Dave, whom we had first encountered on the way to Maidenhead in our very first Orient awayday, back in the National League days three years previously when Kay had tried to convince him on the train that he wanted to swap his Big Mac meal for a couple of cans of lager. He quite sensibly declined our generous offer, but we have tended to bump into him everywhere we have been, apart from this season. As it turned out, his work means that he has hardly been able to go to many home games, let alone any away ones this campaign.

After a bit of a catch up, we bid farewell to Dave hoping to catch him again on our future travels and headed up to the ground. After a longer than necessary search for the right bus stop which involved asking an actual bus driver who didn't seem to have any idea, and then asking the driver of the actual bus we needed, who reassuringly did know, we completed the very short journey. Armed with the knowledge from our previous visit that they don't sell beer in the away end (or in actual fact in any part of the ground as far as we could decipher!), obviously just like Bristol Rovers a clear infringement of our human rights, we headed into the clubhouse bar, the Broadhall Suite, which even at that early enough time was filled with a nice mix of home and visiting fans.

After a chat with some fellow travelling fans and catching the end of Chelsea's 7-0 destruction of hapless Norwich City, which we had been watching earlier back in town, we decided to head inside in search of more solid sustenance. A bit like Salford, this is another ground were the facilities outside of the stands haven't developed at the same pace as the ground itself.

However, even with in excess of 1,300 O's fans in attendance, the queue for the small refreshment stand wasn't too long and we got our "lunch": a pie for Kay, of course, as a newly avowed traditionalist, whereas I opted for a cheeseburger -- not the best thing I have ever eaten, but strangely enjoyable, nonetheless. And we still had plenty of time to take up our seats.

Stevenage unlike most (all?) lower league grounds insist that you take up your allocated seat and remain sitting in it for the duration of the game. That, combined with a travelling support three times as large as usual with many infrequent travelling O's followers, made for something of a more subdued atmosphere in the away end.

After making a real difference to our attacking play in the midweek draw against Forest Green, Dan Kemp kept his place in the starting line-up, but rather frustratingly, Paul Smyth, who had also played a key role in improving our effectiveness up front, was ruled out by another hamstring injury. Tuesday night's goal scorer, Ruel Sotiriou, was given the nod in his absence. Theo Archibald continued at left wing-back where he had played the last half an hour against Forest Green.

From the opening minutes, it soon became very clear that this was going to be another game where the lower in the table opposition sat deep and challenged us to break them down. Annoyingly the space to play wasn't there as it had been against Forest Green, and the O's reverted to aiming long balls in the direction of Harry Smith, who was too isolated and even when he did win the ball was lacking support.

As a result, it wasn't much of a spectacle, as Orient seemed to get up the field well enough, but once again the creativity and the ability to carve out real chances just wasn't there. Harry Smith forced their debutant keeper, namesake Adam Smith, whose signing had been announced just prior to kick-off, to tip a header over the bar and Tom James had an effort blocked just before the goal-line, but that was about all we mustered by means of a threat in the opening 45 minutes. Lawrence Vigouroux had to be alert to block a shot from Stevenage's main attacking threat Elliot List.

The second half started with List forcing another good save from Vigouroux but then settled into the familiar pattern from the opening period with little in the way of goalmouth action, or indeed very much action at all.

Smith had another effort saved 20 minutes from time and then we were denied a penalty when Sotiriou was bundled over in the box. According to Kenny Jackett in his post-match interview, the referee had told him that while there was contact there hadn't been enough. I have to say that is a new one on me, and I have endured the interesting VAR interpretations in the Premier League in recent seasons.

That made it six games without a win for the O's, and there was real frustration that we had managed just four goals in that run and dropped 12 points. The fact that we were still in 9th place, just four points off the automatic promotion places was some consolation, but there was a real feeling amongst the Orient faithful that we needed to get back to winning ways, and soon, or risk creating too big a gap between us and the leaders.

After deciding that it would be quicker to walk the 20 minutes back into town rather than wait for the bus, Kay and I still had time to stop by Greggs (a bit like special forces operatives, awayday fans are trained to eat whenever they can while "in country"!) for a sausage roll each and to grab a quick pint back in the Old Post Office before catching the train.

As we waited in what we guessed was the right spot for our reserved seats, we were shocked to find that the train was absolutely packed with Queens Park Rangers fans on their way back from Peterborough they had apparently taken 4,000 with them. As trying to even find our seats, let alone convince whoever was in them to vacate them, was looking like a complete lost cause, we decided to have a chat with some of them. We covered the usual football-related pleasantries, but once we got onto the subject of Joey Barton (please refer back to Game No. 8 in September if you need a reminder) one of their number, whether as a deliberate attempt to be controversial or not, suggested that he thought Barton was both an excellent player and misunderstood. Sorry, mate, let's agree to disagree on that one!

When we arrived back at Kings Cross, the QPR fans treated anyone around to some songs making it clear exactly who they were, although they were soon greeted by a group of Newcastle fans on their way back from Crystal Palace. Another clear indication of the unspoken bond between travelling football fans, no matter who we support.

Final Score

Stevenage	**0**	**0**	**Leyton Orient**

The referee didn't know what he was doing...but the Orient certainly did!

Game 15: Saturday 30th October 2021, Leyton Orient v Hartlepool

Heading into this match, the disappointment and frustration from the goalless draw at Stevenage and the extension of

Orient's winless run was starting to raise some questions among the O's support, specifically about our prospects for the season and whether we were right to harbour, albeit still guardedly, promotion aspirations. It wasn't so much the case that we were starting to doubt Kenny Jackett or the players, just that after starting the season pretty brightly, Harrogate Town at home aside of course, and picking up 15 of the first 24 points, the recent run of just four points, and more alarmingly scoring just two goals, in the last six games had started to make us worry that we weren't as good as we had hoped.

The Port Vale capitulation at the start of this spell, in which we managed to throw away three points despite going into added time leading 2-1, seemed to have really knocked the squad's confidence, and while still being relatively solid at the back, we seemed overly cautious in our attacking play. Presumably for fear of leaving ourselves too exposed to counterattacks.

Newly promoted Hartlepool, for their part, had enjoyed an impressive start to life back in the Football League after being promoted from the National League via the play-offs. Three wins in their last four matches had seen them climb to 8th place in the table, three points ahead of Orient. This felt like a must-not-lose game for the O's, as with a group of nine teams from 4th place to 12th separated by just three points (Orient and Hartlepool being very much in that grouping), allowing teams to get away from us could prove to be fatal to hopes of an autumn resurgence.

With Arsenal once again having been handed the 12:30 Saturday kick-off slot, it was an early start for Kay and me again as we headed over to Leyton; the only decision needed was where we going to watch the Gunners' trip to Leicester. Because we couldn't make our minds up between the Coach & Horses, Supporters Club and the Leyton Star, we hadn't reserved a table at either of the pubs, and with it being the

"Football for a Fiver" promotion, where all tickets cost £5 to encourage larger attendances, we reckoned the Supporters Club would be packed.

At the very last minute, literally as we were walking up the steps at Leyton Underground station, we opted for the Star based on the logic that it was further away from the ground and less well-known than the Coach. Thankfully we arrived just as the doors were opening and managed to secure one of the two tables that hadn't been booked. (Note to self: next time make up your mind and book a table!).

With it being the day before Halloween, the bar staff were all dressed up ready for the party that evening, which it has to be said made for quite a surreal sight to see a pub full of football fans being served by a selection of ghouls, zombies and other sinister characters (no jokes about how we should be used to it given we have been to Stoke/Port Vale on our travels already this season please!).

Reasoning that the larger crowd at the ground might make it difficult to secure our customary pies and pints before the match, we treated ourselves to some truffle fries (I know, I know, all very civilised and hipster for us!) and enjoyed watching Arsenal, now seemingly recovered from their poor start to the season, win 2-0. When we made our way down and into the ground, the crowd didn't seem anywhere near as large as we had expected and there was only a shortish queue at the bar. Happy Days!

As we headed up to our seats, once again Mark swore he was on his best behaviour with his grandson in attendance. With it being the last home league game before Remembrance Sunday, there was of course the traditional ceremony of poppy wreaths being placed in the centre circle by the captains, the playing of the last post and a minute's silence.

The traditions around remembering those fallen during the wars is even more important at Leyton Orient given that Clapton Orient, as they were then known, were the first English football club to sign up en masse (41 players, staff, club officials and supporters in total) to join the fighting in the First World War. Three players, Richard McFadden, William Jonas and George Scott, made the ultimate sacrifice. The club's O's Somme Memorial Fund Committee has raised money for two memorials: one on the Somme battlefield and the other unveiled just the previous weekend at the National Memorial Arboretum in Staffordshire. The memory remains an intrinsic part of supporting of this oh-so-special club.

With the tributes made, it was time for the action. In order to shuffle his deck and try to spark some life back into his charges, at least in an attacking sense, Jackett opted to bring in tenacious midfielder Craig Clay and also recalled Aaron Drinan to partner Harry Smith up front.

Almost from the kick-off, Orient looked like a team transformed. There was a life and energy around their pressing, with an intention to keep the ball on the deck and try to play football properly, and boy did it work. With 20 minutes gone, Smith laid a ball off that had actually come to his feet for the first time in weeks to Drinan, who rifled the ball into the bottom right-hand corner, and we were off and running.

Quarter of an hour later, Clay won the ball high up the pitch, and it ran to Drinan who set Smith up for his seventh goal of the season but his first since Bristol Rovers six matches previously. When the referee blew for half-time bang on the 45 minutes with no additional time played, no one in the ground thought anything of it.

Having as usual made her way down to the bar nice and early to beat the rush, Kay had bumped into Paul, the guy we had met along with Phil Bailey and the Harry Kane lookalike on the way back from Port Vale. Apparently, he was in the Papa John's dugout – a part of the ground in the northeastern corner where a paying group of up to eight sit and watch the match in an actual football dugout by the corner flag and have pizza delivered to them via a scooter which runs along the touchline in front of the East Stand at the break. Unfortunately, when I met up with Kay, an over-officious steward refused to let me pop along and say hello.

As we headed back to our seats, the teams emerged and then seemingly just started playing without a kick-off, more disconcerting still, Orient were still attacking the north end which they had been in the opening 45 minutes. As the referee and players carried on seemingly oblivious, it started to dawn on us what had happened.

Having forgotten to add on any injury time at the end of the first half and after a complaint by Hartlepool manager Dave Challinor, referee Alan Young (remember that if you do football quizzes!) had decided to add the time on at the start of the second half, play out the four minutes that were judged to be additional, blow-up for "half-time" and then have the players swap ends and kick-off the second half. If I hadn't seen it with my own eyes, I wouldn't have believed. In all my time watching football I had never ever seen anything like it.

Once the second half had actually officially got underway, Orient carried on in very much the same manner in which they had imposed themselves on the opposition in the first half. Just five minutes into the (actual) second period Theo Archibald, continuing at left wing-back, won the ball just inside their half, sparking another sweeping counterattack which saw six O's players driving towards the Hartlepool area. Drinan played it right for Tom James steaming up the right wing, and the

Welshman slotted it home first time for 3-0. #Jacketball seemed to be making a welcome return to E10.

Orient stayed in control for the remainder of the second half, and then less than 10 minutes from time Smith's aggressive pressing forced their goalkeeper Jonathan Mitchell to rush a clearance. The effort went straight to Drinan lurking in the inside left channel, and his looping curling effort over the helpless keeper was the best goal of the afternoon.

In added time, (this time Mr Young had remembered to add it on!), James' cross from the right picked out Smith in the area, and his header was parried by the keeper but fell to Drinan who bundled home his hat trick goal from close range. Brisbane Road was bouncing as the frustration of recent weeks was washed away by renewed optimism.

In the beer garden of the Coach & Horses after the match, we had what is now becoming our customary singsong and then got chatting to a group of lads who had started supporting Orient when former owner Barry Hearn offered free season tickets to teenagers and full-time students. As a few of them were students relatively near to London, they took them up and have continued to follow Orient ever since. One of their number, Tim, is so dedicated that he travels from Norwich for as many home and away games as he can possibly fit in. It flabbergasted us when we agreed to meet him not only at Rochdale but also in Scunthorpe for a Tuesday evening game towards the end of November. It was another humbling experience, one that reminded us that we are relatively new to being dedicated Orient supporters, but also provided reinforcement of the hold that this club can have over you. Similar to me, Tim was finding it less and less attractive to use his season ticket for Premier League Norwich City and much preferred watching Orient.

Final Score
Leyton Orient   **5**   **0**   **Hartlepool**
Drinan 20, 84, 90+6
Smith 35
James 56

League Two table after close of play on 31st October 2021

Pos	Team	Pld	W	D	L	GF	GA	GD	Pts
1	Forest Green Rovers	15	9	4	2	27	13	14	31
2	Port Vale	15	8	4	3	27	15	12	28
3	Northampton Town	15	8	3	4	20	11	9	27
4	Exeter City	15	6	8	1	25	15	10	26
5	Swindon Town	15	7	5	3	22	15	7	26
6	**Leyton Orient**	**15**	**5**	**8**	**2**	**25**	**12**	**13**	**23**
7	Harrogate Town	15	6	5	4	27	20	7	23
8	Newport County	15	6	5	4	25	18	7	23
9	Sutton United	15	7	2	6	23	18	5	23
10	Hartlepool United	15	7	2	6	17	20	-3	23
11	Tranmere Rovers	15	6	4	5	11	10	1	22
12	Bradford City	15	5	6	4	21	18	3	21
13	Rochdale	15	5	5	5	19	19	0	20
14	Walsall	15	5	5	5	19	19	0	20

Pos	Team	Pld	W	D	L	GF	GA	GD	Pts
15	Barrow	15	4	6	5	20	20	0	18
16	Bristol Rovers	15	5	3	7	17	23	-6	18
17	Colchester United	15	4	5	6	12	19	-7	17
18	Crawley Town	15	5	2	8	17	25	-8	17
19	Salford City	15	4	4	7	16	17	-1	16
20	Mansfield Town	15	3	5	7	14	20	-6	14
21	Stevenage	15	3	5	7	11	26	-15	14
22	Oldham Athletic	15	3	3	9	11	22	-11	12
23	Carlisle United	15	2	6	7	11	24	-13	12
24	Scunthorpe United	15	2	5	8	11	29	-18	11

Chapter 7: November 2021

The O's experience a bit of cup success and hold their own in the league, while we do a Tuesday trek to Scunthorpe, but the short trip to Northampton almost proves to be Kay's undoing!

Up for the Cup 2

FA Cup First Round: Saturday 6th November 2021, Leyton Orient v Ebbsfleet United

In the four years that Kay and I had been ardently following the O's, we had never seen them win an FA Cup game. In 2017 they were eliminated away at Gillingham, in 2018 we travelled to Maidstone to see them lose 2-0 in the Fourth Qualifying Round, in 2019 we fell victim to a giant-killing by Maldon & Tiptree then as now of the eighth tier, and in 2020 we could only watch on the live stream as we went down 2-1 to Newport County when fans were locked out of football. Worse still, we had been at the Valley in 2006 to watch Orient lose to Charlton Athletic, and I had been at Arsenal (albeit in my season ticket seat) to watch them go down 5-0 in a replay after a holding the Gunners to a draw with a stunning late equalizer from Jonathan Tehoue in the initial tie. To say we were overdue the chance to witness Orient have success in the oldest cup competition in the world would be something of an understatement.

A lot of the talk in the week had centred on Chief Executive Danny Macklin's decision to only open the West Stand for season ticket holders and to then allocate the East (the stand where Kay and I sit, of course) to what was anticipated to be a sizeable contingent from Ebbsfleet. It is a decision that makes complete sense from a business perspective given the cost savings in terms of stewarding, catering etc. but it irked a number of supporters who were unable to purchase their own allocated seats for the match. More on that one later.

With no early kick-off watching commitments we were able to make our way leisurely over to Leyton pausing briefly at the wine bar. While we were in there, we got talking to some lads from Kent who were obviously here to follow Ebbsfleet but were desperate to find a pub to watch the Manchester derby on TV. I showed huge restraint in resisting the obvious joke about how they must be Man United fans hailing from Kent. While the other three headed off to the Leyton Technical having received reports that the match was on in there, one of their number,

Andy, stayed to have a chat with us. It turned out that he was a Tottenham fan and former referee who had been offered a season ticket in Spurs' recently opened plush new ground, but the time required to travel there and back, the general expense and an increasing disillusionment with the Premier League meant he dedicated more and more of his time to watching Ebbsfleet -- another kindred spirit.

Ebbsfleet United's, or the Fleet's, to give them their colloquial name, recent history is something of a strange one and provides an insight into the way the relationship between football club, supporters and the wider scale spectator market has changed over the last decade and half or so and may continue to do so in the future.

From their birth in 1946 when they were known as Gravesend & Northfleet, they operated pretty much like any other non-league club. The biggest name in their history was a certain Roy Hodgson who made 59 appearances as a player between 1969 and 1971 before going on to forge a notable career in management in Scandinavian club football, on the international stage and eventually in Serie A and the Premier League, before becoming England manager in 2012.

Things were to change drastically in November 2007 when it was announced that website MyFootballClub (MyFC) had entered into a deal in principle to take over the club with the suggestion that members who signed up to the website would have the opportunity to vote on decisions affecting the club in the future. There may, however, have been some exaggeration of the how much involvement these members would have in major decisions like transfers and picking the starting eleven.

Amazingly despite their new structure and approach, the newly named Ebbsfleet United won the FA Trophy at the end of that season. It almost seemed too good to be true, and, in fact, it may well have been. From a peak of 32,000 paying members at the time of the takeover, non-renewals saw that number fall to just 3,500 in September 2010. With financial problems mounting, in April 2013 the MyFC members that remained voted in favour of handing two-thirds of the shares MyFC held over to the Fleet Supporters Trust. Ebbsfleet were relegated to the Conference South at the end of the season.

Almost immediately it was announced that KEH Sports Ltd, a group of Kuwaiti investors advised by a former chief executive of Charlton Athletic, had agreed to take over the club and settle its debts, with a promise to invest in both the squad and the training facilities. The early years of the KEH reign seemed fine, with the club pushing for and winning promotion back to the National League in 2017, along with significant development of the ground and facilities, including the eventual purchase of the freehold.

Then in 2018/19, the playing squad issued three separate public statements about not having been paid on time, and it became clear that the club was in debt to the tune of £2.6 million. They were relegated to the National League South again on a points-per-game basis in the Covid-truncated 2019/20 season, where they had remained ever since.

In terms of the match itself, the visitors' status of being two leagues below us did have the spectre of cup upset déjà vu lingering around it, although the fact that the match hadn't been chosen for live TV suggested that the BBC didn't think a shock was likely. Still, that gave no reassurance whatsoever to those of us who had been badly scarred by the Maldon & Tiptree debacle two years previously. At least Kenny Jackett seemed to be taking it seriously, the only change to the team from the victory over Hartlepool the previous week being to bring in Hector Kyprianou to replace the slightly injured Alex

Mitchell with the increasingly versatile Craig Clay dropping into the back three.

Ebbsfleet looked pretty lively right from the off, as Orient struggled to settle, and their attacking football in particular made them look like a team of a higher pedigree. But after something of a settling-in first quarter of the match, Shad Ogie sent Aaron Drinan racing through the inside left channel with a brilliant ball along the deck from back to front, and the in-form striker made no mistake rifling home his finish across the face of the keeper. It settled my nerves as I am sure it did many others'.

As the first half wore on, we noticed more and more fans being allowed into the supposedly closed South Stand behind the goal where the most vociferous Orient fans are normally located. We decided that after our half-time pint and loo stop, we would go and join them, as the atmosphere in the West Stand was dead. With Kay having departed for the bar to secure the pints before the queue got too bad, I left on the half-time whistle. As I was walking along the walkway at the front of the stand, I ended up next to a certain Danny Macklin, who was clearly displeased that the stewards at that end of the ground had taken it upon themselves to let people through to the South Stand, as there are obviously strict rules on the number of stewards needed and where. When I reported this news to Kay, we concluded that we were probably better off reoccupying our allocated seats.

Ebbsfleet continued to put up a fight throughout the second half and came close to finding an equalizer on a couple of occasions, but we managed to keep them out and secure passage to the second round for the first time in five years, and of course a first Orient FA Cup match win for Kay and me. The draw the following Monday evening saw us paired with Tranmere Rovers at home, a game that always carries a special connection for yours truly as a born Wirralonian.

Final Score
Leyton Orient   1   0   *Ebbsfleet United*
Drinan 24

More Cup progress

Papa John's EFL Trophy: Tuesday 9th November 2021, Leyton Orient v Charlton Athletic

The conclusion of the group stage of the EFL Trophy saw the O's take on Charlton Athletic of League One (most definitely at Brisbane Road and not the Valley!). With the two teams level on points at the top of the group and both therefore certain of qualifying for the next phase, the only issue to be decided was who would go through as group winners and therefore be guaranteed a home draw. While the competition remains regionalised until the quarter finals, there were still potential trips to the likes of Forest Green, Exeter or Swindon were we not to finish in first place.

Having learned our lesson from the previous crazy midweek dash over to Leyton, and with it being a 7 pm kick-off, we left the house as soon as work finished, i.e. as soon as the online meeting Kay was in ended and she could turn off her laptop. Oh the joys of working from home – the one beneficial change to life that the pandemic has brought. Of course, with the way that sod's law operates, where on the way to the Forest Green game we had had to wait longer for each train, this time each one turned up within a minute or so. As a result, we were at the wine bar, pint in hand, before the clock had struck 6 pm.

Given that there wasn't much at stake in this game, that both teams were likely to be made up of squad players, and that many fans (justifiably) look down their nose at this competition, it came as something of a surprise to find that a group of young-ish Charlton fans was already in situ. It seemed fairly evident that they may have been in there for quite some time and were combining Jäger-bombs with their cider and red wine while they watched a quiz show with the subtitles on so they could vehemently shout out the wrong answers. Very bizarre. It was unlike any awayday scene we had ever encountered before.

Once inside the ground it turned out that Charlton had brought a decent away support with them, 762 according to the official attendance figures. Maybe languishing in 18th place in the league, with the manager having recently been sacked, had forced the Charlton fans to concentrate on the cups?

These games are always quite laid-back affairs and relatively free of the intensity of league or the more serious cup competitions, but at a fiver a go they are generally quite enjoyable. The pleasing aspect from an Orient perspective was that the nine changes that Jackett opted to make meant there were a total of seven academy graduates in the starting line-up, proof positive that the club's development policy is really starting to reap benefits these days.

Charlton forced an early save from young goalkeeper Rhys Byrne, but as the O's settled into the game and the much-changed line-up, we started to create a few chances of our own; however, it remained 0-0 at the break.

Orient seemed to have a bit more impetus in the second half, as early on Paul Smyth, all 5-foot-7 of him, rose to meet a Connor Wood cross from the left, forcing Addicks keeper Nathan Harness to palm his effort over the bar. Smyth then broke through and poked an effort goalward from the edge of the area, only to see his effort ricochet off the post.

When youngster Antony Papadopoulos was shown two yellow cards in quick succession, both of which seemed soft, and was sent from the field with 20 minutes left to play, it seemed to galvanise the Orient players and the fans, who started appealing for every minor indiscretion we perceived.

Then with just over 10 minutes remaining, Smyth seized on a loose ball midway inside the Charlton half, drove forward and fired low past Harness for 1-0, his first goal for the club. That would prove to be the winner and the O's would top the group securing the home fixture in the next round.

Final Score

Leyton Orient	**1**	**0**	**Charlton Athletic**

Smyth 78

Rochdale via Leeds (WTF??)

Game 16: Saturday 13th November 2021, Rochdale v Leyton Orient

After the two home cup matches, it was off on another awayday for us, the first that seemed like a proper one, i.e. involving a journey beyond the commuter environs of London, this time to the "picturesque" Lancashire town of Rochdale.

When we were booking the tickets for this trip, it rather surprised us to find out that the best and cheapest way to get there was to go via Leeds and then take a local train through the Pennines to Rochdale. In another concerted effort to be on our best behaviour, we didn't buy any beer for the train, but with half an hour to wait for our connection, we (re)assured ourselves that we would be able to stock up on supplies for that part of the journey. Our hearts sank, however, when we boarded the train to be told that not only was it going to be delayed slightly because of a technical issue, but that it would also be running at a reduced speed. A quick check on our phones, and we realised that there were plenty of trains to get from Leeds to Rochdale, but we probably wouldn't have time to nip to the offie, so we would be beer-free all the way to Rochdale. It was a constructive, if not very welcome, state of affairs for an away day, as behaving sensibly seems much less fun if it is enforced by train delays rather than being by choice.

As we made our way north, I got a tweet from Paul, the Manchester City fan we had met on the way back from Barrow, who sadly apologised that work commitments meant that even with the Premier League enduring another international break, he wouldn't be able to join us on what for him would have been a relatively short hop to catch another Orient game to fill in the time. Maybe he would have fancied this game even before our encounter on a train in Cumbria, but we took it as an indication of how we were managing to spread the Orient word far and wide.

After arriving in Leeds, we just made our scheduled train after a slight panic about which platform we needed to head to. Thankfully we were aided in our search by a local who simply looked it up on his phone and pointed us in the right direction. If only we had thought of that! The journey across the Pennines is pleasant and easy enough, although it is somewhat disconcerting that when the train stops at Bradford Interchange it then leaves by going back the same way we had just come. Thankfully it seemed to be part of the actual planned route rather than the driver deciding to ad lib.

Frustratingly when we arrived in Rochdale, we then discovered that there isn't even so much as a hint of a pub (or anything very much at all!) near the station, so we decided that our best option was to get a cab up to the ground where there are two pubs/bars to choose from which are actually part of the stadium complex (I realise that might be pushing it a bit far as a description of the area surrounding the Dale's ground!). Our 10-minute cab ride revealed the delights of Rochdale, of which there seemed to be precisely zero. As a follower of rugby league, I have been to some grim places in my life, and Rochdale is very much up there, if not the outright winner!

To describe the Ratcliffe Arms, the pub at the ground we opted for simply because that was the first one we found, it is probably best to think back to the Phoenix Club from Peter Kay's (in)famous TV show, although possibly with even less glitz and glamour and an overwhelming smell of vomit, which may have been emanating from the carpet. Still, it was friendly to away fans, easy enough to get served and we could watch the end of Port Vale taking on Bradford. We even had the commentary over the PA until it all went a bit awry with feedback/static. Kay, as a bona fide cockney, was intrigued to discover that Limehouse Lizzy (a Thin Lizzy tribute band from East London, obviously!) would be gracing the stage of this salubrious venue in March, and we only half-jokingly cursed our luck that we would be unlikely to be able to make it.

The club even had what could loosely be described as a "beer garden", and when we ventured out there we ended up chatting to a Rochdale fan who was exiled in Croydon but was up visiting family and friends and thought he would take in a Dale match while he was home. At least that was how he explained it to them, but in truth he admitted he built the visit around watching his team. We continue to be baffled by the dedication of the football obsessives that we meet on our travels. He was less than enthusiastic about their chances against the O's as they had been in poor form, but he was fairly confident that they would stay up.

After five minutes or so chatting away, we were joined by one of the more "interesting" local characters who professed to be a Rochdale fan but was also wearing a hat for Solihull Moors, whom he apparently also supported. Nope, we're still trying to work that one out, as well. As the conversation drifted to some of the grounds we have visited, we started talking about Luton's Kenilworth Road, where you literally have to pass between houses to access the away end. Our new mate, the Rochdale/Solihull hybrid one, then told us a rather scary anecdote about how he discouraged someone from cutting across his garden by threatening to beat him up. Having spent a few minutes in his company, we were 100% convinced that his approach would have ended the issue permanently through sheer unadulterated terror. Not wanting to risk incurring his wrath by saying the wrong thing or threatening his garden, I very unsubtly checked my watch giving the three of us the perfect excuse to flee on the pretext of wanting to get a good speck inside the ground.

Anyone who has conducted any research into Spotland as an away ground will know that there are two specifically highlighted catering options: the apparently excellent Willbutts Lane chippy and the renowned pies at the ground. We opted for the latter, but as we were standing in the queue, I saw something that I have never seen in my entire football-watching life -- they were also advertising kebabs on the menu. We concluded that they must be those horrible microwaveable ones that you get in supermarket freezer sections, so we decided to stick to our guns on the refreshment front.

As we found a perch to rest our beer while we got stuck into the pies, Kay instantly came to regret eschewing the chippy when she discovered that her steak pie, tasty though it was, would have been more appropriately described as a "gravy pie", such was the paucity of meat within it. I took no joy (honestly I didn't!) from reminding her that in the North West, a meat and potato pie is a perfectly acceptable go-to option. You can take the lad out of the North and all that...

I had been to Spotland many years ago watching St Helens take on Rochdale Hornets in a rugby league cup match, but the ground has been quite well developed since then. It is a fairly nondescript but decent enough set-up for this level. The most striking feature from the away side (once again along the side of the pitch, grr!) is the reflective windows on the executive boxes in the stand opposite which are angled and, whether by design or default, reflect the on-pitch action and are, in fact, quite distracting.

Going 1-0 down very early away from home after travelling for a good few hours is always really tough to take, as you start asking yourself why you have bothered, so when Alex Newby opened the scoring for Dale after just 36 seconds, it is fair to say that it sparked a bit of soul searching amongst the travelling support. Thankfully we worked ourselves back into the game, and midway through the first half, man of the moment Aaron Drinan equalized with a goal that even the most-biased O's fans might have suggested had a hint of offside about it.

Just before the start of the second half Lord Dazza messaged me telling me to look to my right and down a few rows where he and the gang were. Having established contact, we, of course, went to join them, as it would have been rude not to!

Orient were very much in control for the majority of the second half, while Rochdale were really poor and could hardly string a couple of passes together. When Craig Clay rifled home from the edge of the area -- an amazing sight in its own right considering the tenacious midfielder had only ever scored five times previously for us, the last of those coming against Bolton the previous October when no fans were allowed in to see it -- just past the hour mark, there only looked like being one winner.

Football however, as we are all only too aware, can be a cruel game, though, especially away from home, so when Newby bundled the ball home after Lawrence Vigouroux had saved a header from a corner in the very last minute, it felt like a real kick in the guts. A point's a point away from home, but it was still tough to take.

Rather than having to undertake the 40-minute walk back to the station, Daz and Co. very kindly created space in one of their cabs for us, including a very opportune stop at the off-licence. We, of course, got the train back to Leeds with them, a journey that was made even more easy by one of our number (who shall remain nameless for security reasons) training for the conductor's job under the guidance of the actual conductor and welcoming passengers on and off the train at each station. Thankfully for the rest of the passengers, he was not allowed to press any of the buttons to open and close the doors.

We had a brief stopover in Leeds, where we bade farewell to the rest of the lads as they were on an earlier train, and we had time to both stop for a quick beer in the very swanky Beer House station bar and to stock up on more than enough supplies for the way home.

When we finally landed back in London, we reflected on another very enjoyable away day. Increasingly we are starting to realise that the result on these adventures is almost irrelevant; it is the fun you have and the people you meet that matters the most. Bring on Scunthorpe on a Tuesday night for our next one!

Final Score

Rochdale	**2**	**2**	**Leyton Orient**
Newby 1,90			Drinan 24
			Clay 66

Back on track?

Game 17: Saturday 20th November 2021, Leyton Orient v Sutton United

After two cup matches in which we were seated in the West Stand and the away trip to Rochdale, it felt like a long time since we were able to take up our usual seats in the "homely" East Stand. Conscious that we wanted to stick to the regular routine as much as possible, and not jinx the O's, of course, we headed to the wine bar.

Once settled outside, we spotted on Facebook that our mate Paul, one of the "Easy Lovers" from the train back from Port Vale, was in the Technical for a pre-match pint with another mate of his, John. Given that we only had a couple of mouthfuls of our pints left and that the Technical is literally across the road from where we were sitting, we decided that it would be rude not to pop over, say hello and have a bit of an Orient-based catch-up.

After a round, the pub was getting busier and busier, so we decided to head back over to the wine bar for another quick round before we all headed down to the ground. Being the complete grown-ups that we are, we of course asked John to show us how to spell out our own names and any swear words we could make use of in goading away fans in sign language. As John is up for coming on an awayday in the future, most likely Bradford in early January, we also made him promise to teach us the words to "Easy Lover" on the way there, to which he, of course, agreed as long as we bought his drinks. Deal done!

For the second match in a row, skipper Darren Pratley started on the bench, meaning that Craig Clay and Hector Kyprianou would be partnered together in the centre of midfield, something that a number of Orient fans (Kay most definitely among them) had been calling for some time. I couldn't help but wonder if this move might be permanent with the captain being relegated to the role of squad player for the foreseeable future. With no changes to the starting line-up at all, it really seemed that after 16 league matches, Kenny Jackett had pretty much settled on his first choice XI.

After the frustration of the last-minute equalizer at Rochdale, and because Sutton were one place and two points better off than us in the table, it felt very much like this was a game that Orient needed to win. So when we went behind to another early goal, this time after 18 minutes rather than the 36 seconds the previous week, it had most Orient fans fearing that we might struggle with this one, too. Shad Ogie, the young centre back, mis-controlled a crossfield pass to him, allowing Sutton's Isaac Olaofe to race clear and fire past Lawrence Vigouroux at his near post. Frustrating but these things happen with young players.

Thankfully it didn't take us too long to get back on terms, as Tom James' long throw was flicked on by Harry Smith for Theo Archibald to prod home at the far post. You could feel the relief in the stands and see the confidence lift amongst the players. Just before the break, Sutton rattled the post to remind us there was still plenty of work to be done to gain a decent result.

If the O's had taken their time to settle in the first half, in the second they were off to a flyer. Archibald tore down the left wing and clipped a cross into the middle, Sutton's keeper Dean Bouzanis spilled it, and Smith was on hand to nod the ball over him and into the unguarded net. From there it was largely one-way traffic, but the result wasn't secured until eight minutes from time when Smith notched his second of the match and ninth of the campaign, hooking home on the volley after Sutton hadn't cleared another James long throw. Then, in added time, Archibald played a clever corner to James driving into the area, and the wing-back rifled home from 12 yards. Job very much done. The win lifted the O's from ninth in the very congested top half of the table to sixth, and the frustration of the previous week evaporated.

With Arsenal kicking off at Anfield at 5:30, we had no choice but to head to the Coach & Horses to endure that in the beer garden. The 4-0 tonking, par for the course for the Gunners up there in recent seasons, was hardly unexpected, but the beers and a catch up with Raj and some of the other lads we have seen on our awayday travels made it a bit easier to tolerate. We even kept the customary Orient chants in reserve until the Liverpool-supporting father and his two young sons, with whom we were sharing a table, left at half-time.

Final Score

Leyton Orient	**4**	**1**	**Sutton United**
Archibald 29			Olaofe 18
Smith 46, 82			
James 90+4			

Oh what a night, up in Scunthorpe on a Tuesday night!

Game 18: Tuesday 23rd November 2021, Scunthorpe United v Leyton Orient

Being completely honest with ourselves, an unusual part of the appeal of Kay's and my season-long adventure watching the O's was that we knew there would inevitably be some fixtures on a Tuesday night in far-flung lower league outposts, where the transport situation would mean that we would have no other option but to stay over. Bizarre as it might seem to people not completely and utterly obsessed with football, the prospect actually adds to the sense of adventure. The luck of the fixture list dictated that the first of these would not come until late November. Having agreed not to even contemplate foreign travel until the end of the season at least and having saved up as much of our holiday allowance as possible, Scunthorpe offered us our chance to make our midweek awayday debut.

A bit of Internet research in the preceding weeks turned up the excellently located (10 minutes' walk from the station and half an hour to the ground) and very reasonably priced 42 Apart-Hotel on Doncaster Road.

Despite having to change at Doncaster after retravelling the majority of the trip to Leeds from a week and a half previously, our Tuesday late-morning/early afternoon journey slipped by easily enough, and we landed in Scunthorpe just after 2 pm. On the walk up from the station, it was very noticeable how many accountancy practices and financial advisers' offices there were on our route, suggesting that Scunthorpe might not be as rough as we had feared. Rochdale it most definitely wasn't.

As we arrived at the hotel and went to check-in, Luke and Jake who together make up the Orient media team were just in front of us, so it felt like we had definitely chosen the right base. For a brief moment due to a mix-up in the name the booking was under, though, we very nearly ended up offering the pair of them the opportunity to crash on our floor. Thankfully it sorted itself out in the end, although I suspect the place may not have been anywhere near fully booked and they would probably have been ok.

Having spotted the Class 6 bar on the way up to the hotel advertising very cheap drinks, handily located approximately 20 yards from where we were staying, we rather obviously decided that this was the perfect place to get our latest awayday adventure underway properly. The bar itself seemed slightly out of place given that it specialised in cocktails and had a layout that was reminiscent of some of the less dodgy nightclubs of our youth. Surprisingly even at this relatively early hour, the place was fairly busy, but with two pints coming in at a most un-

London-like £5.60, we were more than happy with it as a venue for a few pre-match drinks.

After a few rounds in there and with our stomachs reminding us that we hadn't eaten anything on the way up, not helped of course by the lack of a shop on the train, we decided that it was back round the corner to the equally handily placed Wetherspoons for something to eat. After a good feed, we decided it was time to head up to the ground to meet up with Lord Dazza and Co. at the Hungry Horse on the retail park near the ground. Amply fed and watered, though, we decided that the cab office across the road was much more appealing than the half-hour walk. We nearly came to regret that decision when we were originally told it would be a 40-minute wait until the next available ride, until the boss in the back office ordered one of the drivers to end his break and take us up there straightaway. We certainly weren't going to argue!

Once inside the Hungry Horse, or the Old Farmhouse to use its actual title, we got serious accommodation envy when the lads showed us pictures of Daz's lodge (available to rent we believe!) on a site just outside Lincoln, an hour's drive away. It came as no surprise whatsoever when we were told it was officially titled "E10", very much a home away from Brisbane Road.

After a catch-up with the guys, Kay decided she couldn't leave the place without having a go on one of those funfair grabber machines located on the way into the Wacky Warehouse children's play area. Amazingly she won not one, but two prizes, which will provide her with (albeit cheapo!) reminders of our time in Scunthorpe.

Glanford Park when it opened in the late 1980's was the first new league football ground to be built in England since the Second World War, and while it does feel a little bit dated and perhaps in need of a spruce up, it is not completely clear why the club continue to state the intention of developing a new stadium or enhancing the capacity of their current home. Certainly, the average attendances of just under 2,500 don't really merit it.

Even though we had eaten not long before, Kay had deliberately opted for a small plate of scampi in order to save herself for her traditional pie, which although it was nuclear hot was apparently a lot better than the previous trip's option at Spotland. Not only did it have plenty of meat in it, but it was also apparently the best one she had experienced on our travels to date.

For the third match in a row, it was the same starting line-up for Orient, and with the home team sitting rock bottom of the table, even below crisis club Oldham, there was almost a feeling of optimism amongst the surprisingly large (at least for a school night) travelling Orient faithful that this was a great opportunity for the O's to pick up only their second away win of the season.

It was therefore somewhat frustrating that we struggled to impose ourselves on the game in the opening period. We did however seem to spark into life midway through the first half when Alex Mitchell sent Hector Kyprianou charging down the right, and his dipping cross was tucked away by Aaron "Drinaldo" for his 10th goal in all competitions this season.

If we hoped the first goal would be enough to break the home side's resistance, we were to be sadly mistaken, however. Once again Orient seemed to lose their tempo and to play within themselves when really, Scunthorpe seemed very much there for the taking. There seemed to be a timidity about the team on its travels; surely it couldn't still be them feeling the impact of throwing away a seemingly winning lead so late on at Port Vale?

We started the second half in search of a second goal to put the game to bed but were to end up frustrated, wasting very presentable chances through Dan Kemp and Drinan. Just past the hour mark, the O's would rue those missed chances to extend their lead. A corner from the left resulted in an old-school scrappy goalmouth scramble, and Scunthorpe's Jake Scrimshaw was quickest to react to poke home the equalizer.

From there, Orient pushed and pushed for a winning goal but wasted chances with Harry Smith hitting the post, then misdirecting an effort wide from close range when it looked easier to score, and then Paul Smyth, on as a sub for Kemp, was sent racing through the middle by Smith but saw his dinked effort trickle wide. That, put paid to anything other than a solitary point. Back in the Old Farmhouse, the general consensus of opinion was that while drawing matches away from home is no mean feat, if we could have just converted say three of those draws into wins, we would be sitting in the automatic promotion places.

We bid farewell to Daz and Co. as they set off back to the splendour of the lodge, and the bar manager very kindly ordered a taxi for us. A couple of nightcaps back at Class 6 and then it was off to bed, thankful for not having had to try to get home that evening.

The next morning, we treated ourselves to breakfast back in Wetherspoons on the way to the station and made our way home. We even had a bit of positive train irony when the train to Kings Cross that was supposed to be ahead of ours was running late, so our wait at Doncaster was actually shorter than planned. If at the outset Scunthorpe away on a Tuesday evening was a daunting prospect, in the end it turned into a cracking away trip, other than the result of course.

Final Score
Scunthorpe United   1   1   **Leyton Orient**

Ice Station Sixfields

Game 19: Saturday 27th November 2021, Northampton Town v Leyton Orient

When we were starting out on this adventure, or more specifically when Kay was agreeing to come to the away games with me, we always suspected that there might be an occasion when she would "see her arse" on our travels. Among those that we thought might be the most likely candidates were Barrow, Carlisle, Exeter, Hartlepool and actually Scunthorpe. Little did we know that Northampton, around 70 miles from London, on a Saturday afternoon was going to be the first. Thanks to the effects of Storm Arwen, the first named storm of the season, apparently, it was absolutely freezing with a "feels like temperature" of -9.

It all started fairly positively, as despite there having been a Tube strike the previous day, it seemed to have returned to normal service when we were setting off. Even more of a relief was that despite all the cancellations and delays from Euston caused by the adverse weather conditions, our train was one of the only ones completely unaffected.

Having been cocooned on a train for an hour and 20 minutes, we found the wind chill factor was really noticeable when we arrived in Northampton. The obvious and immediate decision was that we didn't fancy the half hour walk in those conditions, so we jumped into a cab to head up to the ground. Plus, I wanted to watch as much of Arsenal v Newcastle in the early kick-off as I could.

When we pulled into the stadium complex, we headed for Carr's Bar, where Football Ground Guide and a number of similar websites had advised us that it welcomed away fans as well as home fans, only to be told by the steward manning the door that it was, in fact, for home fans only. He then told us that we could head up to the Sixfields, another Hungry Horse pub for the second match in succession, which was already filled with a number of Orient fans. That was actually the pub we were told was for home fans only. Whether it had been a recent change in policy or something to stop the sizeable number of travelling O's fans from packing out the stadium bar before the home fans arrived wasn't clear, but it was a strange situation.

After defrosting, albeit only slightly, over a few pints and watching Arsenal get back to winning ways, we decided that we were as ready as we were ever going to be to brave the arctic temperatures again and head down to the ground. Sixfields Stadium is actually based in what looks like a man-made valley but provides very little cover from what was a biting wind.

As we approached the turnstiles, we were then told that there was no beer on sale again, though this time it didn't feel like such a transgression of our human rights given how cold it was. Bovril, the go-to choice for football fans in sub-zero conditions, was a much more welcome option. Things took a turn for the worse, however, when we found out that there were no pies on sale other than cheese and onion ones. Right then was quite possibly the moment that Kay fell out with Sixfields as an away day. How she didn't give up and go back to London from there must have been an extreme test of her dedication to the cause.

As we were drinking our life-saving Bovril and replacement snacks of rubbish microwave burger for me and crap sausage roll for Kay, we remarked how it was probably even colder than when we had been at the Perito Moreno Glacier near El Calafate in the south of Argentina a few years previously. An older guy, Terry, standing near us must have overheard us and told us that we didn't know what real cold was. He had spent years on a ship down in actual Antarctica ferrying various "'ologists" around as they conducted research work in the 50's and 60's. We could only imagine how bad that would have been.

The ground itself is kind of incomplete. The stand down one side and those behind goals are the sort of thing we had encountered at Salford and Stevenage, which are nice and relatively modern but soulless with little to distinguish them from any other newly constructed stadium. The stand running along the east side of the ground, however, was opened to supporters in 2016 but is yet to be completed, and the wide-open upper tier combined with the open corners provide no shelter from the elements at all, obviously more of an issue on a freezing November afternoon than in the early or late stages of the season. From the south end of the stadium, where the away fans are accommodated, you have a clear view of the big hill with the Sixfields pub at the top. Given what was to come from the O's, I spent a not insignificant amount of time dreaming of being back in there trying to get slightly warm.

The only change to the starting XI for Orient was the return of skipper Darren Pratley, as Craig Clay had been ruled out after taking a heavy knock up at Scunthorpe and Paul Smyth was injured once again after playing all of 20 minutes at Glanford Park. The Northern Ireland forward is seemingly either made of glass or just terribly unlucky.

In the opening exchanges, we won an early free-kick in a good shooting position, and wing-back Tom James tested Liam Roberts in their goal with a curling strike that looked like it was sneaking into the top left-hand corner, only for it to be batted away by the keeper at full stretch.

As the half wore on Harry Smith couldn't direct a header on target, and Dan Kemp fizzed an effort on the turn wide, but we weren't able to make our positive start to the half count. Then with half-time approaching, we once again conceded a scrappy goal from a set piece. Mitch Pinnock's long throw aided by the wind was flicked on at the near post, despite the presence of Hector Kyprianou and Smith, two of our tallest players, and poked home by Sam Hoskins.

Despite the relatively early introduction, at least for Kenny Jackett, of two subs just past the hour mark in Ruel Sotiriou and Connor Wood, it did little to improve our attacking impetus. In fact, it could be argued that the removal of Aaron Drinan and Theo Archibald actually blunted our offensive threat. The second half display was one of misplaced passes, aimless long balls and scrambling to try and win back possession. The display coupled with the worsening weather made for a thoroughly depressing afternoon.

On the final whistle, Kay and I clapped the players as much as our frozen hands permitted and headed off back to the pub as quickly as we could. As we thawed out again, we briefly weighed up the option of getting the bus back into town, but when we asked one of the bar staff they suggested that it would only cost a bit more to get a cab. We followed her advice, and our driver even stopped at an off licence en route again so we could stock up on supplies for the train.

Final Score
Northampton Town   1   0   Leyton Orient
Hoskins 41

Out on penalties again

Papa John's EFL Trophy: Tuesday 30th November 2021, Leyton Orient v MK Dons

The prize for topping the EFL Trophy group was a home tie against League One MK Dons, a club that is probably one of the most hated by football traditionalists like yours truly. In case you are unaware of their history, "The Franchise", as we are compelled to call them, came into being in 2004 as a result of the despicable relocation of Wimbledon FC from South London to the new town of Milton Keynes. Once in situ, they rebranded and adopted a new name, colours and badge, essentially killing a club that had been in existence since 1889, had been admitted to the Football League in 1977 and spectacularly rose through the divisions to reach the top division just nine years later. They also famously won the FA Cup in 1988, beating title winners Liverpool in the final.

Thankfully the rise of the phoenix club, AFC Wimbledon, has been equally impressive, and they also now play in League One. However, the controversial move still rankles with many true football fans. In many ways the much-maligned EFL Trophy, which allows the participation of Premier League B teams, seemed like a fitting competition for me to have my first live encounter with the controversial franchise.

After the hoo-ha over the non-opening of stands in the last cup match at Brisbane Road against Ebbsfleet, it came as something of a surprise when I logged onto the Orient ticket portal to discover that we had the option of purchasing tickets in both the West Stand, where we normally have to sit for cup games, and the South Stand, where the most fervent Orient supporters sit. Having never had the opportunity to experience the South Stand up to this point, Kay and I plumped for tickets there.

After a quick stop in the wine bar, we were pleasantly surprised to find that the facilities in our new location were not only way better than in the East (mind you that isn't difficult given the age of our home base!) but also the rest of the ground and many others that we have visited. The refreshment areas are carpeted and a lot more civilised than the concourses in other stands. There is a bar in the middle that is actually a proper bar with tables and seats and draught beer in proper glasses, and it is probably more spacious than the Supporters Club. Having enjoyed these pleasant facilities, Kay and I realised we might face something of a dilemma about whether to relocate ahead of the following season.

As is par for the course in these cup ties, both teams were very much changed from their usual league line-ups. For Orient, the only players returned to the line-up after the defeat at Northampton were Theo Archibald, confusingly deployed at right wing-back when many O's fans have expressed concern about him playing in a more defensive position on his natural left side, Millwall loanee Alex Mitchell, and Hector Kyprianou, who had pretty much played every single game so far. There was, however, significant experience on the bench should it be required.

The scattering of MK Dons fans seated in the usual away section of the East Stand did their best to try and get some kind of atmosphere going and roused some of the younger elements of the Orient faithful in the South Stand. To the young O's credit, or perhaps because it was before their time, they resisted giving them a chorus of "Wimbledon, Wimbledon, Wimbledon!"

Because of the numerous changes, both sides struggled to settle into any sort of pattern, and the game was played at an easy kind of tempo, lacking urgency which suggested that neither club was massively concerned about progressing in the competition. The sum total of first half action was a couple of long-range efforts from the visitors and a shot from Ruel Sotiriou that took a deflection before clipping the bar. A rip-roaring cup tie it certainly wasn't.

In truth the second half wasn't a great deal better, with little in the way of goalmouth action at either end. Teenage striker Jephte Tanga was introduced as a sub to make his debut, and a little while later Harry Smith and Tom James joined the fray, one suspects with more than half an eye on the increasingly inevitable penalty shootout. Smith had a header cleared off the line, Rhys Byrne in the Orient goal had to be alert to palm a looping header onto the crossbar, and right at the death the brilliantly named Troy Parrot was shown a straight red for a clash of heads with Theo Archibald, but in the end, the tie had to be settled from the penalty spot.

Ruel Sotiriou stepped up to take the first kick of the shootout for Orient, not looking in any way confident after missing against QPR back in August, and unsurprisingly fired his shot just over the bar. No one else missed, and Orient were eliminated from another competition on penalties. In the grand scheme of things, exiting the EFL Trophy wasn't a disaster; it proved useful to give minutes to fringe players and youngsters, but ultimately it wouldn't get us promoted.

Final Score
Leyton Orient   0   0   MK Dons
*MK Dons win 5-4 on penalties

League Two table after close of play on 30th November 2021

Pos	Team	Pld	W	D	L	GF	GA	GD	Pts
1	Forest Green Rovers	18	12	4	2	34	14	20	40
2	Northampton Town	19	10	4	5	25	15	10	34
3	Exeter City	19	8	9	2	31	21	10	33
4	Swindon Town	18	9	6	3	28	18	10	33
5	Port Vale	19	9	5	5	32	20	12	32
6	Sutton United	19	10	2	7	28	22	6	32
7	Harrogate Town	19	8	6	5	33	24	9	30
8	**Leyton Orient**	19	6	10	3	32	17	15	28
9	Newport County	19	7	7	5	30	23	7	28
10	Tranmere Rovers	18	7	5	6	15	14	1	26
11	Salford City	19	6	6	7	22	19	3	24
12	Bradford City	19	5	9	5	25	23	2	24
13	Rochdale	19	5	9	5	24	24	0	24

Pos	Team	Pld	W	D	L	GF	GA	GD	Pts
14	Walsall	19	6	6	7	21	23	-2	24
15	Mansfield Town	19	6	5	8	21	25	-4	23
16	Bristol Rovers	19	6	5	8	22	29	-7	23
17	Hartlepool United	19	7	2	10	20	30	-10	23
18	Colchester United	18	5	6	7	16	22	-6	21
19	Crawley Town	18	6	3	9	20	28	-8	21
20	Barrow	19	4	7	8	20	24	-4	19
21	Stevenage	18	4	6	8	15	30	-15	18
22	Carlisle United	19	3	7	9	13	28	-15	16
23	Oldham Athletic	19	4	3	12	16	30	-14	15
24	Scunthorpe United	19	2	8	9	15	35	-20	14

Chapter 8: December 2021

In which I discover that you can go home again – as an away fan! But Kay suffers a bike accident that threatens to derail her Golden Season, while Covid rears its ugly

head again and condemns us to a football-less Christmas and New Year's.

Up for the Cup 3

FA Cup Second Round: Saturday 4th December 2021, Leyton Orient v Tranmere Rovers

The luck of the draw, hey? Having been born on the Wirral and having returned there as a teenager after living in Holland, the States and in Hertfordshire, Tranmere Rovers were a team that I followed for a number of years as they progressed from the Fourth Division (League Two to younger readers) to the verge of the First Division (before it became the Premier League) under the stewardship of legendary manager Johnny King.

In later years, after having relocated to London, I used to go and watch them with a good mate of mine, Paul, who has always been and remains a die-hard Rovers fan, at away games in London and surrounding areas, often with Our Kid (for readers not fully versed in the intricacies of North Western lingo: Our Kid is an affectionate term for one's younger brother or indeed sister) and various other ex-pat Wirralonians. Given the way that football irony/fate works, it came as no surprise to me whatsoever when Orient's prize for just about despatching Ebbsfleet in the FA Cup First Round was a clash against Rovers. Thankfully it was at Brisbane Road, since our away league game at Prenton Park was set for a fortnight later, so at least it didn't mean another December trip to the Wirral to organise – unless, of course, there was to be a replay.

Kay and I, of course, made sure we arrived in good time for a couple of pints in the wine bar before heading down to the ground for our customary pre-match pie and pint deal. After the almost luxurious facilities of the South Stand, it came as a bit of a comedown to be in the cramped concourse area of the West

Stand once again, although as Kay pointed out with ironic glee, the South Stand was open for business. (Note to self: next time wait to see what stands will be open for cup games rather than just buying the tickets as soon as they become available!).

With Tranmere sitting two points and two places behind the O's in the league table but with a game in hand, it always felt as if this was going to be a stern test against a team of comparable ability if we were to progress to the FA Cup Third Round for the first time in eight years.

Rather unsurprisingly, given his consistency in team selection, Kenny Jackett made just one change to his first-choice team with Adam Thompson, building fitness after a shocking injury when he fractured his ankle at Grimsby in March, being given a second successive start. Millwall loanee Alex Mitchell was given the day off. Meanwhile, Craig Clay had recovered sufficiently from the knock that had kept him out at Northampton to recover his place in central midfield, with club skipper Darren Pratley once again dropped to the bench.

After an opening spell, where both teams seemed to be feeling each other out, Orient and the game sprang into life midway through the first half. Hector Kyprianou burst forward from midfield and slid a beauty of a through-ball through the middle to send Harry Smith through on goal, and the tall striker calmly drew the goalkeeper and fired it low past him into the bottom left-hand corner. In the aftermath of the goal, the older gentlemen sitting next to me suggested that he thought I had got up on my feet too early, but I assured him I had every confidence in Smith slotting it home (honestly I did!).

From there, it was pretty much all Orient, and 10 minutes before the break, Aaron Drinan recycled an overhit corner and played it low back into the box where Omar Beckles was on hand to slot it home. Up 2-0 at half-time felt comfortable enough but given Orient's recent propensity to give away sloppy goals, we weren't taking anything for granted.

Orient carried on very much on the front foot from the start of the second half, and Smith had the ball in the net early on, volleying home an excellent Tom James cross, only to be denied by the raised flag of the linesman. As disappointing as it is to start celebrating a goal only to see the raised flag that halts you in your tracks, I still much prefer the old school way to the Premier League's don't raise the flag, wait for VAR and delay the game approach. Football decisions are often a matter of subjective judgement, and arguing about being hard done by is part of being a football fan, rather than killing the action while the officials in Stockley Park deliberate over lines on a TV screen.

On the hour mark, Drinan fired a low cross in from the right only for it to be blocked low by Rovers defender Peter Clarke, and after a brief deliberation referee Mr. Oldham pointed to the penalty spot. Having now seen the replay, I have to say it definitely struck an arm but fell very much into the "how could he have gotten out of the way?" category. Drinan stepped up to take it himself and fired it straight down the middle after the keeper had moved to his left.

Late on, Smith got his second and Orient's fourth of the day, as Drinan drove through the middle and picked out Kyprianou charging up the right-hand side, and his low ball in was perfect for Smith as he slid it home from six yards. Job very much done for the Orient.

In the Supporters Club after the match, we reflected on who we fancied in the Third Round. Obviously most Orient fans wanted a trip away to one of the big Premier League teams, and many fancied the short trip to the London Stadium to play West Ham. Kay fancied a trip to Tottenham's new ground as an excuse to see what it was like, while I secretly contemplated the potential irony of going to the Emirates as an away fan. In the end, Monday night's draw gave us a trip to the Potteries, this time to face Stoke City. Slightly underwhelming, but they are after all a Championship club. The worse news for Kay was that it would now mean that our planned trip to Bradford scheduled for the 8th January would now most likely take place on a Tuesday night, a prospect that very nearly had her supporting Tranmere earlier in the afternoon!

Final Score

Leyton Orient	**4**	**0**	**Tranmere Rovers**

Smith 22,83
Beckles 36
Drinan (Pen) 60

A statement victory for the O's

Game 20: Tuesday 7th December 2021, Leyton Orient v Swindon Town

As welcome as a cup victory and progress to the Third Round of the FA Cup for the first time in eight years is, ultimately it is how a team performs in the league that determines whether a campaign is successful or not. In League Two terms that means being in the promotion argument at the end of the season. Swindon Town were coming into this game only outside the automatic promotion spots on goal difference and on the back of six wins in their previous nine league matches, another seemingly very stern test for the O's.

The UK was being buffeted by another named storm, the second in two weeks, as Storm Barra (honestly who thinks these up?) brought with it a deluge of rain in the late afternoon that had the Orient social media pages going into overdrive with concerns over whether the game would actually go ahead or not. Thankfully the heavy rain eased just before it was time for me to set off, and Orient's much-improved pitch drainage meant that it would be perfectly fine to play on.

Kay was at her work's Christmas Party for the afternoon, which meant that it was easier for her to go straight to Leyton and to meet me in the Coach & Horses, and at any rate, it certainly didn't seem like an ideal evening to be sitting outside the wine bar, patio heaters or no patio heaters. When my darling wife did turn up, let us just say that the three whisky cocktails and several glasses of wine that she had enjoyed over the course of the day were more than evident.

Once we headed into the ground, it became clear that while Swindon had brought a highly impressive 955 travelling fans with them all the way from the West Country on a Tuesday night, a significant proportion of the Orient faithful hadn't shown up. To be fair, anyone due to travel in from Essex (where a high proportion of Orient fans live) or other areas outside of London probably took one look at the weather before setting off and decided that it was better and safer to stay at home.

From the first whistle, it seemed obvious that Kenny Jackett's plan for dealing with a talented and slick Robins side was to try to contain them by defending the halfway line (the "half press" as pioneered by, amongst others, Dynamo Kiev's supremely influential coach Valeriy Lobanovskyi, for any fellow football tactics geeks that might be reading this!). Thankfully the players ignored the fervent encouragement from parts of the East Stand to push further up the pitch and risk leaving themselves exposed at the back. It got me wondering as to whether the greater availability of tactical analysis in the modern game on TV and online has meant that more and more of us regard ourselves as "tactical masterminds" than in years gone by.

The approach worked pretty well to contain Swindon in the opening stages, and when Aaron Drinan opened the scoring after a brilliant cross-field pass from Shad Ogie and an incisive low cross from Tom James, you could feel a renewed belief emanating from all around the ground.

Having gone a goal up, Orient seemed to sit deeper to try to defend what they had. It proved to be something of a dangerous approach, however, and allowed Swindon more of a foothold in the game. Three minutes before the break, the visitors were back on terms when Harry McKirdy, whose ponytail and Jack Grealish-style rolled down socks had already drawn him to the attention of the more vocal Orient supporters, stooped low to head a cross from the left past Lawrence Vigouroux. It felt slightly inevitable and, given recent league form, something of a concern that once again our decent early work might be undone.

Such was Kay's "tired and emotional" reaction to us letting the lead slip that she spent most of the interval threatening to go home. While she was convinced she was absolutely adamant, we both knew deep down that there was no way in this world that she wouldn't be there for the second half. Football obsession dictates that no matter how badly things are going for our teams, walking out simply isn't an option. Besides, as I pointed out to my beloved wife: firstly, we weren't actually losing, and secondly, there was still every chance that we might win.

In the end, Orient's performance in the second half proved me absolutely correct, and it was another display that suggested that things might really be starting to click within the side as they grew to know each other and better understand what the manager wanted them to do. After some early pressure from Swindon, the O's seemed to find their rhythm again, and with a renewed impetus we really took the game to them.

On the hour mark, Theo Archibald fired in a teasing cross from the left and Drinan stretched out a leg to turn home his 13th goal of the campaign. The wild celebrations amongst the 3,000 O's fans who had turned up on this miserable Tuesday evening suggested we recognised that our team was very much in the ascendancy.

A mere matter of minutes later, Harry Smith controlled another Archibald cross and despatched it home to double our lead. You could actually see Swindon starting to rock, unsure of how to deal with Orient's continuing onslaught. Our mate Mark from the row in front took this as an invitation to wander as close to the visiting fans as he could to suggest to them that this might be a good opportunity for them to get a head start on the 80-mile journey home.

The O's wrapped up the match with 10 minutes remaining, as Drinan's shot was parried by the keeper but only as far as Smith, who simply had to nod it home for 4-1 and to draw level with his strike partner on 13 goals for the campaign. Speaking on the club's Fans Forum the following evening, Director of Football Martin Ling suggested that while they had high hopes of both Smith and Drinan when signing them in the summer, 26 goals between them before the halfway point was beyond expectation. Little did we know it at the time, but this was going to be the last positive Orient performance for quite some weeks.

Final Score

Leyton Orient	**4**	**1**	**Swindon Town**
Drinan 19, 59			McKirdy 42
Smith 64, 82			

A bad day at the office for the O's

Game 21: Saturday 11th December 2021, Leyton Orient v Crawley Town

In non-Orient related news Kay, a very keen cyclist in the getting around town rather than the lycra-clad Tour De France wannabees sense, fell off her bike on Thursday evening and managed to not only break her wrist but also at least one of her fingers. I, of course, hasten to add that this was in no way a result of her being pissed, but it did have yours truly frantically researching whether Deliveroo operate on Christmas Day, given my below novice level culinary skills!

As a result of her injury, she was a little bit apprehensive about going to the football for fear of having someone bang into her arm. After careful consideration in which I enthusiastically encouraged her not to spoil her run of Orient attendance over a mere few broken bones, we decided that the best option was to set off much earlier than usual and hope that the DLR and Tube weren't packed with eager Christmas shoppers.

Thankfully as it turned out, the trains were relatively quiet; maybe people's preference for online shopping, as the high street retailers seem only too keen to point out each and every year, really is starting to become a thing? As a result of our decision, we had a chance encounter that we probably wouldn't have had if we had set off as normal. As we were standing on the eastbound Central Line platform at Stratford a guy in an Orient tracksuit came and stood right next to us. After a swift double-take I realised it was none other than midfielder Craig Clay. It's not often that you bump into one of your team's key players on the way to the match. I did, however, read in the programme that ahead of the Swindon match, Harry Smith had struggled to get to the ground on time due to train delays, and we had our previous experience of bumping into assistant manager Joe Gallen on the way home earlier in the season.

There is something refreshing about our players and staff being humble enough to use public transport.

After a few pints in the wine bar (for the pain in Kay's arm obviously!), we made sure we got into the ground nice and early to avoid any crowds on the concourse. Kay even managed to eat her pie without too much difficulty. If that hadn't been possible, I think she may have broken down at her plight completely.

The only change from Tuesday night's stunning win over high-flying Swindon was the introduction of Adam Thompson in the middle of the back three in place of Omar Beckles. Manager Kenny Jackett revealed after the game that Beckles' absence was due to Covid reasons, a worrying first indication that the rapidly spreading Omicron variant of the virus might yet have another impact on the game that we love.

Crawley won the toss and opted to turn Orient round, forcing us to attack the South Stand in the first half, where usually we prefer to play towards our most vocal supporters in the second half. I am "sensible" enough to realise that the direction the teams play in in a given half shouldn't have any impact whatsoever on the performance, but it is something that I always find strangely disconcerting when my team is forced to do this on our own ground. Even I'm not sad enough to carry out a statistical analysis on this to see if it results in more defeats, but it never seems right.

Right from the off, Orient looked out of sorts, and the crispness of the passing and the slick movement that had been a joy to watch against Swindon just four days previously was gone, seemingly having been replaced by a ponderousness that thankfully hadn't been too prevalent at Brisbane Road this season. As a result, it was the visitors that forged the early chances, as we really seemed off the pace.

Just past the half hour mark, from a long ball forward, their right wing-back Mark Davis found midfielder George Francomb surging into the box, and he fired past Lawrence Vigouroux first time for 1-0. It hurt because it was the sort of sweeping goal that Orient had scored when at their absolute best in performances earlier in the season.

Minutes later right wing-back Tom James, who had been one of Orient's standout players through the season so far, went down after what looked like a tough tackle and had to be replaced by Dan Happe. As the Welshman was helped from the pitch, I felt a nagging fear that he might be out for quite some time. Speaking on the O's Fans Forum the previous week, Director of Football Martin Ling had suggested that cover at right wing-back/full back was a priority area for the January transfer window, and that sadly seemed even more the case now. Not long later the referee called a halt to what had been a fairly depressing opening half for the Orient faithful.

Rather than come out with a point to prove after an underwhelming first half, the O's started the second half very much in the same vein. Harry Smith and Aaron Drinan were starved of decent service up top, and we really didn't look like a team that was going to come storming back into the match. Eventually we got the ball in the net, somewhat fortuitously it has to be said, as Theo Archibald overhit a cross that rebounded back off the upright and in off the keeper for 1-1.

If we were hoping this was the cue for the O's to spring into life and push for the win, we were sadly to be mistaken. Just five minutes later, Crawley were back in the lead from another sweeping move that saw Kwesi Appiah slot home. The goal very much took the wind out of our sails, and we never looked like stealing even a point. Right at the end, skipper Darren Pratley was shown a second yellow card, an indication of how frustrated the players were feeling, perhaps.

It was a gutting display because it was so much poorer than what we had been producing at home in recent weeks. After the match, Kay and I went to drown our sorrows/wait for the crowds to clear a bit in the Coach before heading home, reality check most definitely acknowledged.

Final Score

Leyton Orient	1	2	Crawley Town
Morris (OG) 62			Francomb 32
			Appiah 66

Covid, injuries and suspensions hit the O's as I return "home" as an away fan

Game 22: Saturday 18th December 2021, Tranmere Rovers v Leyton Orient

By now, you will be fully aware that I have something of a connection with Tranmere Rovers from my youth, and with the league fixture at Prenton Park being scheduled for just three days after my birthday (no, I am not telling you how many years are on the clock for this football obsessive!), that offered the perfect opportunity for a brief staycation up on Merseyside ahead of this fixture. There would be some further bad news with regard to Kay's injuries, however.

Having struggled her way to Euston, Kay could hardly walk when we got off the train at Liverpool Lime Street (no, it was nothing to do with the medicinal beers on the train!), but thankfully our hotel was only a 10 minute (or 20 at Kay's amended pace) walk away. Once checked in, we met up with Our Ian (the cousin who turned me into an Arsenal fan all those years ago and whom I am in constant text message conversation with every time Arsenal play) and his partner Liane. We had booked a table in the excellent Lunya tapas restaurant (which features amongst other delights Catalan Scouse – a take with a twist on the city's famous stew), which thankfully for Kay was across the road from the hotel. The restaurant is so good that Kay and I went back on Friday and Saturday evening, as well, so if you like Spanish / Catalan food and ever find yourself in Liverpool...

On Friday morning, Kay's leg had got worse, so we decided that the best option was for her to take her second trip of the week to Accident and Emergency, where she was diagnosed with a delayed strain of her groin/upper thigh. Initially we had ruled her out of taking the trip over the Mersey for the match the following day, but after a few pints in various pubs within very close proximity to the hotel and another excellent tapas meal, Kay's bravado had increased to such an extent that if we could get her over to Birkenhead in a cab, there was no way she was going to miss our 11th away match of the season.

On match day, we met up with my dad and his wife for coffee, but with the hotel bar being closed we decided that there was no other option but to head back to, yes you guessed it, Lunya, for a Catalan breakfast. Back in the days before the pandemic changed the world, most years Kay and I would celebrate my birthday in Spain, most frequently in Barcelona, to take in a La Liga match and enjoy the excellent cuisine, so in a funny way we were almost re-creating that. Costa Del Mersey if you like!

As my dad still lives over on the Wirral, he very kindly offered to drop us off at Prenton Park, and one suspects he may have even come along to the match if he had been free! While the ground has changed significantly since the late 80's and early 90's, there are still two excellent pubs in very close proximity: The Mersey Clipper and the Prenton Park Hotel, the latter of which is now immediately opposite the away turnstiles, so the choice was simple for us.

Just as I was about to message Lord Dazza to see where he and group were going for a pre-match drink, he walked through the door, presumably having reached the same conclusion on which of the two pubs was better. After a catch-up and a round of shots -- paid for by Daz but ordered by some of the younger members of the crew who had got the one thing that Daz can't stand, Sambuca -- a long-standing friend of mine from school, partner in World Cup adventures and Tranmere Rovers die-hard Paul arrived as planned. He fitted easily into the conversation in which we discussed how much more real football at this level is than the money-driven world of the Premier League.

In the build up to the match, more and more players were being ruled out as a result of Covid on top of the injuries and the suspension of skipper Darren Pratley that we already knew about. As a result, we cobbled together a line-up that included three left-backs, Matt Young making his full league debut in the middle of the park and just four subs named on the bench, although amazingly one of the subs was the rarely fit Paul Smyth.

The handy location of the pub meant that we were able to leave just 20 minutes before kick-off, share a quick beer and be in our seats before play got underway. Once inside, I took stock of the surroundings, having only been to the redeveloped ground once previously. With a capacity of over 16,500, the most dominating feature is the Kop Stand, which replaced the previous open terrace and now houses the home fans behind one goal. This means that the Cowshed Stand (so named after it replaced the previous covered terrace that looked very much like a home for livestock and often smelt similar!) now accommodates the travelling support, a factor that was especially disconcerting for yours truly.

For the second match in succession, the team that won the toss opted to turn the teams around; however, this time it was Orient forcing Tranmere to attack their favoured end in the opening half. Bizarrely, I have no issue when it is my team doing this away from home.

Despite the depleted nature of the side, Orient got off to a promising start, establishing themselves well in the game. After an early ball fizzed across the face of our goal, Dan Kemp tested Ross Doohan in the Rovers' net with a curling free kick, and Lawrence Vigouroux was forced to save low from Josh Hawkes, but that was about it in the way of goalmouth action in the first 45 minutes.

After a half-time pint and a catch-up with Raj, whom we see at most away games and after home games in the Coach, we were back in situ and hopeful that the O's might secure an unlikely point out of this one. Those hopes were crushed on 58 minutes, when Jay Spearing, once of Liverpool, rifled home from the edge of the box. Paul later confirmed back in the pub that may have been the only thing of note he has ever done for Tranmere.

Credit to Orient, we stuck at it, and despite having to scramble to clear on a couple of occasions, had two great chances from Drinan and Smith at the death to sneak a draw but it wasn't to be. However, given the circumstances, it was an admirable performance and definitely an improvement on the previous week.

After the match, Kay and I treated ourselves to a cab back to Liverpool to watch most of Leeds v Arsenal before our final Catalan feed-up slightly disappointed about the way things had worked out but having enjoyed a fantastic pre-Christmas trip to Merseyside.

Final Score
Tranmere Rovers   **1**   **0**   **Leyton Orient**
Spearing 58

Christmas 2021 & New Year's 2022: They only went and took our Orient away!

Anyone reading this who has attended even just a few English football matches will be familiar with the terrace song set to the tune of "You Are My Sunshine", originally released by Johnny Cash, in which the word sunshine is replaced by whichever team is the subject of the chant, in our case Orient. The motivation behind this is that to us football obsessives, taking our football team away from us is the equivalent of stripping away the main source of joy (or too often misery, in reality!) from our lives. With the exception of those who lived through the war years and supporters who have suffered the utter devastation of their club going out of business (or indeed being moved up to Buckinghamshire – hello, MK Dons!), this was never a situation most of us would have to contemplate. But last season's suspension of fixtures due to the coronavirus was but a precursor to what was about to happen to our O's.

After being forced to scramble together a squad to fulfil the fixture up on the Wirral, Orient were then to suffer the cruel twist of having their next four league matches called off as a result of Covid issues within the opposition camps. The new Omicron strain of the virus was proving to be highly transmissible, if not as deadly. The rapidly increasing number of cases across the whole country, coupled with the requirement to self-isolate if testing positive, meant it was always going to have a significant impact on our lives, football most definitely included.

First to go was the scheduled Boxing Day fixture at Colchester United. Originally this match had posed a significant challenge for Kay and me, due to no trains running through to Colchester on Boxing Day itself, and even worse, for reasons to do with the holiday period, there wasn't going to be a Supporters Club coach as a fall-back plan. At one point it looked very much as if we would be spending Christmas itself there.

In the end, being the resourceful types that we are, we had found a very early National Express coach service from Stratford which would get us there in plenty of time for the match and a suitable hotel for the evening before being able to return to London via rail replacement bus and then train.

As if that wasn't bad enough, on Boxing Day itself we got the news that the home game against Newport had also been postponed due to a number of positive Covid cases within the visitors' squad, meaning that they wouldn't be able to fulfil the fixture. That was doubly disappointing given that we had planned to meet up with John Paul (the Newport fan who is exiled in Leytonstone but still travels to watch them as often as possible) for a few pints beforehand.

The worst was still to come, however. Up until 10am on New Year's Day it looked for all the world as if the home match against Bristol Rovers was going to go ahead. However, as I was scrolling through Twitter just to make sure, the news hit me like a sucker punch -- that one had gone as well. Yes, you guessed it, Rovers were claiming they didn't have sufficient available players to fulfil the fixture. With Arsenal due to host Manchester City in the daunting early kick-off, I was literally about to start getting myself organised and out the door to head down to the Coach & Horses for that one.

Of course, as disappointed (if not downright p**s**d off!) as I was, the postponements did come as something of a relief for Kay, whose ongoing injuries from her bicycle accident had put her attendance and the completion of her part of our unarticulated target of a "Golden Season" (in which you attend every one of your club's league matches home and away for the entire season, a concept I first discovered in the chapter on

Belarus in Matt Walker's excellent book: "Europe United: 1 football fan. 1 crazy season. 55 UEFA nations.") in serious jeopardy.

League Two table after close of play on 31st December 2021

Pos	Team	Pld	W	D	L	GF	GA	GD	Pts
1	Forest Green Rovers	20	13	5	2	43	20	23	44
2	Northampton Town	21	12	4	5	29	17	12	40
3	Tranmere Rovers	22	11	5	6	20	14	6	38
4	Sutton United	22	11	3	8	33	27	6	36
5	Port Vale	21	10	5	6	35	23	12	35
6	Newport County	22	9	7	6	35	29	6	34
7	Swindon Town	21	9	7	5	29	24	5	34
8	Exeter City	21	8	9	4	32	24	8	33
9	Mansfield Town	22	9	5	8	27	28	-1	32
10	**Leyton Orient**	**22**	**7**	**10**	**5**	**37**	**21**	**16**	**31**
11	Harrogate Town	22	8	6	8	35	31	4	30
12	Walsall	21	7	7	7	25	24	1	28

Pos	Team	Pld	W	D	L	GF	GA	GD	Pts
13	Salford City	21	7	6	8	24	21	3	27
14	Rochdale	22	6	9	7	30	30	0	27
15	Hartlepool United	22	8	3	11	24	34	-10	27
16	Bradford City	21	5	11	5	27	25	2	26
17	Bristol Rovers	21	7	5	9	27	33	-6	26
18	Crawley Town	20	7	4	9	23	30	-7	25
19	Barrow	22	5	8	9	22	26	-4	23
20	Colchester United	20	5	7	8	16	25	-9	22
21	Stevenage	22	4	8	10	16	34	-18	20
22	Carlisle United	21	4	7	10	15	29	-14	19
23	Scunthorpe United	22	3	10	9	19	37	-18	19
24	Oldham Athletic	23	4	5	14	22	39	-17	17

Chapter 9: January 2022

The transfer window opens and reinforcements arrive, but the O's form dips alarmingly after a long Covid-enforced layoff and Kay grits through her injuries to keep her home-and-away streak alive.

The end of the FA Cup run and yet another postponement

The FA Cup third round draw saw us paired with Stoke City away, while Port Vale, the other team from Stoke on Trent, would face Premier League Brentford at home. Of course, according to strict football rules, the two ties were not permitted to take place at the same time, so our game was pushed to the Sunday and given a 2 pm kick-off.

Anyone who has had the "pleasure" of using British public transport on a Sunday will know this is the time that is used for engineering works, and often, if trains are allowed to run, they are diverted and take much longer than on the other six days of the week. So it was to prove for travel to Stoke, with trains being re-routed via Northampton and taking at least an hour longer than they usually would. With Kay still struggling to walk any further than our local pub, and then only on special occasions, the earlier start and the longer journey meant we decided that we could skip this one, reckoning that cup matches didn't form part of a Golden Season bid.

Rather impressively 940 Orient fans did make the trip up there and were in fine voice from what we could hear, once we eventually got the audio stream working; draconian Football Association regulations, of course, meant that this match could only be viewed if you lived abroad.

Reportedly the O's gave a decent account of themselves against the Championship (second division) club and but for wasteful finishing could, and maybe should, have run the hosts closer. Eventually going down 2-0 thanks to goals from Paul Ince's son Thomas and Kevin Campbell's son Tyrese, as if that wasn't surreal enough, Ian Wright's grandson D'Mario Wright-Phillips came on as a sub to make his professional debut.

Back into routine after that match the following Monday, we gave Kay a fitness test to judge whether she would be able to make it to Oldham for the planned resumption of our adventure. There was good news and bad news, the good being that she felt strong enough to be able to go to the match, the "bad" being that she didn't want to push herself too hard and felt that a wiser option would be to go up to Manchester on the Friday afternoon, stay over and get a cab to and from the ground on the Saturday and then come back to London on the Sunday, just as we had for Salford on the opening weekend.

An impromptu staycation in Manchester again? It took me all of two and a half minutes to agree and for us to book the trains and hotels. Then on the Thursday came the news -- yep you guessed it, Oldham announced that they wouldn't be able to field a team and the match was off. Thankfully, it was fairly easy to cancel the hotel and get a refund for the train, but the damage that could be done by our fifth week in a row without Orient was altogether more difficult to quantify!

At long last the adventure resumes!

Game 23: Saturday 22nd January 2022, Leyton Orient v Port Vale

Finally, after an absence of 34 very long days and some frantic checking of the Orient website and every relevant social media page on almost an hourly basis, just in case it was going to be called off yet again, we were off to watch our beloved Orient once more.

Since the last time we had played, we had managed to bring in two new players: another loanee from Millwall in the form of right back Dan Moss and then the signing of Otis Khan from Walsall on an 18-month deal, a player who could reportedly fill the right wing-back role in the ongoing absence of Tom James but who could also intriguingly apparently operate as a midfielder. These two positive moves were somewhat tempered by the news that after surgery to address a long-standing issue, Craig Clay would be joining James on the sidelines for the remainder of the season.

Kay was on the mend from her own injuries, but again was fearful of getting the DLR and Tube in case she set herself back, so we treated ourselves to a cab up to Leyton. Because we had once again set off in plenty of time in case there were traffic issues (this is London, when aren't there traffic issues? says yours truly: a staunch non-driver!), this meant that we arrived at the wine bar with plenty of time for a few pints and to make sure we headed into the ground early enough to make it easier for Kay. I briefly toyed with the idea of having a beer and burger deal for what seemed like a reasonable 12 quid (well it is for London!), but in the end decided that this was no time to stray from tradition, and I would save myself for a pie at the ground.

We got to the ground just after 2pm and bumped straight into Jamie, co-editor and lead distributor of esteemed publication "The Leyton Orientear" (what do you mean you have never heard of it?), of which I am a regular contributor. I left Kay with Jamie as I went in search of a copy of the other Orient fanzine "Pandemonium", which was apparently available round the other side of the ground outside the club shop. It is a key feature of my football geekery that even in this day of almost unlimited amounts of online content for any club you can think of, I am still a stickler for fanzines and have been ever since I used to buy "When Saturday Comes" outside Prenton Park as a teenager, in the days long before it became a nationwide publication sold in actual bona fide retail outlets.

With my copy of the other fanzine and the matchday programme safely tucked into my coat pocket, when I rounded the corner, I was in no way surprised to find the missus was helping Jamie to sell the 'Ear and even managed to flog one to an away fan. She may well have to augment the salesforce going forward, although I am not sure how she will balance that with her pre-match drinking commitments, unless she combines the two and hawks them round the local pubs. Two birds with just the one stone and all that!

Once inside and refuelled with the usual pie and pint combo, we got in our seats in plenty of time to pay our respects to the O's and Port Vale fans who had passed away in the previous 12 months, as the club had planned to do on New Year's Day but for the postponement. This included the father of Paul, who sits in front of us, featured movingly in a piece in the programme.

Out of the two new signings, Moss was given the nod to start at right wing-back while Khan had to content himself with a place on the bench. I suspect this may have been based on who had been signed first, but it would prove interesting to see if the latter becomes the go-to option in coming weeks, or whether a role higher up the pitch might be more suitable.

After five weeks off other than the cup defeat at Stoke, it was probably always somewhat inevitable that Orient might be a bit rusty in trying to get back into the swing of the season. As tiring as lower league schedules are, there is no substitute for playing week in and week out to keep the players at the highest level of competitiveness. Clubs can do many things in training, and the extra time for Kenny Jackett to work with the players could be of benefit in the long run, but there is no substitute for playing in terms of fostering intensity. Orient looked very much like a team that had played just the one competitive game since the middle of December.

The fact that the three most memorable pieces of action were a fox appearing on the pitch in the first half and then making a mad dash for the gate in the north east corner of the ground, a flock of parakeets circling above the ground in the second and a slightly heated altercation over what would have been a generous penalty for Orient late on, probably tells you all you need to know about this match as a spectacle. If we had been hoping that the O's would hit the ground running after their prolonged hiatus, we were to be sadly disappointed. This match, all being well with the pandemic, started a run of seven matches in three weeks, and we could only hope that it served to blow the cobwebs away ahead of better performances in the next six.

Final Score
Leyton Orient	**0**	**0**	**Port Vale**

More frustration for the O's!

Game 24: Tuesday 24th January 2022, Leyton Orient v Newport County

Another seven days of the transfer window and another couple of new players. After the signing of two right wing-backs the previous week, the focus this week seemingly was on young central midfielders, with the club announcing on Monday the addition to the squad of Jordan Brown, an 18-year-old on a free transfer from Derby County, and Ethan Coleman, a defensive midfielder from Kings Lynn. Suffice to say the entire Orient faithful was very much looking forward to the end of the week and the unveiling of two 20-plus goals a season strikers, in our dreams at least!

In other major news, Kay was fit enough to brave the train to Brisbane Road for this one on the premise that we gave her sufficient time to recover from her travails in the wine bar before the match and that we would in all likelihood be getting a cab home. Who was I to disagree with either of her perfectly logical and justifiable demands? In another break from tradition, the missus then decided that she would save getting a pie until half-time. I, however, am way too much of a traditionalist and was in actual fact too hungry to follow suit.

Generally speaking, in recent clashes with Newport, Orient have tended to fare quite well, even though the Exiles have a tendency to feature towards the upper end of the table and always seem prepared to come to play, so after the frustration of Saturday afternoon against Port Vale, while optimism may not have been running rife through Brisbane Road, there was the hope that this might provide an ideal opportunity to get a result, stimulate some momentum and get our season back on track. Oh, how wrong we were.

Of the new signings, Otis Khan was given his first start at right wing-back, with Millwall loanee Dan Moss dropping to the bench and Jordan Brown featuring in central midfield in place of skipper, and recently much-maligned, Darren Pratley.

In fairness, there was some football played, in the first half at least, but the O's attack, which had looked so potentially prolific in the earlier part of the season, was once again blunt. We controlled the ball fairly comfortably when in possession but were so slow and ponderous in trying to progress it forward that a goal for Orient scored by one of our actual players for the first time since Swindon on the 7th December still looked a distant possibility.

Kenny Jackett tried to shake things up a bit in the second half, bringing on Paul Smyth, who after his less than sporadic appearances in the first half of the season was now almost a bona fide regular, having featured in the last three league games, for Aaron Drinan, to partner Harry Smith up top.

Smyth was lively from his introduction, his diminutive stature allowing him to turn sharply and drive at the opposition backline, a facet that we hoped could prove important in sparking Orient's creativity and incisiveness again. Later on in the half, forward Ruel Sotiriou replaced Dan Kemp, who had been playing in the space behind the two frontmen, and Smyth dropped a little deeper, which suggested another potential role for him, if, of course, he could stay fit.

With time running down and it looking for all the world that we were going to have to settle for yet another draw and a second goalless game in a week, the mediocre turned to the disappointing when we allowed a corner to be flicked on at the near post toward an unmarked Cameron Norman, who nodded home for 1-0 to the visitors. It was another goal from a set piece that we failed to clear, a state of events that was becoming a bit of an Achilles heel for Orient.

We roused ourselves for a late push for an equalizer and very nearly got it when first Moss, on as a late sub, and then Khan were denied by goalmouth clearances in the same spell of pressure. In the end, it wasn't to be, and we went away from the ground disappointed, once again.

That match made it more than six hours of league football since Orient had managed to score a goal in their own right. That and the continued dropping of points had perhaps for the first time started to raise some doubts about the squad's play-off credentials. It felt very much as if somehow Kenny and the boys needed to find a spark to get a result and shock themselves back to life, and with trips to 7th placed Mansfield and then 11th placed Bradford in the next two games, it felt like we were approaching a critical juncture in Orient's season.

After consoling ourselves with a pint back in the wine bar, then finding out that the mini-cab office near the station shut before 10 pm (nope I have never seen that before: a cab company that shuts before the pubs!), we opted to order an Uber, despite having family and friends who are black cab drivers in London. In one of those middle-aged moments, we actually had to ask a fellow football fan (a Manchester City season ticket holder who lived in Kew but had been to watch the O's with his mate, no less!) to read out the reg number, as Kay had forgotten her reading glasses and I am way too stubborn to admit that I need them. We got home safe and sound in the end, however.

Final Score

Leyton Orient	0	1	Newport County
			Norman 85

Orient get battered, everywhere we go!

Game 25: Saturday 29th January 2022, Mansfield Town v Leyton Orient

After having to endure two disappointing home games and more than a month since our last awayday adventure, it is fair to say that Kay and I were both absolutely raring to get underway on this one.

Mansfield were coming into the match on the back of seven straight wins, and from what we were led to believe, were a very different prospect from the anti-football incarnation of the side that had niggled and shirt-pulled its way to a goalless draw at Brisbane Road back in September. In many ways, that team had been surprising from the point of view that they seemed way too far away from a smooth passing side for a team managed by someone bearing the surname of Clough. No matter how we looked at the match in the build-up, it looked like it was going to be a big ask for an Orient side very much in the doldrums of uninspiring form. Still, sometimes in football when you think you have no chance is exactly the moment when things click back into form.

With Kay continuing to recover from her injuries, we were able to take the Tube up to St Pancras, showing great restraint by refusing to go in the rather posh (and expensive!) bar at the station. Our good intentions went out of the window, however, as soon as we got underway, when we realised that there was an onboard trolley service which sold beer. As Kay said, it was the perfect accompaniment to the jalapeno and nacho cheese crisps that I had bought to follow my customary sandwich, and I certainly wasn't going to argue with logic like that.

After a brief change of trains at Nottingham, we arrived in Mansfield pretty much bang on 1 pm with two hours to kill before kick-off. As per usual, I had gone to great pains in researching appropriate local hostelries, but given the effects of yet another storm that was buffeting the country with high winds, alongside Kay's relative lack of mobility, we headed straight towards the town and into the nearest pub.

It is probably fair to say that the Wheatsheaf is far from being the most glamourous and salubrious drinkery you will even happen across, but with cheap beer and three shots for £5.50, what was not to like? Given the cheap shots and the experience up on the Wirral on our last trip, we wasted no time whatsoever in sending a picture of them to Lord Dazza, who instantly replied with his appreciation of our efforts.

Mansfield may not exactly be a heaving metropolis (in all honesty I would have struggled to find it on a map prior to going), but with Field Mill being a 10-minute walk away from the station (or 14 minutes from the Wheatsheaf), it is another ground that is perfectly set up for the travelling football fan.

The ground itself is fairly modern on three sides, including a spacious away stand behind one of the goals, which almost mirrors that for the home supporters at the other end. On one sideline however is a long abandoned wooden stand that is plastered with advertising hoardings. Presumably it used to add character to the place but now it just looks like a badly maintained (if rather large) garden shed.

Having eschewed a pie in favour of a Catalan breakfast up on Merseyside, and then having had the trips to Colchester and Oldham postponed, Kay was more than keen to get back to her pie-rating scale and opted for a steak one, which it has to be said was very tasty, definitely up there with Scunthorpe, Rochdale despite the lack of meat, and much to her insistence/bias Brisbane Road as the best she has had through the campaign so far.

Perhaps the least said about the O's performance in this one the better. For about 20 minutes or so, we matched a lively looking Mansfield side; however, as the half wore on, the home side took more and more control. Just before half-time, Jordan Bowery went through in the area, looking for all the world as if he had controlled it with his arm, and fired past Lawrence Vigouroux for 1-0. Despite vehement protests from the O's players, the goal stood, another tough one to take.

As the teams emerged after the break, it became apparent that Paul Smyth had gone off injured yet again, to be replaced by Matt Young. It later transpired that this time, the forward had suffered a collapsed lung. He really must be the unluckiest player anyone has ever known.

The second half was one in which the Stags were very much in control and we struggled to contain them, and it came as little surprise to the travelling O's faithful when Ollie Clarke made it 2-0 and sealed the game on the half volley with just over quarter of an hour left. The home support to our right entertained us with continued choruses of "Orient get battered everywhere they go!", and it was difficult to do anything but agree with them given our current run of woeful form.

To make matters worse, on the train back to London there was no buffet car or even a trolley, not only another clear infringement of our human rights, but it also meant that we -- well, when I say "we", I mean me -- had to spend the entire journey sulking about another defeat without even being able to drown our sorrows.

Final Score
| **Mansfield Town** | **2** | **0** | **Leyton Orient** |
Bowery 44
Clarke 72

League Two table after close of play on 31st January 2022

Pos	Team	Pld	W	D	L	GF	GA	GD	Pts
1	Forest Green Rovers	26	17	7	2	55	21	34	58
2	Tranmere Rovers	27	14	6	7	28	19	9	48
3	Newport County	28	13	8	7	46	35	11	47
4	Sutton United	27	14	5	8	43	33	10	47
5	Northampton Town	26	13	6	7	33	24	9	45
6	Mansfield Town	26	13	5	8	37	31	6	44
7	Swindon Town	26	11	9	6	41	32	9	42
8	Exeter City	26	10	11	5	37	26	11	41
9	Port Vale	25	11	6	8	37	27	10	39
10	Salford City	28	10	7	11	31	28	3	37
11	Bradford City	27	8	12	7	34	32	2	36
12	Bristol Rovers	25	10	6	9	34	36	-2	36
13	Crawley Town	26	10	5	11	31	36	-5	35

Pos	Team	Pld	W	D	L	GF	GA	GD	Pts
14	Harrogate Town	25	9	6	10	38	38	0	33
15	Leyton Orient	25	7	11	7	37	24	13	32
16	Hartlepool United	27	8	7	12	25	37	-12	31
17	Stevenage	28	7	10	11	28	42	-14	31
18	Rochdale	25	6	11	8	30	32	-2	29
19	Walsall	27	7	8	12	30	37	-7	29
20	Carlisle United	27	6	9	12	19	35	-16	27
21	Barrow	27	6	8	13	27	35	-8	26
22	Colchester United	26	6	8	12	23	36	-13	26
23	Oldham Athletic	26	4	7	15	22	42	-20	19
24	Scunthorpe United	28	3	10	15	21	49	-28	19

Chapter 10: February 2022

Kenny Jackett gets the dreaded vote of confidence from the board…and then gets sacked anyway, as we watch Leyton Orient sink down the table, and the winter weather spoils our trip to Harrogate.

I was there when Pratley scored!

Game 26: Tuesday 1st February 2022, Bradford City v Leyton Orient

Orient's progress in the FA Cup and the subsequent moving of this game to a Tuesday night meant that Kay had to dip out of this trip due to work commitments. Not only did this bring an end to her bid for a league Golden Season, but it also meant that I would be flying solo for our visit to Yorkshire. Reassuringly, my northern accent and well-developed knowledge of rugby league would provide me with the perfect cover story, should I require it while "in country".

With the previous day having been the last day of the transfer window, Orient fans were surprised by the unveiling of two more recruits, both on loan: George Ray, a defender, came in from Exeter in anticipation of Alex Mitchell needing an unspecified operation in the near future, and Frank Nouble arrived from Colchester to replace the now definitely out injured Paul Smyth.

I arrived about 2:30pm and thought the best option was to go and see if I could check into the hotel, despite it saying on my booking confirmation that check-in was at 4pm. Seriously, how busy could the Holiday Inn Express on a February Tuesday night in Bradford be? Thankfully the answer was not very, and I was safely installed in my room after a brief chat with the guy on the desk about the match that evening. He suggested that Bradford's current form saw them throwing away leads on a regular basis, but I told him not to worry, as scoring a goal would be seen as a sign of progress for Orient at the moment!

Once I had got myself settled into my room and unpacked, which took all of two and a half minutes, I decided to go for a bit of a wander to see what the place was like. Amazingly for someone who hails from just over the Pennines, I have only ever been to Bradford to watch St Helens play at Odsal Stadium, which is on the outskirts of town, and so I had no idea what the city centre itself was like.

The effects of the storm that had hit us in Mansfield were still causing problems across the north, and thus I made the rather swift decision that I would askew my planned visit to a couple of local hostelries and do my pre-match drinking back at the hotel.

After a quick check-in with Kay, in which I took no pleasure at all in winding her up that she was missing the trip of a lifetime(!), I steeled myself for heading back out into the wind and towards the ground.

With Kay back in London and unable to change pub options as she tends to do, I headed straight for the Bradford Arms, which is literally no more than five minutes away from the ground. As soon as I had walked in and bought myself a pint, I turned to my right and there were Matt, Michael and Co., some of the lads who had very kindly shared their cab with us on the way back from Rochdale. Owing to a lack of annual leave, they had had to come by coach with another dedicated dozen or so brave souls. I was in no way jealous of the prospect of arriving back in East London in the wee small hours. The Holiday Inn in central Bradford may not be the most luxurious hotel in the world, but it was only 20 minutes' walk away.

Valley Parade is a ground that I had always fancied visiting, and it didn't disappoint. It may be a bit run down these days, but it feels huge, cavernous almost, with steep sloping stands around two of the sides including the corner, a main stand and a small double-decker stand behind one of the goals that looks a tad out of place. Obviously as a venue it carries the sad memory of the fire there back in 1985, but also reminds us that Bradford's ground didn't look too out of place during the couple of seasons that the club featured in the Premier League way back at the turn of the millennium.

Whether in response to our recent run of very poor form, or maybe Kenny Jackett had been plotting it for a while, but we changed from the 3-4-1-2 system that simply hadn't been working to a more traditional 4-3-3, with Theo Archibald pushed higher up the pitch more like a traditional winger, and it has to be said that it worked to an extent, making us look much more of an attacking threat than we had for a good few weeks. We looked much more in control of the game and more like a team that understood what it was trying to do.

Despite the improved performance, first half chances were few and far between. Just past the half-hour mark, Lawrence Vigouroux had to be alert to pounce on the ball after Matt Daley had driven towards goal, then Omar Beckles weakly headed straight to their keeper, Alex Bass, from an Otis Khan free kick from just inside the Bradford half, but that was about it in terms of attacking action.

With Kay not in attendance to run her expert rule over the pie offerings, I decided that the least I could do was to try one of them on her behalf. For a brief moment I was contemplating another chicken Balti one, as Bradford is more than famous for curry, but in the end I stuck to my northern roots and went for meat and potato. While I think it was pretty tasty, I cannot confirm 100%, as it was so nuclear hot that my mouth was still burnt the following day and most of the rest of the week.

It was the home side that started the second half with more intent, as Andy Cook, a prolific marksman wherever he has played, steered a header from a corner just wide, but Orient gradually gained control once again.

It is an oft-used cliché in football that when a team or player is struggling for goals, they just need one to go in to spark them.

So it was to prove for Orient when we took the lead through an unlikely source. The Bradford defence half-cleared another Khan searching ball into the box from a free-kick, and it rolled to much-maligned skipper Darren Pratley, who slammed home from the edge of the area. If, as I suspected at the time, that was likely to be his only goal contribution in the whole season, I was half-tempted to get a t-shirt printed with "I was there when Pratley scored" on it, if only to wind up Kay! (Update: It did prove to be Prats' only goal of the campaign, and even now, as immature as I am, I do actually regret not having the t-shirt made!).

Of course, as per usual when going ahead the challenge for Orient was going to be holding onto the lead, something that we had proven largely ineffectual at, especially on our travels, for the majority of the campaign to date. It came as little surprise, but was nonetheless annoying, when Elliott Watt's half volley from the edge of the penalty box was deflected past Vigouroux with just seven minutes to play.

Despite an improved performance, we had to be content with yet another draw. It was no consolation that it was another frustrating result for the home team, who had almost unbelievably drawn more than we have.

Final Score

Bradford City	1	1	Leyton Orient
Watt 83			Pratley 69

Will it ever come good for Orient again?

Game 27: Saturday 5th February 2022, Leyton Orient v Colchester United

Back in London and reunited with Kay, and now the games truly were coming thick and fast at this juncture. As he had been over in the UK for a belated visit, Chairman Nigel Travis took the opportunity to host an "Ask the Chairman" session on the club's YouTube channel on the preceding Wednesday evening. During the course of this, he was at pains to point out in response to the ongoing poor performances that the board still had every confidence in Kenny Jackett as the manager and that they hadn't given up on qualification for the play-offs this season. But above all, he wished to respond to some criticism of the club's moves in the transfer market.

Going into the transfer window, Nigel had said that the club were going to be "aggressive", but there was a feeling amongst some (most/all?) of the support that three loan signings, two inexperienced youngsters and the admittedly impressive Otis Khan didn't meet the expectation he had created. He pointed out that the loan signings were to cover for Tom James, Craig Clay and Paul Smyth, who would be out for most of the rest of the season, and that Ethan Coleman, Jordan Brown and Khan represented an investment in the future. In football, however, what happens on the pitch is the only true way to judge a team.

As positive as the session was, to then follow it up with such a poor performance, probably the worst of the season, and to lose to a team sitting in 20th place in the table, only fuelled the complaints about how things were going and the mumblings about the manager from a large chunk of the Orient faithful.

I do not profess to be any sort of tactical genius, but after the relative improvement in performance at Bradford using the 4-3-3 system, why Jackett then went back to the three-at-the-back approach that had been so hard to watch over recent games was beyond me. Granted, Theo Archibald was ruled out, but surely we could have found someone else to operate on the left flank?

Annoyingly, Colchester won the toss and opted to turn us around, and maybe I should have read the writing on the wall then and gone home. We did have an early chance when Aaron Drinan's leaping header tested Sam Hornby in their goal, but they swept up-field on the counter from that, cutting through us like a hot knife through butter, and eventually the ball rolled to Freddie Sears on his own in the area, who slotted home. There were less than four minutes on the clock. You could sense the resignation and sinking feeling around the ground, as it dawned on us all that a team that had managed just two goals, only one of them scored by an Orient player, in its last six matches was going to have to chase the game – not something we had proven particularly good at.

Understandably after taking the lead, the visitors settled into a deep shape, conceding the flanks but challenging Orient to try to play through the middle. You really didn't need to have watched a lot of Orient over the course of the season to guess that we resorted to launching the ball forward in the general direction of Harry Smith and Drinan but without it sticking. Our attacking play looked clueless and miles away from the team that we had seemed to be back in the earlier months of the campaign.

Drinan's industriousness allowed him to get a couple of shots in from decent enough positions, but our belief seemed to have deserted us, and it was actually Colchester that threatened to notch a second. Kay and I consoled ourselves with a pint back in the Coach & Horses after the game and met up with Raj and the boys, but as disappointing an afternoon as it was, we all knew we would be in Exeter on Tuesday night.

Final Score

Leyton Orient	**0**	**1**	**Colchester United**
			Sears 4

Another Tuesday, another awayday

Game 28: Tuesday 8th February 2022, Exeter City v Leyton Orient

Even before the season got underway, a trip to Exeter on a Tuesday night in early February was always going to be a big ask. With the O's form moving from poor to dreadful with the defeat by 20th placed Colchester on the preceding Saturday, any semblance of a result would have been more than gratefully received by the Orient faithful.

With Kay now free of work commitments, she was back in harness for the trip, and we were both looking forward to what promised to be a nice train trip and a couple of days off work down in Devon. We certainly weren't expecting very much at all from our beloved O's.

Upon arrival at Exeter St David's, one of two mainline stations in Exeter, we were somewhat relieved that Kay had been thorough enough in her research to pick the St David's location rather than the city centre option, as our hotel was literally across the car park from the station. Once again, it was empty enough that we were able to check-in early, and once installed in the room Kay indulged herself in a recovery nap (nothing at all to do with the beers on the train, of course, she insisted!), while I watched the Winter Olympics on TV and read my book.

After Kay's power nap, we decided that we might as well go and explore the local area a bit while heading in the general direction of the ground, with the intention of stopping on the way at a couple of pubs to break up the half hour walk, given the missus was still short of full fitness. It will surprise none of you reading this that we made it as far as the nearest

Wetherspoons, a mere five minutes away, although admittedly up a rather steep incline.

The Imperial, to give it its official title, is one of the most impressive pubs I think I have ever been in; to describe it simply, it looks like a country manor house. It made complete sense once we discovered it was originally Elmfield House, which the Internet reliably informed us was previously a private house that was built by the county surveyor, who built the Exeter canal basin, before it was turned into a hotel in the early 1900's. Eventually it was purchased by the pub chain but with the character and grounds kept intact. Its most striking feature is the part of the bar that used to house the orangery -- a huge conservatory that looks like an old-world railway station. If you ever find yourself in the area, it is a lovely spot to have a pint.

After catching up with Raj and some of the other travelling O's faithful, we decided that our best option was to head back down to the station and get a cab up to the ground. In a similar way to Salford, our driver knew where the ground was but had apparently never heard of the St Anne's Well pub recommended on Football Ground Guide. Thankfully, he had heard of Well Street on which it was located. After a pint in there, we decided to get ourselves in, as neither of us had eaten since the train was still in the London suburbs.

Amazingly on our way through the turnstiles, we were offered a couple of vouchers for a free tea or coffee by the lady on the turnstile. She had either mistaken us for the sort of people who had driven up or decided that we might prefer a non-alcoholic drink. We decided that we would pass them onto fans who were actually driving and headed for the bar.

Annoyingly it was a cash-only till (note to self: always make sure you have sufficient cash on you for such eventualities in the future!), but thankfully Kay had wisely got some money out and could cover two bottles of lager and, to our utmost delight, two Grecian steak pasties, which were huge and very tasty and a suitable alternative to the usual pie options. When in the South West and all that.

After exchanging pleasantries with other travelling O's, we decided to go and secure ourselves a decent spot on the terrace. Any fears that Kay had originally had of it being a bit crowded and precarious for her were soon soothed when we realised there was plenty of room. St James Park has recently undergone refurbishment work, and while I never had the "pleasure" of visiting in its previous state, which was apparently pretty grim in the away end, it now seems like a decent ground. The away terrace behind the goal has a decent view but is dwarfed by the terrace at the other end which houses the home supporters. The "Big Bank", as it is known, can house around 3,950 fans and is apparently the largest terrace left in the English Football League. Along each sideline are decent sized and fairly modern stands, although one definitely looks more modern than the other. It does feel like a ground that has managed to keep its true character while being modernised.

Once again, there was a change to the system for Orient, as Kenny Jackett tried once again to spark some form of life into a team mired in a woeful run of form. This time it was a more traditional 4-4-2 line-up, with new loan signing Frank Nouble partnering Aaron Drinan up front. Harry Smith was left out of the squad all together, reportedly due to illness, but us cynical, seasoned football watchers might have suggested that it may well have been to do with his tantrum when being subbed off against Colchester, in which he threw his shirt to the floor.

Right from the start of the game, it seemed as if Orient were going to try to stifle their opponents and hope to nick a goal, and as a result, it was something of a timid performance, although we could have taken an early lead when Drinan raced through on goal, only to fire wide when it looked easier to hit the target. I didn't see it, but Drinan apparently raised his fingers to his lips to "shh" the travelling support, not something that endeared him to anyone, given his poor current form.

At half-time, we bumped into Tim, the O's fan that travels from Norwich for every game he attends, who we had first met outside the Coach a few months back. As I went back for the start of the second half, Kay stayed chatting and even came to Tim's mate's rescue when she offered to buy him a beer, as he had no cash on him either. Tim would later go on to ensure that he paid us back on his mate's behalf.

The second half continued with the O's looking fairly resilient but without threatening the Exeter goal. We were then treated to a sighting of the lesser spotted Callum Reilly, who came on for a well overdue 25 minutes or so after not having featured since an EFL Trophy game in mid-September, replacing Matt Young.

Orient just about looked to be holding on for a point, until in stoppage time Omar Beckles was adjudged to have committed an off-the-ball foul and Exeter were awarded a free kick. As it came into our penalty area, Cheick Diabate was left largely unchallenged to nod home for the hosts, securing all three points and condemning us to our eighth consecutive match without a win.

The biggest consoling factor in following a team away from home, especially in midweek when you are staying over, is that the craic and catching up with familiar faces helps you to get over the pain even of an added time winner for the opposition. So it was that Kay, Tim and I headed back to the St Anne's Well to cheer ourselves up. Unbelievably, however, it was apparently off limits due to not one, but two functions going on (yeah, right, on a Tuesday night?). Determined to buy Kay the pint that his mate owed her, Tim led us back up the road to the Bowling Green, where he had been pre-match.

Rather amazingly, there was a band on, and the place was pretty full, so maybe Tuesday is actually the night to go out in Exeter. Of course, we couldn't just leave it at one round, so we had another before calling a cab back to the hotel, leaving Tim in the capable of hands of the group of Exeter fans that he had just met.

After the now compulsory Wetherspoons breakfast, Kay and I made our way home the following day, reflecting on another disappointing result but another cracking awayday. Perhaps the best way to handle these going forward is to ignore what happens on the pitch and to just enjoy the trip.

Final Score
Exeter City   **1   0   Leyton Orient**
Diabate 90+2

Another Saturday, another home defeat

Game 29: Saturday 12th February 2022, Leyton Orient v Salford City

As a football obsessive, when your team is on a bad run, you find yourself just hoping and praying that their luck changes and they can manage to turn a corner every time you go and see them. As Kay put it so succinctly, you keep going because if they did manage a win (or to even score a goal, in Orient's case!) you wouldn't want to miss it.

In the morning, we listened to an interview on the LO Down podcast with Chairman Nigel Travis, which, just like his Q&A the previous week gave you the feeling that this was intended to reassure the fanbase that while things might be at a very low ebb on the pitch, the future looks positive. With a background in the commercial world at Dunkin' Donuts, Blockbuster video and Papa John's pizza, Mr Travis certainly has a smooth way of accentuating the positive and reassuring the fan (customer?) base. When we left the house, in the lovely February sunshine, I think both of us hoped that today would be the day that the O's turned things around.

After a brief stop at the wine bar, we headed down to the ground, puzzled by the lack of a Salford supporters' coach. I only half-jokingly suggested that Salford, as a newly moneyed club prepared to splash the cash to climb the leagues, didn't have that many fans. However, given Orient's recent mind-numbing performances and poor form, there weren't that many home fans knocking around either.

Just before kick-off, Mark and Kevin came wobbling in, looking very much as if they had been in the pub for quite some time before the match. As it turned out they had arrived at their favourite Lion & Key in Leytonstone at 10 to 10 in the morning. Mark later showed us his bar bill which totalled in excess of £100, spent mostly on pints of lager and, to be fair, a bit of breakfast. Quite some going.

For this one, Kenny Jackett opted to stick with the 4-4-2 debuted at Exeter, but Theo Archibald's return to fitness after injury/illness meant that we had him on one flank and Otis Khan on the other to hopefully provide some decent service to our front two of Aaron Drinan and Frank Nouble.

For 20 minutes, Orient looked like a team reinvigorated, as there was a new impetus and much quicker movement when we had the ball and aggressive pressure on the opposition when we didn't. Maybe they had been listening to the chairman before the match, as well? However, as the game wore on,

Salford gained more and more of a foothold as we tired, and consequently the intensity of our work started to die off. We did, however, keep it goalless until the break, thanks in no small part to a sharp reaction save by Lawrence Vigouroux in our goal.

In the opening exchanges of the second period, Drinan wasted another glorious chance to give us the lead we were so desperately hoping for and most definitely needed, again pushing the ball wide of the right hand upright when bearing down on goal through the inside left channel, just as he had done at Exeter.

A mere matter of minutes later, the killer blow came: Brandon Thomas-Asante, who had been a thorn in our side throughout the first half, played the ball across the face of goal, where Liam Shephard was sliding in unopposed to turn it home. You could feel the resignation to our fate all around the ground and almost see the confidence drain from the players' faces. It truly knocked the stuffing out of all of us.

Ten minutes later our fate was sealed when Theo Vassell headed home a corner, once again largely unopposed. As bad as we had been in attack, to make matters even worse, we also seemed to have added an ability to concede soft goals over our recent matches.

Orient couldn't seem to raise themselves for the remaining half an hour, and we were consigned to our third consecutive home defeat and ninth game without a win. If we hadn't reached crisis point just yet, we could surely see it coming into view.

Final Score

Leyton Orient	**0**	**2**	**Salford City**
			Shephard 50
			Vassell 60

Does it count as an awayday if you go but the match is postponed?

Game 30: Saturday 19th February 2022, Harrogate Town v Leyton Orient

All during the week we had been bombarded with the news that yet another named storm was going to batter the nation, Storm Eunice as it was titled. It was predicted that the impact was going to be so major that a "red" weather warning was issued for London and the South East, apparently for the first time in history. I just knew that the havoc wreaked by Eunice would disrupt the trains to Harrogate and that we wouldn't be able to go to the match, even if it went ahead.

Trying to put a brave face on things, Kay and I resolved that we would proceed as planned until such time as going would be impossible. We got up nice and early had a quick flick at the news which warned anyone contemplating travelling by train to stay at home unless their journey was absolutely essential. Typical sensationalism, obviously, but we stuck to our plan and headed to the station, our judgement being that going to a match is essential travel for hopeless football obsessives. We did fear, however, that we might end up having a "day out" around Kings Cross.

To our utter amazement, not only were the trains running, but they were reportedly on time without any suggestion of disruption. So much for staying at home! We arrived in Leeds, where we had to change for the train through to Harrogate pretty much on time, but as we were pulling into the station, we noticed the first flakes of snow starting to fall. We reassured ourselves that it was way too wet for it to stick, and it wouldn't impact the game. Oh, how wrong could we be?

All the way on the half-hour journey, the snow seemed to be intensifying, and, worse still, it was clearly starting to settle on the fields that lined the route. We weren't the only ones starting to flap, as a number of O's fans and Harrogate supporters were starting to check their phones. Harrogate Town had put out a call for volunteers to come and help clear the pitch, never a promising sign.

When we arrived at the station it is fair to say that we were greeted by a very wintry scene, and our hopes that the match would go ahead took a further dent. We decided that the best (only?) option was to head to the rather posh but excellent Harrogate Tap, which is part of the station building, to see how things shaped up before trying to get a taxi up to the ground. As soon as we walked in, there was Keren from the Supporters Club with family and friends, as it seemed they had had the same idea.

With just over an hour to go to kick-off came the news that the match had officially been called off, bad news for pretty much everyone in the pub, as most seemed to be football supporters. At least Kay and I had booked a hotel, as we were due to meet one of her colleagues who lives nearby for dinner that evening, so we didn't have to face the long journey back to London without having been to a match. We had another pint or two bid our farewells and headed in the direction of our hotel, apparently just 10 minutes' walk away.

As we were halfway up the hill, we spotted a familiar tall figure in an Orient hoodie coming towards us -- it was none other than O's frontman Harry Smith. We stopped for a brief chat, and he told us that he was off to Leeds for the Leeds v Manchester United match the following day. He also pointed us in the general direction of our hotel, where the team had stayed the previous couple of evenings. Reassuringly, he said it was very good.

After a slight wrong turn (thanks, Google Maps!), we eventually found the place without any further issues, checked in, unpacked and were in the bar ready to plot the rest of our day and evening in Harrogate. Checking on Facebook, we discovered that Paul (he of the "Easy Lovers" fame from Port Vale) was having a drink in town and had happened across a bar called Trotters, which is exactly what you might think it is: an Only Fools & Horses themed bar. We decided that this was the only place to catch up with other stranded O's fans. Sadly, Kay's colleague, Leslie, decided that it wasn't worth risking the 10-mile drive from Ottley so wouldn't make dinner, but we decided that we might as well use the reservation however.

By this time the snow had stopped, but it was starting to turn a bit slushy and slippery, not a great situation given how hilly Harrogate is and that Kay was still on the mend after her accident. After a quick McDonald's pit stop, we started to look for Trotters, but couldn't locate it (thanks again, Google Maps!) so decided to sack it off, as Paul would be heading for home soon, and find somewhere else to base ourselves. The first pub we chose was a craft beer brewery place, which always presents something of a challenge for us more traditional drinkers. Suffice it to say that my choice of New Zealand Pale Ale didn't turn out to be an undiscovered gem.

Thankfully, the next place we happened across, The End, was much more to our liking. It is essentially a sports bar with pool tables and TV screens everywhere, so much so that it really confused a young and very drunk fellow patron who couldn't make up his mind which match to watch given the choice. I resisted the temptation to tell him that out of the 10 screens, nine were showing Man City against Tottenham and the other was on Sky Sports News.

After a few minutes, we got talking to some lads who had just arrived and looked very much as if this wasn't the first pub they had visited. It turned out that they were both avid football fans, one of whom was a Leeds supporter but who had also developed a soft spot for Orient after driving a mate from university to Hull to watch the O's in 2010. The other was an Arsenal fan, despite being from Yorkshire. As a result, the conversation flowed smoothly between us four football obsessives, and before we knew it, it was time for Kay and me to head off for dinner. If you ever find yourself in Harrogate in search of food, the Tannin Level (once you are able to find it!) offers quality food and plenty of it, as well as great wine, at un-London like prices. Definitely worth a try.

After dinner, having had enough of slipping around everywhere and using Kay's injuries (which the previous week were confirmed as fractures in her pelvis) as an excuse, we treated ourselves to a cab back to the hotel for a few final drinks and to watch Match of the Day.

In the morning, we headed down to the town again for the customary trip to Wetherspoons, whose grandeur rivals the one in Exeter, although we opted to have lunch courtesy of McDonald's in a very tense-feeling Leeds station, given that the game against hated rivals Manchester United, the first encounter to be played between the two in front of a crowd since Leeds returned to the top flight, was kicking off at 2pm. On the train on the way home, we reflected on what looked like a very nice town and despite the lack of a match to watch were both keen to return, work permitting.

Final Score
Harrogate Town   **P**   **P**   **Leyton Orient**

No Jackett required

Game 30: Tuesday 22nd February 2022, Leyton Orient v Bristol Rovers

When a team is in a slump, which make no mistake, Orient definitely were at this stage, you end up going to the matches in the hope that something, anything, will spark the team into life and turn its fortunes around. Each time it doesn't, things just feel stale, and you start to wonder where the next goal or point is going to come from. Unfortunately for Orient, two home games in a row did little to give us any fresh hope. The first was the visit of Bristol Rovers on another February Tuesday evening.

Kay and I did our usual and got to the wine bar as early as we could, probably as much to steel ourselves for what we feared might be another disappointing and difficult-to-watch match. When we headed down into the ground, there was an overwhelmingly subdued atmosphere around the place, almost as if everyone brave enough to drag themselves along was expecting little but fearing the worst.

In an attempt to try to change things, Kenny Jackett brought Ruel Sotiriou in on the left-hand side, and Matt Young started in midfield. Unlike against Salford, though, the O's really didn't seem to start with any impetus. It was almost as if the players themselves lacked any belief in their ability to turn things round.

Two first half goals in quick succession, one a curling effort from range by Antony Evans, the other rolled into an empty net by Aaron Collins after Lawrence Vigouroux had made a decent save, sealed our fate. Try as we did in the second half -- and we did create a number of chances -- we couldn't take one and slumped to our fourth consecutive home defeat without scoring. Alarming, to say the very least.

In the Coach & Horses after the match (well, we needed to drown our sorrows, of course!) while we were chatting to Raj and the lads, the news broke on Twitter that Jackett had been sacked. The only surprise was that the board had finally had enough after very publicly backing the manager in recent weeks.

As we digested the news, we started to wonder where it had all gone wrong and how we now faced the very real prospect of being dragged into a genuine battle for survival in the Football League (again!). That might seem somewhat overdramatic, but when our team was sitting just five points above the relegation places and hadn't won in its last 10 games, mustering just a solitary goal scored by one of our players, it was pointless trying to kid ourselves.

The loss to Bristol Rovers was sickening because it was so far away from that sunny afternoon at the Memorial Stadium back in September, when Orient put Rovers to the sword with all three of Harry Smith, Theo Archibald and Aaron Drinan getting themselves on the scoresheet. Now, none of them looked like scoring any time soon. Worse still, Orient had picked up just 17 points since that day.

Thinking back to Jackett's appointment in the summer, it is fair to say that there was genuine optimism amongst the Orient faithful. Most fans seemed to think that a manager with experience and a good track record of securing promotions in the lower leagues was exactly what we needed to push us towards promotion contention, if not this season, then almost certainly the next. Instead, we now found ourselves in a worse position than when previous manager Ross Embleton lost his job almost exactly a year previously.

Maybe we didn't think it at the time, but the mass transformation of the squad over the summer that saw very few players remaining from the season before, let alone the National League title-winning squad, may have posed a bigger issue than we perhaps realised. While we were reassured that those coming in were all of at least League One pedigree, it was always going to be the case that they would take time to gel as a squad and for Jackett to settle on his best side and the right system to bring the best out of those selected. While it seemed to be coming together in September with some good results at home, Orient's later form suggested that may have been something of a false dawn.

As we moved into winter, the injuries to Tom James and Craig Clay, which robbed us of probably our two best performers of the season, the Covid outbreak that depleted the squad to its bare bones ahead of the trip to Tranmere, and the postponements over the festive period and beyond had certainly not helped our cause. But we really should have mustered more than two points and two goals in 10 matches.

Many O's fans had suggested that the January transfer window was poor and that the players we brought in may not have been those that Jackett felt he wanted and we needed, despite the assurances to the contrary coming out of the club. Obviously, we will never know what goes on behind closed doors, but the new arrivals seemed to have confused Jackett's line-up selections further.

Ahead of the Carlisle game, it was announced that former players Matt Harrold and Brian Saah would take interim charge while the search for a new manager got underway. A whole variety of names were doing the rounds, but we just had to wait for news once an appointment was made.

Final Score
Leyton Orient	**0**	**2**	**Bristol Rovers**
			Evans 34
			Collins 37

The dawn of a new era?

Game 31: Saturday 26th February 2022, Leyton Orient v Carlisle United

On the Thursday ahead of this game was the fateful day that the world woke up to the news that Russia had invaded Ukraine. Since then, we had seen the saddening scenes coming out of a country that seemed to simply want to develop as a modern nation, but whose neighbour simply couldn't let that happen, instead preferring to send in troops to destroy the country and remove its hard-gained sovereignty. Events like these, as awful and tragic as they are, serve to remind even us hopeless football obsessives just where football sits in the grand scheme of life and the world. As renowned Italian manager Arigo Sacchi so succinctly put it: "Football is the most important of the least important things in the life."

Nevertheless, football can provide us with great comfort, to give us a distraction and something to focus on away from the tragedy unfolding in Eastern Europe. In a very real sense, football has always been my insulation from the world and from difficult, upsetting and trying times. While I realise that I should probably be much more grown up about life, for me there is immense comfort and solace in losing yourself in the minutiae of the game and the day-to-day happenings at your club. So, with apologies for my not being brave enough to make more of a statement upon the Russian invasion, back to all things Orient and the things that don't really matter in life.

A new manager, albeit only on an interim basis, and another sunny late February day reminding us that spring was on the way, and it is fair to say that we headed to this match with renewed optimism and positivity that Orient might finally turn the corner in terms of their performances and results, after having been in the doldrums for so long.

Because we had a couple of errands to run in Stratford on the way, and as Kay needed to get a refund for her ticket for Harrogate as she would be unable to make the rearranged game, we opted to have our pre-match pints in the Supporters Club. Even though the club is a real gem of a place with a superbly friendly atmosphere and very supporter-friendly beer prices, it does tend to get very busy as kick-off approaches. However, as we were in situ pretty much bang on 12:30, this match afforded us a perfect opportunity to sample its delights once again.

Even at that relatively early time, it was pretty much standing room only as most fans kept half an eye on Tottenham battering Leeds at Elland Road in the lunchtime kick-off. However, we found a perch out on the terrace at the front in the sunshine, which it has to be said is not an unpleasant way to prepare for a match.

As we headed for our seats, Kay was relieved to spot that Mark and Kevin had brought little Tyler with them again, as in that way that football obsessives read superstition and signs of fate into all kinds of absurd associations, she remained convinced that Orient's recent poor form could be explained by Kevin's son's absence from recent matches. She was, however, going to have to revisit that hypothesis approximately an hour and three quarters later.

Matt Harrold's first team selection didn't deviate too far from the line-up the previous Tuesday against Bristol Rovers save for bringing in Hector Kyprianou and Connor Wood for Ruel Sotiriou and Shad Ogie, the system remained the 4-3-3 that for me still seemed to be the best deployment of our current personnel.

Carlisle had been struggling even more than us in recent weeks, languishing just above the bottom two and having on Wednesday morning sacked their manager and director of football, although unlike Orient, they had moved to appoint Paul Simpson, for the third time, pretty much immediately.

Any optimism that had built up around the ground at the prospect of a new dawn was cruelly punctured after just four minutes when Carlisle striker Omari Patrick went racing down their left, cut inside Ethan Coleman, and fired home for 1-0. You could feel the deflation amongst the crowd and the players on the field.

In response, our new mate Harry Smith managed to head an effort into the ground and over the bar from close range, when in actual fact it looked easier to score, but it felt like we might be about to witness another huff and puff performance, where despite creating chances, we would struggle to take one -- something we had had to endure all too often in this campaign. Other than that, and despite sustained pressure, we really didn't threaten any further.

Early in the second half, Theo Archibald was involved in a clash on the edge of the box, and just as Kay and I were pondering who might be best suited to take the resultant free kick (the left-footer Archie or the right-footed Otis Khan), the ref produced a second yellow (just two minutes after having issued the first) followed swiftly by a red for our wide man. Admittedly we didn't have the greatest view of what took place up in front of the South Stand, but we were flabbergasted, as were most of those around us, not that we are in anyway biased of course.

Down to 10 men and a goal down was always going to be an uphill battle for the O's, but they actually seemed to play with a bit more impetus after the dismissal. To be fair to Carlisle, they had a couple of gilt-edged chances to seal the victory and looked dangerous on the break. In the end, it was another bitterly disappointing home defeat without scoring, the fifth in succession -- worrying, if not quite alarming, times, indeed!

Final Score

Leyton Orient	0	1	**Carlisle United**
			Patrick 5

League Two table after close of play on 28th February 2022

Pos	Team	Pld	W	D	L	GF	GA	GD	Pts
1	Forest Green Rovers	32	19	9	4	62	27	35	66
2	Northampton Town	33	16	8	9	38	26	12	56
3	Tranmere Rovers	34	16	8	10	36	27	9	56
4	Exeter City	31	14	12	5	46	31	15	54
5	Sutton United	33	15	9	9	50	39	11	54
6	Mansfield Town	31	15	8	8	42	33	9	53
7	Swindon Town	33	14	10	9	55	40	15	52
8	Newport County	33	14	10	9	54	44	10	52
9	Port Vale	31	13	10	8	45	31	14	49
10	Bristol Rovers	32	13	9	10	45	40	5	48
11	Salford City	32	13	8	11	37	30	7	47
12	Hartlepool United	33	12	8	13	34	43	-9	44

Pos	Team	Pld	W	D	L	GF	GA	GD	Pts
13	Crawley Town	31	12	7	12	39	42	-3	43
14	Harrogate Town	32	11	9	12	50	49	1	42
15	Bradford City	34	9	13	12	37	43	-6	40
16	Rochdale	31	8	14	9	39	40	-1	38
17	Walsall	33	10	8	15	35	45	-10	38
18	**Leyton Orient**	**31**	**7**	**12**	**12**	**38**	**32**	**6**	**33**
19	Stevenage	34	7	12	15	30	52	-22	33
20	Barrow	32	7	11	14	30	39	-9	32
21	Colchester United	33	7	11	15	30	47	-17	32
22	Carlisle United	32	7	10	15	24	45	-21	31
23	Oldham Athletic	31	7	9	15	31	47	-16	30
24	Scunthorpe United	34	4	11	19	24	59	-35	23

Chapter 11: March 2022

Richie Wellens arrives to turn Orient's fortunes around, but will a nasty experience in Nailsworth derail our season-long adventure following the O's? Spoiler: No. But it takes Orient's first win since early December to fortify our spirit.

We scored a goal...we scored a goal...we scored a goal!

Game 32: Tuesday 1st March 2022, Colchester United v Leyton Orient

Having been to Colchester before, a bit like Stevenage and Northampton, I don't really count it amongst my favourite away trips. This is nothing to do with the people, the place or even the facilities at the stadium. It is just one of those grounds that has been built quite far outside of town (half an hour walk from the station, which is, in turn, another 20-minute walk in the other direction into the town centre), and therefore with nothing in the immediate surrounding area other than roadways, they feel soulless.

As you may have gathered over the course of these pages, I much prefer old-school traditional grounds that you can get to easily from the station with plenty of nearby pubs to choose from and the ability to get a feel for the place. These new identikit stadiums on the outskirts of their towns are basically interchangeable, lack character and could be anywhere. Give me Valley Parade, Exeter or any of the older more traditional grounds any day of the week.

As covered earlier, this game had originally been scheduled for Boxing Day, which at the time gave Kay and I perhaps the biggest potential challenge of this journey when we discovered that due to engineering works, there would be no trains at all to

Colchester, or anywhere nearby, on the day. We actually contemplated heading over there on Christmas Eve, staying for Christmas and then going home on the 27th. If you haven't realised so far, there is very little that we wouldn't be prepared to do to carry on our Orient adventure (yes, we really were that far gone with this whole obsession!).

In the end, Kay found an early Boxing Day morning National Express coach from Stratford (East London) and a more than suitable hotel for us (it was a converted pub!) in which to spend the evening. I was actually quite looking forward to the whole trip, until the match was called off due to Covid issues within the Colchester camp.

This time around, as the trains were running fine, we decided to do the whole trip over the course of an afternoon and evening. Having taken the afternoon off work, we rocked up in Colchester, well, at the station, that is, with almost exactly four hours to kill until kick-off. By now, you will have realised that in these situations, Kay's and my natural response is to find a suitable pub (or in many cases pubs, plural) to base ourselves in, which was exactly what we opted to do.

Following the signs towards the town centre, we made it as far as the Magnet on North Station Road all of 0.2 miles from the station. Well, it was drizzling, as it had been all day, and Kay had an injured leg, lest we forget! The pub turned out to be quite intriguing, as it looked like someone's converted house in a very modern style and with a fully functioning chippy next door. The barman and the locals who were in on a wet Tuesday afternoon, proved very friendly, and it was a lovely way to pass on an hour or two.

After a round or three, we decided that we probably ought to do a bit more exploring of the surrounding area, if not the town itself. This time, we made it is far as the excellent and traditional Victoria Inn another five minutes down the very same road. So much for exploring the place! We spent another hour or so in there chatting away with some more locals before ordering a cab up to the ground. When we had been here before, it had been in the September sunshine and was a very pleasant stroll with a pub approximately halfway there. This time with the drizzle and Kay's injuries, a taxi was the only real option, and fatefully, we decided we would worry about getting back later on.

When we arrived at the ground, having once again not managed to eat since the train was leaving Liverpool Street, the first order of the day was to get some food on board. It was the usual pie for Kay, while I had one of those burgers that you seem to exclusively find at sports grounds that very much look like the real thing but taste of virtually nothing. Assuming there were actual calories in it, then it probably did the job.

As a result of the strict protocols for Covid safety that Colchester had put in place, getting a ticket for this match had proven to be something of a rigmarole involving creating a social bubble (Kay and I, of course, decided to title ours: "The Orient Nerds"), paying for a match permit and then completing a declaration that you were Covid-free the day before the match, before your e-tickets were sent to you. Of course, it also meant that we had to stay in our allocated seats, but thankfully ours were a few rows from the back, and the two chaps in front of us and the group of lads behind were all going to be standing throughout.

In his second match in charge of the team, Matt Harrold went with a similar 4-3-3 set up to that which he had used against Carlisle. This time, however, Otis Khan was pushed higher up on the right-hand side and Ruel Sotiriou came in on the left, Aaron Drinan dropping out of the 11.

Orient had a very early shout for a penalty when Sotiriou went down in the area, although I have to admit, it was at the far end for us and through the swirling drizzle, so I didn't get a particularly great view, so will have to assume that the ref called it correctly in denying it, despite the vehement protests from some of the O's players and some of those around us who clearly got a better view than we had managed.

There were a couple of chances at either end, especially when Colchester hit the post and then had the ball in the net, only for it to be ruled out for offside. For Orient, it was Sotiriou that looked the most likely, however neither side was truly dominant, and yet another goalless first half was probably a fair reflection of the action thus far.

At the break, Kay's leg was really starting to hurt her, and she was becoming increasingly concerned about the trek back to the station and being able to make it in time for our train, which was pretty much the last one back to London that evening. We asked a steward how easy it would be to get a taxi after the match, and he simply confirmed what we already suspected: that it would be very difficult, and we may well have a bit of a wait. Not wanting to take the risk, Kay decided to go to reception, where the friendly staff helped her get a cab back to the Magnet, and we agreed that I would watch the second half (did you really expect me to leave?) and then we would meet up at the station at 10:15, with quarter of an hour until our train home.

As I got back into position for the second half, the surprising news was that Paul Smyth was on as a sub, having recovered from the collapsed lung he suffered at Mansfield. It was a real shock to me, as I must have missed his name being read out as being on the bench.

About 15 minutes or so into the second half, Kay messaged me to say that, rather disappointingly, the pub was shut, but the driver had kindly dropped her at the station, and she was going to head home. I could follow her, as planned, after the match. A mere matter of minutes later, midfielder Ethan Coleman seized onto a miskicked clearance from the Colchester keeper and played it forward to Sotiriou, who worked space for a shot and rifled home from the edge of the area. It was Orient's first goal since Darren Pratley had scored at Bradford exactly a month before, and there was pandemonium amongst the 900 or so traveling supporters.

I, of course, being the caring husband that I am, wasted no time in messaging Kay to tell her what she had just missed. Her annoyance was even more heightened than expected, given that she had been forced to pay an additional £30, as she wasn't on the right train, and I wasn't with her, so she couldn't use our Two-Together Railcard. Rather than displaying any sympathy whatsoever, the conductor told her to be thankful she wasn't being fined £75! Only the fact that this is intended for family reading prevents me from expressing my true feelings on overly officious train personnel!

Back to the action at the Community Stadium, though, and Orient being Orient, I just knew that there was no way they would be able to see the remaining 24 minutes out. Sadly, I was proven to be absolutely correct, as first Myles Kenlock equalized for the home side on 75 minutes and then Joe Edwards put them 2-1 up just four minutes later. Absolutely typical of Orient, version 2022!

For the remaining 10 or so minutes, I kept anxiously checking my watch. I almost never leave a match early, on principle, but I was also mindful of the mad dash that I would have back to the station if I didn't want to end up stranded in Colchester for the evening. As added time approached, I thought I would pop to the loo to make sure I was under starters orders as early as possible. When I was ready, I briefly contemplated leaving, but strangely something was drawing me back. I went back through the entranceway just in time to see a goalmouth scramble from a free kick right in front of me, which saw Coleman poke home the equalizer in the third added minute. I was so glad I had gone back!

As soon as the referee blew for time, I made for the exit and half ran/half walked back to the station, frantically checking Google Maps every step of the way to make sure I was on course. Amazingly I rocked up at precisely 10:14. If only Kay had been able to stay in the pub, we could have avoided her incident with the inspector. Of course, no one checked my ticket for the entire journey back to London.

Final Score

Colchester United	**2**	**2**	**Leyton Orient**
Kenlock 75			Sotiriou 66
Edwards 79			Coleman 90+3

Another (small) step in the right direction.

Game 33: Saturday 5th March 2022, Leyton Orient v Stevenage

Planned engineering works meant that the Central Line was suspended from Bethnal Green out to Essex, a major inconvenience for a significant chunk of Orient's support, given how many live out that way. Thankfully for Kay and me, it just meant that we would have to get the bus from Stratford, just as we had the previous Saturday, rather than the one stop on the Tube.

Having based ourselves in the Supporters Club the week before, we decided to share our custom around and felt that we were due a pre-match drink in the wine bar for this one. Although the weather was nowhere near as pleasant as it had been the previous week, we even sat outside, thanks in no small part to the patio heaters.

As we headed down to the ground, we stopped for a quick chat with Orientear editor Jamie about the new edition, which once again had full details of our travels following the Orient right up to Harrogate in the snow. Jamie suggested that sales had been so good this season that he was hoping to squeeze in a bonus edition towards the end of the season. Very much music to my ears, not just because it would allow me to ramble on about our Orient adventure once more, but because as something of an old school traditionalist (or just old git!), a strong printed fanzine -- or in Orient's case two -- keeps it very much real.

If it had been disappointing to find ourselves trailing going into stoppage time on Tuesday night in Colchester, that was in some way eased by the snatching of a point (also our first for a month) with a last gasp equalizer and managing two goals in a match for the first time since early December. Things were far from perfect in the Orient camp, and the search for the next permanent manager was looking like stretching into another week, but it was a lift for the fans if nothing else.

In his third game in charge, Matt Harrold went for what looked like a 4-2-3-1, with young midfielder Matt Young being pushed forward into the Number 10 role, presumably with the intention of him making way for the returning to fitness Paul Smyth early in the second half.

Of course, while there may have been some signs of improvement in recent games, especially at Colchester, the players' confidence still looked very fragile, and when

Stevenage, languishing in 21st place although menacingly just a single point behind us, opened the scoring midway through the first half, it was difficult to hold onto any strand of positivity that had come from the comeback on Tuesday night.

Thankfully, Ruel Sotiriou seemed to have at long last found his shooting boots in recent matches, and he equalized on the half-hour mark, slotting home after latching onto a looping ball over the top from Darren Pratley. Finally at long last, Kay and I could celebrate seeing an Orient player score a goal together for the first time since the game against Swindon on 7th December.

Alas, the joy of the equalizer was to be somewhat short-lived when Luke Norris raced through the inside right channel onto a long ball forward from their keeper and rifled past Lawrence Vigouroux. You could almost feel the deflation around the ground. It stayed 2-1 at the break, giving us the perfect chance to moan about Orient's ongoing poor form over a half-time beer.

Sure enough, at the start of the second half, on came Smyth to replace Young and try to play off big Harry Smith, who was winning a few of the long balls aimed at him but struggling to find a teammate in support when he did so.

Stevenage, for their part, seemed content to try to stifle us and make the game as disjointed as they possibly could. Smyth and Archibald looked the most dangerous for the O's, but as the half wore on, it started to feel like we were going to lose yet another game. However, cometh the hour, cometh the birthday boy (yes, according to the programme it was actually Archie's birthday), and in the fourth minute of added time, Archibald picked up a loose ball on the edge of the penalty area and curled a beauty into the top left-hand corner. The ground went nuts with relief that our lads had somehow found a way not to lose. It may have only been a couple draws against two of the fellow bottom-of-the-table sides, but it felt like a step in the right direction.

In the Coach & Horses after the match, the atmosphere was very much one of relief, if not outright joy. There was still work to be done to save Orient's season, but at least we had stopped losing, started to score goals and were now picking up some points.

Kay and I got talking to a Dutch guy, Edwin, an FC Utrecht fan, who along with a set of mates had been coming to watch Orient each year for the last 20 years. Given my time growing up in Holland and still being a Feyenoord fan, we had a good old chat. Just as we were about to leave, Edwin asked us if we had a spare cigarette, which as we were trying -- and failing for the most part -- to pack in we didn't. His face was a picture when I nipped to the offie while Kay ordered a cab and then handed him a cig. As we are continuing to experience on our madcap adventure, it is the people that you meet and the universal language of football that is the most important thing.

Final Score
Leyton Orient	**2**	**2**	**Stevenage**
Sotiriou 30			Prosser 24
Archibald 90+4			Norris 32

Welcome to the Orient, Richie Wellens!

After a rather drawn-out 15-day process that had some Orient fans on social media comparing it to the selection of a new pope, Orient finally announced that Richie Wellens had been appointed as head coach after the sacking of Kenny Jackett.

The 41-year-old Mancunian had a playing career that started as a youngster at Manchester United but then was for the most part based in the lower divisions. As a manager, he had led an impressive Swindon Town to the League Two title on a points-per-game basis in the Covid-curtailed 2019/20 season, before leaving for a new challenge at first Salford City and then Doncaster Rovers, but without being able to recreate the success he had had at the County Ground. Most importantly for Orient, given how stale the football had become over the end days of Jackett's reign, he described his approach and philosophy as all about playing "attacking football, believing long ball and defensive-minded football to not be suitable to long-term success."

Of course, this being Orient, there was no way they could resist letting a good-news story dominate the build-up to the game, and a mere day or so later, they announced the controversial appointment of Paul Terry (yes, that's right, John Terry's brother!) as one of his assistants alongside Matt Harrold, who had led the team on an interim basis over the previous two weeks. Terry had been an Orient player between 2007 and 2009 but had an affair with the wife of his teammate, Dale Roberts, while at Rushden & Diamonds, which it was alleged contributed to Roberts' suicide. He had also been fined for a reported 209 breaches of betting regulations in 2020 and had also apparently been involved in illegal approaches to Orient players while in a coaching role at West Brom. Nothing like an uncontroversial appointment!

As a hopefully fair-minded judge of all things football, I resolved to base my assessment of him in support of the new boss by results and performance on the pitch, rather than for what had happened in his personal life/off the field.

Richie Wellens' Red n' White Army!

Game 34: Saturday 12th March 2022, Hartlepool United v Leyton Orient

Rather amazingly, there were no direct trains from London to Hartlepool scheduled for Saturdays and, from what we were able to gather, very few during the week. As a result, we were left with the option of changing trains at least twice and a total journey time of more than four hours. The recommended route was to change at York and then again at somewhere called Thornaby to get the train through to Hartlepool.

Not fancying an eight-hour-plus return trip, Kay looked into other options for breaking up the journey, as well as researching where we might stay. After briefly considering an evening in Newcastle, where all the hotels seemed to be very expensive, even though we couldn't find anything of note happening in the city that weekend, we concluded that this may well be the impact of people opting for staycations in this country rather than travelling abroad, despite the regulations around Covid being all but relaxed. In the end, she played a blinder in discovering that there were direct trains to Darlington, where the usual budget hotels weren't overpriced, and we could get to Hartlepool in just over an hour, albeit having to change trains en route.

Of course, due to the sheer distance and time involved, it was another very early start for us, and with the Bank branch of the Northern Line being out of action for a few months yet, it was a bus to Mile End and then the Hammersmith and City line from there. A daunting journey only adds to the sense of adventure on these trips, though.

After a brief stop at Greggs, in which I briefly flirted with the idea of sausage roll and/or steak bake to go with my coffee, in the end deciding that a pain au chocolat was probably both a more sophisticated and healthier option, we got on the train.

Once again being on our absolute best behaviour, we decided that there would be no drinking until 11 am at the very earliest, roughly when we were due to arrive in York.

Little did we know that the LNER staff would actually help us to stay teetotal for the entire trip by first closing the bar ahead of a change of staff and a wait at the station, and then ensuring that the card machine wouldn't start so that the only option was to order from your seat and hope the one lady serving would be able to bring our stuff to us before we arrived in Darlington. Not wanting to pay for beer and then leave it on the train, we decided that our best option was to use the 50 minutes changeover time to source some beer, and if they had a pub at the station, even better.

When we arrived, our hearts leapt with joy when we discovered that there was not only a Pumpkin café (anyone who has spent any significant time travelling by train in England will know what these are!), but that it also had draft beer available. The patron saint of travelling football fans had come to our rescue in the nick of time.

The rest of our journey was a 20-minute train ride to Thornaby, a 20-minute or so wait there and then 20 minutes on to Hartlepool. At Thornaby, we met a group of younger O's fans who had chosen this route like us, but also had to face it on the way back. We also got talking to some Hartlepool fans who advised us that the Corner Flag bar did let away fans in for a small donation, which I thought was worth verifying after the disappointment at Sixfields. Having confirmed this fact, we then arranged to meet Paul, whom we had met on the way back from Port Vale, and his mate Gary there. Of course, those were the two we had failed to meet in Trotter's in Harrogate.

The Corner Flag has a real traditional feel to it as a supporters' club bar, very similar to our own at Brisbane Road, but this one is set on two floors, each with their own bar. After ordering a couple of pints, Paul and Gary came up to meet us and catch up on all things Orient. They confirmed that Trotter's hadn't actually been that nice and we hadn't missed much, but it did still make me want to go when I was due to be back there in a couple of weeks' time for the rearranged fixture, though.

Victoria Park is a very old-school feeling ground, which given my opinions on the newer ones that are all very similar, went down especially well with yours truly. It is quite compact, but that only makes it feel more real. The home fans get an actual terrace behind one goal, and while the away fans behind the other (another plus point, of course!) have seats, the stewards aren't officious about making you sit in your actual seat or even about standing, as long as it is ok with the fans behind you.

Obviously as a result of the new hope generated by Richie Wellens' appointment, there was a real buzz amongst the 175 brave (beyond hope?) souls who had made their way up. It felt like it was time for a bit of a restart to our season. Even though he had just two days to work with the players in the run-up, there was a noticeable difference in our play, as we looked to keep the ball on the ground more and to stretch play when we had possession. It is obviously easy to get carried with a new manager or coach, but there were some encouraging signs.

We had a couple of good early chances, one from a free kick from Theo Archibald after Paul Smyth was brought down on the edge of the area, and another when Harry Smith couldn't quite reach a ball in from Connor Wood. For their part, the home side had a good opportunity to open the scoring 10 minutes before the break, only for youngster Joe White to fire wide. Just before the break, Omar Beckles was adjudged to have conceded a foul in an off the ball incident, for which he was booked, and then nearly got himself in further trouble as he continued to argue his point as the teams left the field. Thankfully, his teammates managed to calm him down before he talked his way into a second booking.

Right at the start of the second half, midfielder Hector Kyprianou had an effort cleared off the line and Smyth forced a good save from Hartlepool goalkeeper Ben Killip, but that was the most the O's were going to threaten for the remainder of the match. Hartlepool had another glorious chance through Omar Bogle, but he shot straight at Lawrence Vigouroux, and from there it always looked like ending in share of the spoils. A point's a point, as they say, especially away from home, and it was a more positive performance from Orient, definitely something to build on.

After the match, we bade farewell to Paul and Gary and headed back to Darlington, which if you ever find yourself there on a Saturday night isn't the worst place to be. There are a number of good pubs, some which offer excellent music and others some rather more amateur karaoke; however, the beer is almost as cheap in the pubs as it is in Wetherspoons, which is remarkable for those of us who live in London.

Next up for the O's was a trip to table-topping Forest Green Rovers, with their sustainability focus, vegan food and quirky-sounding ground in the small Gloucestershire town of Nailsworth. It was an experience I have to say I was really looking forward to as something completely different. Sadly, it was to turn out to be an awayday experience that we are likely never to forget, for all the very wrong reasons.

Final Score
Hartlepool United   0   0   **Leyton Orient**

The less said about it, the better

Game 35: Tuesday 15th March 2022 Forest Green Rovers v Leyton Orient

Many of the Orient faithful, especially those whom we have met on our travels, will already know what transpired when we tried to gain access to The New Lawn for this match. Some I know witnessed it. Not wanting to rake over old coals, I won't go into further details; however what I will say is that out of the 23 different grounds that I visited over the course of this adventure, this is the only one to which I will never ever return, and I would urge caution to any other fans planning to visit.

As we left Nailsworth the following morning, it is fair to say that both of us were questioning whether we wanted to carry on with our whole travelling adventure, or even to go to the away games for which we already had tickets, trains and hotels booked. Throughout the whole experience, the Orient family, as we have become to feel part of, were immense, and it made us realise just what an extremely special club and bunch of supporters our football obsession had led us to find.

In one of the strangest quirks of footballing fate, on the train back to London, we bumped into Arsenal's legendary captain and one of my heroes during my teenage years, none other than Mr Arsenal himself: Tony Adams, who was on his way to the Emirates for the game against Liverpool that evening, a game I was going to myself, as it was too late in the evening for Kay's dad to go.

While it was good to be back at the place where I had spent a significant part of the last 12 seasons (of course us football obsessives measure our lives in seasons, not years, like the rest of the world – just as Nick Hornby, author of the seminal "Fever Pitch" famously confirmed!), it also felt strangely disconcerting. It was a lot like visiting an old house, of which you know every nook and cranny but strangely it no longer feels like home.

Fantastic stadium though it is, like many (all?) of the new grounds, it lacks soul and character, and strangely I found myself missing the much less salubrious facilities of Brisbane Road. The one inescapable familiarity was Arsenal getting beaten 2-0 by Jurgen Klopp's men, although at least this time they put up a bit more of a fight than they had for some time.

Orient finally win a game!

Game 35: Saturday 19th March 2022, Leyton Orient v Rochdale

With Arsenal featuring in the lunchtime kick-off, we decided that the best option for this one would be to watch it back in the safety and comfort of the Supporters Club, very much back amongst the Orient family.

We managed to find a perch on a table with an O's fan who also supported Manchester United (well, we'll have to forgive him for that one!) and Rolf, a Norwegian who was over for Tottenham v West Ham the following day but could think of no better way of spending a Saturday afternoon than by taking in a match at Brisbane Road. A little way into the game, we were joined by Chris, whom we had first met in Bristol after the 3-1 win back in September. The five of us spent the rest of the match chatting away about all things football, although admittedly I still had at least one eye on the TV screen for the rest of the game. It provided a much needed and very timely reminder of the true spirit of football fandom.

After the end of Arsenal's hard-fought win at Villa Park, we headed back round to the East Stand to take up our seats. After two creditable away performances and results, it was fair to say that the famed "new manager bounce" was definitely in evidence in E10 as we got ready for Richie Wellens' first game in charge at Brisbane Road. However, that wasn't to last very long.

With six minutes on the clock, Alex Newby (him again!) opened the scoring for the visitors, and you could almost feel the puncturing of the feel-good atmosphere as the ball hit the back of the net. The conceding of an early goal really seemed to have become something of an issue for the O's this season, especially in recent weeks. The players looked to slump themselves and seemed to lose the confidence with which they had started the match.

We struggled to impose ourselves from an attacking perspective, except for an Aaron Drinan header from a cross that would have been a goal if he could have directed it anywhere but straight at the keeper. That was until Paul Smyth conjured up a moment of individual brilliance. Picking up the ball midway inside the Rochdale half, he cleverly worked space for himself and let fly from fully 30 yards. His effort rocketed past the keeper and nestled in the top left-hand corner. It may not have been especially deserved, given the team's display up to that point, but it gave us a much-needed foothold in the game.

After the break, Orient looked like a team transformed and burst fully into life when Ruel Sotiriou fired a loose ball in the penalty area home for his sixth league goal of the season and his fourth since Kenny Jackett's dismissal. It is always amazing how different managers get different performances out of different players. The way the outfield players celebrated as an entire team by the corner flag showed just how much it meant to them, as well, and there were long-missed celebrations amongst the Brisbane Road faithful that matched it.

With 10 minutes to go, Harry Smith, on as a sub for his impressive almost namesake Paul, put the result beyond doubt, reaching a looping ball from a Theo Archibald blocked shot ahead of the goalkeeper and nodding home his first goal since early December.

After seeing out the remaining time plus the six added minutes, "Rocking All Over the World" finally rang out around the ground, and we departed with a spring in our step that had been missing for quite some time.

We popped into the Coach after the match to see if Rolf had taken us up on our offer of meeting him in there, but alas he hadn't and presumably was either distracted en route, or he had been put off by all the rugby fans in the place for France v England in the Six Nations. From our point of view, the whole day had rekindled our love for football so badly dented by events of the previous Tuesday evening, helped of course by a good second half performance and a promising victory. That was five points in three matches for Wellens, a very decent start to his reign.

Final Score
Leyton Orient   **3**   **1**   **Rochdale**
Smyth 40   Newby 6
Sotiriou 58
Smith 80

Harrogate away – take two!

Game 36: Tuesday 22nd March 2022, Harrogate Town v Leyton Orient

With this game having been rescheduled after it was originally snowed off the previous month, Kay's work commitments once again meant that she wouldn't be able to make it and I would be flying solo to Yorkshire once more. From my point of view, I was keen to get another awayday under my belt and to prove that the previous week was just a one-off isolated incident that wouldn't dampen my enthusiasm for the crazy adventure that we had been on. Besides, Harrogate is a beautiful town, and I would highly recommend visiting if you haven't before, although believe me it is a much better experience in the early spring sunshine than it was in the snow.

This time, my selected route sent me via York rather than Leeds, although regrettably I only had 13 minutes between trains so didn't have enough time to have a little wander round the Roman city and stretch my legs. Upon arrival in Harrogate after half an hour or so, I was relieved to find that the weather we had been experiencing down in London was the same up in Yorkshire, so I decided that I would have a stroll around the place to see what it looked like when it wasn't covered in an inch or two of the white stuff, before checking into the hotel. Of course, one of the first places that I happened across was the infamous Trotter's bar as "enjoyed" by our mates Paul and Gary back in February.

There was clearly something going on at the conference centre, as when I looked to book the hotel the Premier Inn was sold out, the Cedar Court where Kay and I had stayed last time had doubled in price and I was left with no other real option but to pay north of £150 for a room in the Travelodge (yes, you read that right, the Travelodge!). It seems I had actually been more organised than some, as when I arrived at the hotel reception, the old couple in front of me were asking for guidance on other hotels they might try, given that this one was now also fully booked. When the receptionist gave them the directions to the Premier Inn, I didn't have the heart to tell them that it might be booked up, as well. I hope they found somewhere.

When I popped into the Wetherspoons, The Winter Gardens, where Kay and I had failed to have breakfast last time, handily placed virtually next door to the hotel, the reason for the demand on hotel rooms became all too apparent, as the place was full of mainly men wearing those identification badges on lanyards that give away the fact that they had all been on a conference. It was almost standing room only, even outside.

After a pint and a catch up with some of the Orient travelling faithful, I decided that it was probably time to stroll up to the ground. The first part of the walk was basically the same route that Kay and I had become familiar with on our previous visit, although obviously a lot more pleasant without having to slip and slide everywhere. One thing about Harrogate is that for the most part, whichever direction you are heading in, you are by definition going up or down hill. If you stand still anywhere for too long, you have that strange feeling of leaning to stand up straight.

Once you reach the area where we were staying last time, it is then a lovely stroll across the park, the Stray, to reach Wetherby Road. I am not sure I have been to a match in a more picturesque setting. The ground itself betrays Harrogate's quick rise to the Football League and their non-league roots, as they were only promoted to the National League (fifth tier) in 2018. It is small and compact but well-appointed and very reminiscent of some of the non-league grounds I have visited, both with Orient and others. Unlike Forest Green, it feels like a genuine community-based football club. Away fans are given a choice of a small six-step covered terrace behind the goal, some seating and some more terracing to the side, though by now I am sure you will be able to guess where your author stood.

Having gone into the ground relatively early and with the lack of beer on sale (there simply wasn't room on the concourse!), I decided I would watch the players warming up while waiting for kick-off. Anyone who has been into a football ground early enough to watch shooting practice can't fail to have noticed how many shots from professional players miss the target badly. With this going on I decided that I would leave getting any food until half-time for fear of having it knocked out of my hands by one of the many wayward efforts from the O's players. Some brave (foolish?) fans opted to run the gauntlet and have the full works of pie, chips, gravy and mushy peas (well we were in Yorkshire) within striking range, but the exercise passed off without major incident.

In terms of team news, Otis Khan kept his place in central midfield to partner skipper Darren Pratley, who had recovered from a bout of Covid. Orient started the match with a real impetus and really took the game to Harrogate, a clear indication that the new manager bounce was very much still in effect and that Saturday's win, our first in 15 matches, had boosted confidence within the players.

Theo Archibald hit the foot of the post with a low strike, and we seemed to pen them back towards their penalty area for large parts of the opening period but without being able to find a breakthrough. At half-time, some of the home fans booed their players off, a good indication of how we had imposed ourselves on the game. Of course, though, if you are dominant without scoring there is always the worry that they will nick one and undo all the good work.

Thankfully even though we didn't play anywhere near as well after half-time, we crucially managed to take some of the chances that we created. First, it was Aaron Drinan that tore through the centre of the Harrogate side, steadied himself and fired home. Then just 10 minutes later, Drinan was on hand to turn home a flick on by Omar Beckles from a Shad Ogie long throw. The second goal seemed to very much break the home side's spirit, and with just over quarter of an hour to go, striker of the moment Ruel Sotiriou put the result beyond any doubt, latching onto a lay-off from Drinan and netting his fifth goal in six games, sending the 206 travelling Orient fans either home or into Harrogate or Leeds for the night more than happy. As I scrolled through the Orient social media pages back at the hotel, it was all too clear how happy the fanbase were already with our new gaffer and the way that he was turning the club round in double quick time, even without the benefit of significant work on the training ground.

Final Score

Harrogate Town	**0**	**3**	**Leyton Orient**
			Drinan 51, 57
			Sotiriou 73

The Orient feel-good factor continues at Brisbane Road

Game 37: Saturday 26th March 2022, Leyton Orient v Barrow AFC

After the trip up to Harrogate, we were back at Brisbane Road for the second Saturday in a row, and for this one we were treated to another one of those sunny spring days that remind us that we are on the way out of winter, and we could hopefully look forward to some nicer weather for the rest of the season.

With it being the latest international break for the two top tiers, the club decided that this was going to be another "Football for a Fiver" day, with fans encouraged to wear retro jerseys and the return of the O-Nut (yes, that is exactly what it sounds like: an Orient-themed Dunkin' Donut). Kay and I were due out for a family dinner, so we had to turn up in our relative finery, rather than sporting our old football tops. The promotion did, however, mean that one of our friends Gina, who is a steward at Tottenham, had decided that she was going to come along to watch the O's, although sadly had got tickets in the West Stand. Still, we arranged to meet her for a pint in the Coach & Horses before the game.

As we were going to be seeing our niece Amiee's young children Ada and Archie that evening, Kay decided that it would be a wise move to nip to the shop before the match to see if we could pick up some presents for them. Even though their dad Reiss is a committed West Ham fan, we thought we might as well try and get in as early as possible to show them the correct team to support in their formative years. We managed to get a wyvern (the dragon-like creature featured in the Orient badge and now de facto mascot for Orient) soft toy and a cuddly dinosaur, and Kay also picked up a retro shirt, the braces kit from the lockdown season, for just a fiver, although sadly she decided against wearing it to the meal later on.

When we arrived at the pub, we were somewhat surprised to find that it was pretty much empty, but then it dawned us that given the sunny weather everyone would be outside, and so it was to prove. We managed to find a perch on a barrel where Kay could put her shopping down and we could put our jackets, which were definitely not needed at this point.

We caught up with a few of the regular faces and also got talking to an Orient fan who lived in the block of flats between the South Stand and the away fans and who had invited her uncle and parents over to watch the match from the comfort of her first-floor balcony. I only half-jokingly suggested that Kay wouldn't let me move into those flats, and even if she did ever relent, knowing me I would probably still go to the pub before the match, keep my season ticket and watch the game from my usual seat.

When Gina arrived, she was resplendent in last season's home shirt and all set for the game. She also suggested that if the O's won this one well enough, she might be tempted to get a season ticket next season, as she was unlikely to be returning to her Tottenham Stadium stewarding commitments. Another potential recruit to the Orient cause.

After finishing our drinks, we walked back down to the ground, bade farewell to Gina and made our way inside. Usually for the promotional games like this one, the ground can be quite busy with people who don't come on a regular basis and aren't fully up-to-speed with how things work, but thankfully we had arrived early enough to minimise the disruption. We had a chat with Len, the older guy who sits on the end of our row and is always so accommodating in letting us in and out. When he went up to his seat, I warned him not to bother sitting down, as we would be up ourselves in a minute and would only make him stand up again.

Maybe I was being carried away on the wave of optimism that seemed to have taken hold of Orient fans since Richie Wellens came in like a complete and utter breath of fresh air through the club, but it really felt that there was a buzz of anticipation and excitement around the old place after so long in the doldrums. It is amazing how much difference a few positive performances and results can bring.

The only change to the team from Tuesday was the introduction of Paul Smyth for Otis Khan in the midfield. After the latter's display up in Harrogate, it could have been judged as being somewhat unfair for him to lose his starting berth but given how many matches we had had to play recently, I chose to view it as squad rotation.

Maybe it was the sheer number of minutes that the squad had endured throughout the preceding few weeks, but we didn't seem to start with the same impetus as we had in midweek. Our cause wasn't helped by Barrow, under new manager Phil Brown (yes, he of Bolton, Hull and many other clubs infamy), encouraging his charges to press us high up and try to stifle our newly developed possession-based approach. Also, the opposition had won the toss and opted to make us attack the South Stand in the first half, which as discussed previously makes me feel uncomfortable, as I'm sure it does the team.

In the opening stages, the rejuvenated Aaron Drinan forced a block from the keeper, and Ruel Sotiriou rattled the crossbar with a wicked free kick and then forced another save with a bullet of a header. However, we went in at the break goalless.

Right after half-time for the second week in succession, it was Smyth that produced an individual piece of magic to open the scoring for Orient. This time, he beat the keeper to a hopeful ball through the inside left channel from Connor Wood, turned and from an almost impossible angle, almost on the by-line, curled the ball home. As always with goals like that, there was a debate on whether he actually meant to do what he did, or whether there was a healthy slice of good fortune involved. Having watched it a number (ok, ok, a lot!) of times on the replay the following day, it looked very much to me as if he lifted his head, spotted the space, calculated the angle and executed a perfect finish. Biased me? Never!

Ten minutes later, Sotiriou continued his hot streak, notching his sixth goal of the month by slotting home a loose ball in the area. The second goal was enough to secure our third consecutive league win for the first time this season and to send the bumper crowd of 6,032 home happy. All of a sudden, things were looking very rosy in the Orient camp after some dire months. Of course, it couldn't last, could it?

Final Score
Leyton Orient   **2**   **0**   **Barrow AFC**
Smyth 52
Sotiriou 62

Attempted squad refreshment halts the O's momentum

Game 38: Tuesday 29th March 2022, Oldham Athletic v Leyton Orient

Orient's fourth Tuesday night awayday in March was also to be the last one of the season (barring any further postponed and rearranged games due to Covid, inclement weather or the coming of the apocalypse, given how things had worked out this season!). This one also coincided with Kay's and my anniversary of meeting; little did we realise when we got together that we would be celebrating 19 years together watching Leyton Orient up in greater Manchester.

It was another nice lunchtime train journey that had us arriving in Manchester in the middle of the afternoon, where we had decided to base ourselves, having enjoyed it so much for the Salford match way back at the start of the season. We opted for the Travelodge near Victoria Station with the vague intention of getting up to Boundary Park by tram. It seemed we weren't alone in our choice, as we saw a few familiar faces around reception, and Keren from the Supporters' Club later told us that there were 45 travelling Orient fans staying in the same hotel.

We decided that the best way to celebrate our day was to have a late lunch in the local area before heading up to Oldham. After extensive research of Spanish tapas restaurants nearby (well, it had been a very long time since one of our Spanish/Merseyside football trips!) we found a couple of options less than five minutes' walk away. Our choice of which one to go for was made all the easier by the fact that one was open in the afternoon, while the other didn't open until the evening. Evenu NQ on the artisan Tib Street turned out to be an excellent choice and very good value.

After a hearty feed-up, we reached the rather easy conclusion that we couldn't be bothered with a fairly lengthy tram trip followed by an estimated 20-minute walk, so popped into the also excellent Tib Street Tavern to watch a bit of Denmark v Serbia, a game in which I was utterly amazed to see Christian Eriksen captaining Denmark on the very same pitch on which he had suffered a cardiac arrest a mere nine months previously, and then order an Uber. During the course of the half-hour journey, we congratulated ourselves on the right decision as going by car took long enough. Just don't tell any of our black cab-driving friends or family!

With the stadium located on the outskirts of the town, there aren't too many pubs to choose from nearby, so for the sake of ease we opted for the Brewers Fayre, the Clayton Green, as it was a mere 200 yards away from the entrance to the away turnstiles. The pub serves a Premier Inn; however, given the lack of things to do in the surrounding area, it was easy to see why most of the O's fans who were staying over had chosen central Manchester in preference.

Boundary Park is another of those grounds that I had visited in the past to watch St Helens. It may not be the most salubrious of stadiums, but it is positively palatial compared to the now gone but most definitely not mourned, Watersheddings, where the rugby league team had played prior to moving in to share the football ground. Football fans with a long memory will remember first and foremost that they used to be one of a quartet of clubs to have an artificial pitch (bonus points for all of you who instantly named the other three without looking it up!) and that the club was in fact a founder member of the Premier League back in 1992 where they stayed for a couple of years before being relegated. Of course, your author wasted no opportunity in boring anyone with this knowledge if they displayed even the slightest bit of interest.

The place hadn't changed very much since my previous visit back in the mid-90's. There is the modern enough Joe Royle Stand (named after the club's most successful manager, the one who led them during their time in the Premier League) running along one touchline and the less modern but characterful main stand, with the tunnel positioned so that the players have to come down some stone steps to access the pitch. Behind each goal are stands that are converted terraces. The home fans were moved from the Chaddy End to allow it to be solely for visiting supporters, a move which I believe still rankles fans of a certain generation.

The biggest talking point for Orient fans ahead of kick-off was the five changes that Richie Wellens had opted to make from the team that started against Barrow, something that his mum (yes, she was in the away end!) used as mitigation for the poor performance the team put in while talking to Kay and some other fans at half-time. Out of the team went Darren Pratley, Aaron Drinan, Shad Ogie, Theo Archibald and Adam Thompson, to be replaced by Otis Khan at right back, Ethan Coleman, George Ray, Harry Smith and Frank Nouble.

One of the key features of the much-improved performances under the new coach had been the way we had been able to play the ball out from the back and through the midfield to create opportunities for the forwards. The changes stifled that, and we struggled to progress the ball forward with any security, and as a result, our attacking players ended up fairly isolated or chasing lost causes when the ball was played in their general direction.

After an opening half an hour that saw Oldham threatening but frustrated by last-ditch defending or wayward finishing, Orient centre back Ray opened the scoring for the home team steering a supposed clearing header past Lawrence Vigouroux and into our net.

Things didn't get much better from there on, and a frustrating night was made complete in added time at the end of the match. With Vigs up for a corner in a desperate attempt to salvage something from the evening, the ball of course broke to a couple of their forwards with only Khan between them and our open goal. As the move was unfolding, I said to Kay, "I know how this ends…" I took no joy whatsoever from being proven right, as the pair of them easily bypassed Khan, leaving Callum Whelan to roll it into the unguarded net. In the end, we just had to put it down to a bad evening at the office.

In fairness, given how the team had been performing prior to Jackett's dismissal, it was never ever going to be plain sailing for the new coach. Equally, he will have wanted to have a look at the full squad ahead of planning for the following season. The main takeaway from this one was probably that while we may have had a decent enough starting XI supplemented by a couple of options, the rest of the squad were far from convincing that we had enough depth.

Final Score
Oldham Athletic   **2   0   Leyton Orient**
Ray 33 OG
Whelan 90+5

League Two table after close of play on 31st March 2022

Pos	Team	Pld	W	D	L	GF	GA	GD	Pts
1	Forest Green Rovers	37	20	12	5	66	32	34	72
2	Exeter City	38	18	14	6	56	36	20	68
3	Northampton Town	39	19	9	11	47	33	14	66
4	Port Vale	38	17	12	9	57	36	21	63
5	Newport County	39	17	12	10	62	49	13	63
6	Bristol Rovers	39	18	9	12	53	43	10	63
7	Tranmere Rovers	39	18	9	12	44	34	10	63
8	Mansfield Town	37	18	9	10	52	43	9	63
9	Swindon Town	38	17	10	11	62	48	14	61
10	Sutton United	39	17	10	12	58	46	12	61
11	Salford City	38	16	11	11	48	35	13	59
12	Hartlepool United	39	14	10	15	41	52	-11	52
13	Crawley	39	14	9	16	49	55	-6	51

Pos	Team	Pld	W	D	L	GF	GA	GD	Pts
	Town								
14	Bradford City	39	11	14	14	43	47	-4	47
15	Harrogate Town	39	12	11	16	56	61	-5	47
16	Walsall	39	12	11	16	42	51	-9	47
17	**Leyton Orient**	**39**	**10**	**16**	**13**	**51**	**40**	**11**	**46**
18	Carlisle United	39	12	10	17	34	52	-18	46
19	Rochdale	39	9	16	14	43	51	-8	43
20	Colchester United	39	10	12	17	37	52	-15	42
21	Barrow	38	8	13	17	33	45	-12	37
22	Oldham Athletic	39	8	10	21	39	61	-22	34
23	Stevenage	38	7	13	18	34	60	-26	34
24	Scunthorpe United	39	4	12	23	26	71	-45	24

Chapter 12: April 2022

The new manager resurrects the O's, as a winning Easter weekend restores our faith – and, he earns points in my book for his verdict on pie and mash! But the onset of spring means our season of Orient adventures is entering the home straight.

We just can't seem to get enough of Richie Wellens!

Game 39: Saturday 2nd April 2022, Walsall v Leyton Orient

After the disappointment of how we played and the result at Oldham, the majority of Orient fans were keen for the first-choice team to return, in the hope that we would put in a much better display. It was, of course, yet another awayday in quick succession.

Kay and I had briefly flirted with another stopover to enjoy a night out in Birmingham but instead decided that given the relatively short duration of the train trip (well, at least on the way there! More on that later), we might as well get home on the same day and have Sunday to ourselves rather than having to trek back.

Reaching the Bescot Stadium is fairly straightforward, as it has its own station at the ground, which is only 20 minutes or so from the centre of the Birmingham. Anyone who has been there, or indeed spent any time travelling along the M6, will know exactly where it is, as it is literally right next to the motorway, so much so that there is a huge double advertising hoarding at the entrance to the car park targeted at motorists. When you get off the train, it is a strange feeling as you cross over a stream via a bridge, suggesting you are almost in the countryside, but with the constant noise from the motorway to remind you that you most definitely aren't.

As a result of its location, there isn't very much in terms of local amenities, especially now that the apparently previously very popular Supporters Club bar has closed down. There is reported to be a pub approximately 15 minutes' walk away, but there is also a hotel with a bar literally next door to the ground. Rightly or wrongly, we decided that this was probably the best option for us. It seems we weren't alone in our thinking, as there were quite a few familiar Orient faces already installed when we arrived, including Tim, who had apparently survived in Exeter when we had left him in the pub a few weeks back.

While the staff were friendly enough, it isn't being too harsh to suggest that they weren't the swiftest or most efficient we have ever encountered, not helped by the fact that even though there were at least four people on hand most of the time, they all had to queue up at the single till to put the different orders through. A mate of ours, Jonny, had great difficulty in explaining that he would actually like some beer in his glass rather than the half a pint of froth they had just served him. They also deigned it necessary for us to have plastic glasses despite the outdoor seating options being minimal at best. Still, it was a pleasant enough place to pass on a bit of time before the match.

As we headed into the ground, it soon became clear that the reputation that the club enjoys of being incredibly friendly is most definitely deserved. Even the lady who was checking bags at the turnstiles told us not only to enjoy the match, but that she hoped we'd win. I did just check whether she meant it, and she was adamant she did. Maybe she supports Villa, Birmingham City or West Brom and only works there?

Having been off the pies thanks to our Spanish meal in Oldham, Kay was keen to try the local fayre once again. While it may not have been the warmest offering we have encountered, it was very tasty, and she also treated us to a bag of the local delicacy of traditional pork scratchings. This was something of a poignant reminder to her dear husband that I had failed to bring her back any from a trip to the Hawthorns a good few years back; it seems in matters of food my missus doesn't forget easily.

When the team news came through, there was a breath of relief from the travelling supporters as it became apparent that we were going with the best available XI (Aaron Drinan, Darren Pratley, Shad Ogie and Adam Thompson returning to the line-up and Otis Khan moving back into central midfield) and deploying them in the 4-3-3 system that had been working so well until the numerous changes at Oldham. The opposition featured former O's frontman Conor Wilkinson, and those of us well-versed in how football fate tends to work were utterly convinced that he would, of course, score in this one.

As proceedings got underway, it soon became apparent that my initial fears were mainly based on nerves, as we took the game to Walsall and pretty much had it settled as a contest after just quarter of an hour. First Khan, facing the club Orient signed him from in January, opened up Walsall with a diagonal driving run from left to right, picking up a pass from Drinan en route before beating his man on the right wing and picking out Harry Smith with a teasing cross. All the striker had to do was control his header and put us a goal to the good.

A mere matter of minutes later, Khan picked up on a loose ball from a corner on the edge of the penalty box and with the aid of a wicked deflection made it 2-0. It may have been very early, but the leading candidate for man of the match had already emerged. For the rest of the game, you could feel the relief amongst the O's supporters, as Walsall rarely troubled us, and it just felt like a case of seeing out the match, securing the three points and moving onto the next one. Late in the second half, we were treated to a snow shower (yes, in April -- what was it with the weather this season?) that caused most of those fans in the front few rows to seek shelter a bit further back. The fact that this is what a lot of fans will remember of the second half shows you how in control Orient were. The threat of a Wilkinson goal thankfully didn't come to fruition, and he was reduced to a largely bit-part role, as he often had during his days in E10.

Despite the disappointment of Tuesday evening, this win took Orient to two draws, four wins and just one defeat in the seven games since Richie Wellens took up the reins, quite some turnaround since the dark days of winter.

After the match, Kay and I headed back to the hotel, as we had booked the 18:04 train and had about an hour to kill. Amazingly when we arrived, the staff informed us and the handful of other Orient fans that they were only serving hotel guests or those attending the wedding reception that was starting in a few hours. I am not sure how it happened (honestly!) but when I returned from a quick call of nature, all the O's fans had now been served. I imagine the hotel may have thought they were on for a bumper attendance that evening's event.

The train ride back into Birmingham was easy enough, and I revelled in the utter football geekery of excitedly pointing out both Villa Park and St Andrews, to which Kay managed to feign some semblance of interest. However, when we boarded the London-bound train at New Street, we were greeted with the news that our driver hadn't turned up yet, and we would be stuck there for at least 40 minutes. A brief trip to the off-licence made that more bearable. We got underway eventually and arrived into Euston an hour or so late, but thankfully the relatively short journey meant it wasn't too bad. On arrival we bumped into Paul and Gary, whom we had last seen up in Hartlepool, but after a relatively long day we decided against a trip to the Signal Box, as besides, Paul had promised his other half he would come straight home this time.

Final Score

Walsall	0	2	Leyton Orient
			Smith 10
			Khan 16

Orient not at the races on Grand National Day

Game 40: Saturday 9th April 2022, Sutton United v Leyton Orient

Another match and another awayday, and this time we faced the "mammoth" trek to Sutton, handily a mere half hour on the train out of London Bridge to Greater London/Surrey depending on your disposition. A lot of Orient fans don't like going to Gander Green Lane, having visited it a couple of times while we were exiled in non-league; however, I was actually quite looking forward to it for a number of reasons. Firstly, in the deepest realms of my football obsessive memory, I can recall watching them giant-kill Coventry City (yes, for younger readers, Coventry City were in fact in the top division a while back and had actually won the FA Cup a year and a half previously) back in 1989 on Match of the Day and being intrigued by the look of this quirky-seeming small ground.

More recently, I had watched Arsenal play there on TV in a game that was made infamous by reserve team goalkeeper Wayne Shaw eating a pie in the dugout as part of a betting promotion. Finally, the last time Orient had played there during the National League title-winning season, almost exactly three years to the day, not to show off (well, alright, to completely show off our football obsessive tendencies!), Kay and I had actually been at the Westfalenstadion watching Borussia

Dortmund on one of our previously regular football tourist trips. We had caused bemusement amongst the German fans when we danced gleefully round the concourse on hearing the news that Macauley Bonne's late penalty had secured all three points for Orient and helped them take a significant step towards securing our return to the Football League.

This match also coincided with the Grand National, in which it is traditional for people who know absolutely nothing about horse racing, or betting, for that matter, to stake money that could be most likely be put to better use and bet on horses based on some apparent tenuous connection. Having wasted my money year on year since I was old enough to go into a bookmakers, I finally decided that I wouldn't be bothering this time around. Kay, of course, called into our local bookies on the way to the station, where she restrained herself to a £9 outlay on three horses to win and each way. Nothing like hedging your bets!

Once we boarded the train at London Bridge, we got talking to a couple of Dutch guys who were in town to watch Fulham play Coventry the following day but despite a whole variety of options to entertain themselves in London on a Saturday afternoon had rather bizarrely chosen this match. They asked us what they could expect from the Skylines Grandstand for which they had bought tickets. I could only honestly respond that I couldn't say for sure but that I suspected the "grand" bit might be stretching the description of it.

The closest station to the ground is West Sutton, but having conducted our usual extensive research (yep, having a quick flick at Football Ground Guide!), we decided to get off at the main station in town, as it offered plenty of food and drink options on the relatively short walk up to the ground. We made it all the way to the Old Bank, literally next door, where we settled in for a couple of pints and to watch most of Everton v Manchester United, although we had to leave early in the second half as we were on a mission on behalf of a fellow football obsessive.

Paul, the Manchester City season ticketholder we met on the train on the way back from Barrow, had contacted me to ask if I could help him out, as while he had been to Gander Green Lane a few seasons back, now that they were in the Football League he needed a photo of the main entrance and an official lapel badge for his collection. We football obsessives really are a very strange bunch.

Getting to the ground takes you through outer London suburbia, which feels very surreal when you remind yourself that you are actually there to watch a football match. Upon arrival, I went straight round to what I presumed was the main entrance based on the sign that said "Welcome to Sutton, the home of football" (strangely I think there may be a few grander stadiums with more of a claim!), while Kay headed for the official club portacabin to pick up the badge. With our mission completed, we decided to head inside.

Once inside the ground, it is fair to say that it lived up to its non-league pedigree, and why anyone would decide to start the refurbishment/alleged improvement of the facilities while the season is still going on is beyond me. I am not 100% sure what the plans involve, but surely whatever work they had in the pipeline could have been completed efficiently enough over the summer? The ongoing building work meant that the away "end" was a complete mishmash; there was a half-completed stand to be accessed via a small path in front of a building site, a small temporary stand on the corner and a standing area, which was essentially a flat section of ground. Very bizarre, indeed.

This was another changed line-up (all enforced, reportedly) with Paul Smyth and Theo Archibald coming in in the wide positions,

Aaron Drinan playing through the middle and Jayden Sweeney and Dan Moss occupying the fullback roles.

Not helped by the home side's robust and physical tactics, Orient never really got going in the first half and actually had to be thankful for Lawrence Vigouroux for a couple of good saves to keep Sutton out in the opening stages. Then midway through the first half, we failed to deal with an in-swinging corner, and Joe Kizzi turned it home to give the Sutton the lead. There was some evidence to say that there had been some shirt pulling and blocking in the area, but in truth it was no more than the home side deserved.

While Orient seemed to get their act together a bit more in the second half and had better control of the ball, we couldn't find the breakthrough that our improved display possibly merited. After recent decent results, it was disappointing to lose for the second time in three games, but sometimes you just have to admit that you failed to deal with the opposition's approach.

On the way back through town, we managed to find a pub to watch the Grand National, in which Kay revelled in having picked the third and fourth place finishers for a total of win of a whole £5. As we headed for home, with Kay adamant that she would not be coming back to this ground, that soon changed when we reflected on how easy it is to get to, the decent pubs in town and because we are intrigued to see what it looks like when they have finished the supposed improvements.

With just two more away trips to go until the end of our season-long adventure, we both didn't want it to end and were looking forward to next season's trips with perhaps a slightly less hectic schedule. However, every time we started to discuss which ones we weren't going to do next time around, it was incredibly difficult to rule any out.

Final Score

Sutton United	**1**	**0**	**Leyton Orient**

Kizzi 20

Orient return to form in the Good Friday sunshine

Game 41: Friday 15th April 2022, Leyton Orient v Scunthorpe United

One of the great traditions of the English Football League centres on two scheduled fixtures for each club over the four-day Easter weekend. For Orient, the fixture gods determined that it would be at home to almost relegated Scunthorpe on Good Friday, and then off on a relatively short trip to Wiltshire to face play-off chasing Swindon Town on Easter Monday.

As sometimes happens in the UK, a relatively late Easter meant that we were treated to nice and sunny weather through the whole weekend. It was, in fact, perfect weather for a couple of pre-match pints in the wine bar before heading into the ground. As we strolled down Leyton High Road, it soon became clear that we weren't alone in our thinking, as most of the outside tables were already occupied, while inside it was almost empty, but thankfully we managed to find a spot outside with enough sunshine for Kay and enough shade for those of us who hail from the north of the country and need to be extra careful even in relatively mild sunshine.

Despite the recent loss at Sutton, there was an air of optimism as we entered the ground, which the sunshine and extended weekend no doubt contributed to, as well as the on-the-whole encouraging results since Richie Wellens had taken charge. Scunthorpe, for their part, were in desperate straits: rooted at the foot of the table knowing that they had to win all of their remaining four matches to have any chance whatsoever of remaining in the Football League for another season. It was a plight that Orient fans needed only to think back five years and our own relegation to have great sympathy with.

With the need to manage players through two matches in four days, there were a few changes to the recognised first choice starting line-up. Most notably, 20-year-old January signing Jordan Brown was given his first start under the new gaffer, partnering Hector Kyprianou in the centre of midfield.

Orient made light work of the visitors with three goals in the opening half an hour, effectively ending the contest before we even got to half-time. The first came from Paul Smyth, who once again showed his individual quality, picking up the ball on the right-hand touchline, driving infield leaving the full back in his wake and firing low past the goalkeeper. It was perhaps the most incisive play we had seen from Orient in a long while and made us to start to wonder how things would have gone if only the diminutive creative force could have stayed fit for the majority of the season.

Just nine minutes later, Theo Archibald doubled our lead, as he, too, cut in from the right and fired home left-footed from the edge of the area. It was then rejuvenated striker Ruel Sotiriou's turn to get his name on the scoresheet again, with a diving header from a Brown cross that clipped the upright before nestling in the net.

Despite hitting the frame of the goal three times in the second half and going close on another couple of occasions, we couldn't add to our lead and had to be content with a 3-0 victory. Still, it was a comfortable win and a return to form for the O's. However, there was a tinge of sadness that having thoroughly enjoyed our trip to Scunthorpe on a Tuesday evening back in November, it may well be some time before we might be able to do it again.

Final Score
Leyton Orient   **3**   **0**   **Scunthorpe United**
Smyth 15
Archibald 24
Sotiriou 30

We've got Super Richie Wellens…he knows exactly what we need!

Game 42: Monday 18th April 2022, Swindon Town v Leyton Orient

After a slightly surreal seeming non-football watching Saturday, which seemed to confuse both of us, despite the fact we had only been to Brisbane Road the previous day, and then a traditional Sunday roast dinner with Kay's dad, it was back on our football travels on Easter Monday to Swindon for the penultimate awayday of the season. Once again, the sun was shining, even if it wasn't quite as warm as it had been earlier in the long weekend.

To our amazement when we had travelled to the likes of Newport, Bristol and Exeter, we had realised that Swindon wasn't anywhere near as far away from London as we had initially thought. In fact, it takes just under an hour by train from Paddington, which made it easily doable in a day.

Even better, though, is the fact that once you arrive, it is only a 10-to-15-minute walk from the station to the ground (which you actually see as the train is pulling in), and there are two very hospitable-looking pubs -- The Queen's Tap and the Great Western Hotel -- immediately across the road before you even get underway. We opted for the former simply because it advertised that it showed live sport, and it had what looked like a decent garden.

When we walked in, there were already a few of the familiar Orient travelling faithful in situ, so we said hello and decided where we wanted to sit. Our first instinct was to go outside and enjoy the sunshine, until it soon became clear when the people on the table behind us moved, that not only was it a few degrees cooler in Wiltshire, but that we were also sitting in something of a wind tunnel created by the natural breeze but also the pub's air conditioning fans kicking into life every few minutes. Suffice it to say that after a few minutes, we decided we were better off finding a perch inside.

It turned out that the ground was both well signposted and very easy to find, and we were on our way inside no more than quarter of an hour after we had left the pub. The away fans are housed at the far end of one of the stands, the Arkell's Stand, and while obviously this annoyed me as it wasn't behind the goal, it offers a decent view of the proceedings and has a strange food kiosk/bar that caters for both the away fans and the home fans on either side. From my point of view, though, the metal bars and a huge door that wouldn't be out of place in a bank vault seemed a tad over the top. The external wall of the concourse is also covered with a kind of red plastic panelling that casts a surreal red glow, making it feel even more weird.

It has to be said that the food offerings were pretty impressive, the cheeseburger was one of the tastier ones that I have had, and Kay seemed pretty happy with her pie. However, with fizzy tasteless Carling lager being the only beer available, it also has to be said that the catering facilities lost a few marks on that alone.

The rest of the ground is very much another of the old traditional ones that feels like a proper football ground. There is a small, covered stand behind one of the goals that houses what is presumably the most fervent home support, although you would never have guessed given the lack of noise that emanated from there or any other part of the ground for that matter. Opposite the Arkell's Stand is the more modern Don Roper Stand, and behind the other goal is an uncovered stand that is presumably only ever needed if Swindon host a team with a large away following in one of the cups. Most importantly for us traditionalists (nerds?), it has proper floodlight pylons, rather than the spotlight-on-the-roof variety that seem so popular these days.

In the lead up to this game, despite our recent improved performances and results and the fact that we had dispatched Swindon 4-1 back at the start of December before we descended into the footballing doldrums for the next three months, I was far from confident going into this one. The hosts were sitting in 10th place but only two points off seventh and the final play-off spot. In our pre-match analysis, Kay and I had both reached the conclusion that a point away from home would definitely be a more than acceptable result.

The only changes to the Orient line-up from Friday were the return of Darren Pratley and Shad Ogie after being rested and the late withdrawal of Adam Thompson through injury, meaning that once again Otis Khan had to fill in at right back.

The opening stages were pretty even, but on 20 minutes, that was to change. Paul Smyth won a free kick after being hacked down on one of his trademark forward surges, and Theo Archibald swung it into the area where big centre back Omar Beckles was on hand to nod it home. If the travelling Orient fans had been in good voice before the opening goal, we were in raptures now, with a series of new songs including, "We've got super Richie Wellens, he knows exactly what we need, Beckles at the back, Drinan in attack, Orient going up the Football

League", which crept through the entire away section until literally almost every single one of the reported 351 (there seemed to be a lot more than that!) of us was joining in.

Just four minutes later, young centre midfielder Hector Kyprianou was shown a second yellow card for a late lunge at Louie Barry, which at the time seemed harsh, although admittedly it was up the other end of the pitch. I think the majority of Orient fans probably feared the worst, as it became a case of trying to hold onto what we had. Wellens made a quick tactical switch, bringing on Ethan Coleman, but it was the fighting spirit, commitment and attitude of those left on the pitch that stood out the most.

Just past the half hour mark, there was a bit of a scuffle that broke out after Pratley was bundled over on the sideline, and the way the players all joined in sticking up for the skipper and each other showed the togetherness that had been fostered over the previous five weeks. As commentators always tell us, these are the scenes we are not supposed to like to see, but all fans know deep down that we really do. As things died down, the referee brandished several yellow cards, including one for our flabbergasted gaffer, who hadn't seemingly been involved at all.

Going in at the break with the lead intact was vital to boosting the spirit of our lads ahead of the second half. Just eight minutes into the second period, Beckles scored again, this time poking home a loose ball after a long throw from Ogie.

While Swindon did manage a late goal, we saw the game out with an impressively resolute performance. Even though there was little at stake from an Orient perspective, it felt like a significant step forward in the evolution of the team. The celebrations which were shared between the fans, coaching staff and players revealed a new belief that was really starting to grow throughout the whole club.

We headed back to the station with plenty of time ahead of our 6 pm train, so decided that we might as well see what the other pub, the Great Western Hotel, was like. As soon as we walked in, we could feel a tension in the air. There was only one other person in there who had quite evidently had more than enough to drink, and we later heard that he had brandished a knife, in truth just a penknife, in the direction of the bar staff. Even though he had already left when asked to do so, we decided that a seat out the back in the garden might be the safest option. When Keren and Co. from the Picnic Crew passed by and we told them what had happened, they decided that they would try the Queen's Tap instead!

Final Score

Swindon Town	**1**	**2**	**Leyton Orient**
Davison 78			Beckles 20, 54

Richie dishes on pies and Orient

On the following Thursday evening, the club had organised a Q&A Pie & Pint session with Richie Wellens, new Chief Executive Mark Devlin, formerly of Brentford, and assistant coach Paul Terry. Kay and I, of course, could think of nothing better to do and booked ourselves in.

It was a really nice way to spend an evening and suffice it to say that we left the event feeling even more positive and optimistic about the direction of our club. Its future seems to be not only in safe but very much expert hands. Plus, Kay was able to definitively ask Richie the vital question that as official pie enthusiasts we were desperate to know: what were my fellow North Westerner's feelings on the local delicacy of pie, mash and liquor which the club sells and is very popular in East London? Without wanting to betray any confidences, I will just officially state that I was much happier with his opinion than Kay was, and that proper lumps of meat in your pie and gravy are far more preferable!

Final Score

Steak pie and gravy	**1**	**0**	**Minced beef pie and**
Wellens 1			**liquor**

Back down to Earth with a bump!

Game 43: Saturday 23rd April 2022, Leyton Orient v Northampton Town

Even after the two decent results over the long weekend, doing the same against high-flying Northampton was always going to be something of a big ask. Going into the match, the visitors were in fourth spot, just two points behind Port Vale and very much still in the race for automatic promotion. I consoled myself that the game would provide a useful measure of our recent progress to face one of the better teams in the division.

It was another one of those days when Arsenal had been allocated the early kick-off spot, so it was off to the Supporters Club to watch it in there. Rather pleasingly, as a result of a slight delay to our train on the way over, the Gunners were already 1-0 up against European qualification rivals Manchester United when I walked through the door. They eventually went on to win 3-1. The first part of the footballing day had gone well, now for the big Orient match. After Kay failing to win the raffle for two bottles of expensive-looking vodka despite buying five rows of tickets and catching up with some familiar faces, it was time to make our way in.

As we headed round the back of the South Stand, we bumped into Lord Dazza, who revealed that he hadn't been to many away games over recent weeks as he was taking his boxing training seriously with a potential bout in the offing. He then asked Kay to test his stomach muscles by giving him a punch, but when she pointed out that it may not be the best idea given she was still recovering from her broken hand, the honour fell to yours truly. Let me just say that the results of his intensive training were very noticeable, and my hand was still sore later that day.

There was only one change to the Orient line-up: Ethan Coleman replacing the suspended Hector Kyprianou after his dismissal on Easter Monday. Whether it was us playing badly or the visitors getting off to an absolute flyer, we found ourselves 3-0 down after just 38 minutes. We simply couldn't get near them, and everything seemed to click for Northampton. Even though Theo Archibald pulled a goal back for us in added time at the end of the first half, the Cobblers scored again before the players left the field.

When Jordan Brown managed to pull another goal back just five minutes into the second half, there was a brief flurry of hope amongst the Orient faithful, but Northampton were able to see out the game comfortably. Shad Ogie was shown a red card on 83 minutes for an alleged headbutt after he had been scythed down by a nasty-looking challenge. The officials had been poor throughout the match, and it seemed a harsh decision. The sending off basically ended any lingering hope we had of salvaging anything at all from the match. It was a tough one to take, as it was something of a reality check that showed us the level we need to get to if a serious tilt at promotion is to be a reasonable target in the next campaign.

Final Score

Leyton Orient	2	4	Northampton Town
Archibald 45+1			Pinnock 19
Brown 50			Guthrie 32
			Eppiah 38, 45+3

The Easy Lovers reunited in Crawley

Game 44: Saturday 30th April 2022, Crawley Town v Leyton Orient

For the final away trip of the season (seriously where had the last eight months gone?), it was another fairly straightforward journey for us, as, just like for Sutton, all we had to do was to get ourselves to London Bridge for the relatively short train ride of just under an hour to Crawley.

As the end of the season approaches, it always feels a bit melancholic for us football obsessives who, if we are totally honest, only truly feel comfortable following the rhythm of the fixture list, and we start to realise that the matches are running out. The summer of 2022 looked even "tougher" to endure than recent ones, as the moving of the World Cup in Qatar to the autumn/winter left a gaping hole on the calendar where the four-week fiesta of football should usually sit. The one saving grace is that it did mean that the start of 2022/23 would be earlier than usual; in fact it was scheduled for the last weekend in July for EFL clubs.

We arrived in Crawley just before 1 pm and decided that rather than "explore" the town centre, no offence to the residents of this Sussex town but once you have seen one new town you have seen them all, we would head up towards the ground. To our utmost joy, once we had negotiated the level crossing over the train line, we discovered the rather excellently placed Railway pub at the very start of the 20-minute or so walk up the hill. With the sun shining once more, this provided the perfect place for a leisurely pint or two in the beer garden.

Just as excellently strategically placed as the Railway, there is another pub up at the top of the road, the New Moon, where we had arranged to meet Paul and the rest of the "Easy Lovers". After a catch-up while watching the end of Newcastle v Liverpool in the lunchtime kick-off, we decided to head under the underpass and into the ground.

Broadfield Stadium, (or the People's Pensions Stadium, as the sponsors would, of course, prefer that we called it!) like a number of the other grounds that we had visited across the season, is fairly modern and well set up but lacks the real character of the older grounds. Also, like Stevenage and Northampton (what is it with these new towns?), there is no beer on sale inside the ground for away fans. In fact there isn't very much of anything available at all. All we had to choose from were sausage or cheese and onion rolls from the kiosk just inside, although the guy serving said there were burger and chips options on the far side of the ground but that they had probably run out by now. And we think the catering at Brisbane Road is limited! In the end, we settled for cold sausage rolls that Kay is still convinced may not have actually been cooked in the first place.

There was a slight surprise to Orient's starting line-up with young academy prospect Zech Obiero being given his first team debut in central midfield and usual midfielder Jordan Brown coming in at right-back. The match itself was the very definition of a game of two halves: Orient took an early lead thanks to a cute lob from Theo Archibald after he had latched onto a flighted long pass from Lawrence Vigouroux after just eight minutes and were in control right through the opening half. We had a glorious chance to double our advantage approaching the midway point of the first half, when we were awarded a penalty, but the fact that Aaron Drinan had his shot comfortably saved surprised none of the Orient faithful, given that our last successful penalty conversion in a league game was in January 2020 by former midfielder Josh Wright, although in fairness we don't get given that many.

The second half was entirely different, as the Orient players seemed to conclude that a single goal was sufficient for them to take it easy for the rest of the match. As a result, it was pretty much all Crawley for the second period, as they upped their game and kept us very much penned back. As the game neared its end, James Tilley fired an effort goalward for the hosts, only to see his effort hit the bar and bounce straight down. From our vantage point at the opposite end of the ground, I was obviously 100% sure that it hadn't crossed the line; however a Crawley fan in the pub after the match and the TV replays showed that it had been in by quite some distance. Thankfully there is no goal-line technology at this level.

Maybe that proved something of a late wake-up call for the O's, as Aaron Drinan burst through the inside right channel but seemed to want too many touches of the ball to steady himself and ended up dragging his shot tamely wide. However, moments later, Drinan broke through the other channel and curled his effort home to settle the match once and for all.

After the match, we headed back to the New Moon to catch up with the Easy Lovers and celebrate the end of the O's campaign away from home. None of us were in a rush to get back to London, as we didn't want to admit that this would be the last trip for a good few weeks.

Final Score

Crawley Town	**0**	**2**	**Leyton Orient**
			Archibald 8
			Drinan 90+5

League Two table after close of play on 30th April 2022

Pos	Team	Pld	W	D	L	GF	GA	GD	Pts
1	Exeter City	45	23	15	7	65	40	25	84
2	Forest Green Rovers	45	23	14	8	73	42	31	83
3	Northampton Town	45	22	11	12	57	37	20	77
4	Bristol Rovers	45	22	11	12	64	49	15	77
5	Port Vale	44	21	12	11	65	44	21	75
6	Mansfield Town	44	22	9	13	63	48	15	75
7	Swindon Town	45	21	11	13	74	54	20	74
8	Sutton United	45	21	10	14	67	53	14	73
9	Tranmere Rovers	45	20	12	13	52	40	12	72
10	Salford City	44	19	12	13	56	40	16	69
11	Newport County	44	18	12	14	65	55	10	66
12	Crawley Town	45	17	9	19	53	63	-10	60
13	Leyton	45	14	16	15	62	46	16	58

Pos	Team	Pld	W	D	L	GF	GA	GD	Pts
	Orient								
14	Bradford City	45	13	16	16	51	55	-4	55
15	Walsall	45	14	12	19	47	57	-10	54
16	Hartlepool United	45	14	12	19	44	62	-18	54
17	Harrogate Town	45	14	11	20	64	73	-9	53
18	Carlisle United	45	14	11	20	39	60	-21	53
19	Colchester United	45	13	13	19	46	60	-14	52
20	Rochdale	45	11	17	17	49	59	-10	50
21	Barrow	45	10	14	21	43	54	-11	44
22	Stevenage	45	10	14	21	41	66	-25	44
23	Oldham Athletic	45	9	10	26	43	72	-29	37
24	Scunthorpe United	45	4	14	27	29	83	-54	26

Chapter 13: May 2022

Our adventure draws to a close, and we provide our verdicts and ratings on awayday food, proper pubs and stadium settings.

A disappointing result to end a season of "what might have been"

Game 45: Saturday 7th May 2022, Leyton Orient v Tranmere Rovers

For the majority of fans, the final game of the season is always slightly bittersweet, as you want to celebrate the season just gone, but there is also the full realisation that you will be out of the usual routine for a good few weeks (12 to be precise, not that it is etched into my brain of course!). In many ways, it is about catching up with the people you know from going to the matches ahead of the summer break.

Having used both the wine bar and the Supporters Club as our go-to pre-home-match drinking spots, Kay and I were a little bit undecided as to which one we should go to for the last game. That was until Kay came up with the brainwave that if we set off early enough, we could in fact have a couple of pints in each. So it was that we walked into the wine bar just as they were opening up.

After an hour or so enjoying the sunshine outside, we headed down to the Supporters Club. As soon as we had we said hello to a few people, bought our drinks and headed outside onto the "sun terrace", we discovered Orient vice chairman and principal investor Kent Teague had started a bit of an impromptu meet and greet with the fans gathered around. Of course, it provided the perfect opportunity for us all to grill the affable Texan on transfer targets and which players we were likely to keep, etc. Kay, for her part, played the perfect role as unofficial football journalist by asking him if there was any truth to the rumour that former fan favourite Macauley Bonne, scorer of 45 league goals in our 2 seasons in the National League and now at QPR but whom had been on loan at Ipswich for the season, might be returning to the club on loan next season. We took the fact that he didn't rule it out at all and his confession that he was in a WhatsApp group with Macca and his dad as clear indications that it might happen. You read it here first as they say!

Just before we were leaving, I noticed a familiar figure in a Tranmere sweatshirt -- the rather infamous, soon-to-retire Premier League referee Mike Dean, who as a fellow Wirralonian is a staunch supporter of Rovers. Although never truly being one for the social media self-promotion spotlight, I couldn't resist the perfect photo opportunity. As Kay was taking the picture, I only half-jokingly told Mr Dean that I had pretty much called him every name under the sun from my seat at the Emirates over previous seasons. To his credit, he smiled.

The game was another advertised sell-out (although once again not all seats were filled, rather frustratingly) which makes trying to get any food or drink in the East Stand an overly long and drawn-out process, and with the end of season awards due to be handed out on the pitch from 2:30 pm, we decided that the easiest option was to go to our seats. For the record: goalkeeper Lawrence Vigouroux won Player of the Season and Manager's Player of the Season, while big Omar Beckles won Players' Player of the Season and Community Player of the Season, and Aaron Drinan was selected by Darren Pratley as Captain's Player of the Season. It was difficult to argue with any of the selections, while Paul Smyth's wonder strike from virtually on the goal-line against Barrow won Goal of the Season.

Going into the match, there was an outside chance that Tranmere could still make the play-offs if they could beat us and the teams above them were to drop points. From an Orient perspective, the highest we could finish was 12th if we won and Crawley lost. The better news from an Orient point of view was the return of right back Tom James, who had been out injured since the middle of December. The Welshman's performances in the early part of the season had seen him emerge as one of the most rated of all the new signings but whose contract was due to come to an end at the end of the season. Hopefully Kent and Co. would be able work their magic and convince him to extend his time with the O's.

From the outset, Tranmere seemed to set up to try to contain Orient and stifle our attacking play. As a result, when we did have possession, we played in front of them and struggled to create any meaningful chances, save for a header from a cross that Smyth did well to get to given his size but which sailed well over the bar and a free kick from James that Rovers keeper Joe Murphy turned onto the post.

With less than 10 minutes to go to the break, Kane Hemmings produced a diving header from a cross from the right that left Vigouroux with no chance whatsoever, and it was 1-0 to the visitors.

Orient seemed to lose what little impetus they had in the second half, and chances were even fewer and farther between than they had been in the opening period. We were given a brief flicker of hope with quarter of an hour to go, when there appeared to be a handball in the midst of a tangle of players competing for a high ball and referee Seb Stockbridge pointed to the penalty spot. After a brief consultation with his linesman, he then overturned the decision, and we consoled ourselves with the not-unreasonable thought that we probably would have missed it anyway. With that, any hope of salvaging a point was gone. Sadly for Tranmere, Swindon's win at Walsall meant that they couldn't make the play-offs and were consigned to another season in League Two.

After applauding the players after the match for their efforts throughout the season, Kay and I headed to the Coach & Horses for a final post-match drink. While it was relatively busy, none of the usual people we know from the awaydays were in there, although we did get talking to a Polish guy who was literally the size of three fellas welded together and who told us that his favourite English teams were Millwall and West Ham, as they were proper hooligans like back home. We kept our disagreement on what constitutes a "good" football fan hidden, although there was a very interesting moment when he went to the bar and a group of 20-somethings decided to take his seat, despite our advice to the contrary. I don't think I have ever seen people move so quickly when he came back!

Given the lack of the usual gang in the Coach, we decided to head back round to the Legends Lounge in the West Stand, which was open on a first-come-first-served basis to all fans after the match. We bumped into James outside and a few other people, before heading back to the Coach where Raj, Darin, Johnny, Jack and a few of the other awayday regulars were now in situ. It was almost as if no one wanted to leave, as that would be admitting that the season was over. When we did eventually arrive back on the Isle of Dogs, Kay and I spent the evening half-watching Liverpool v Tottenham on telly but mainly reminiscing about the whole season-long adventure and what we were going to do for the next 12 weeks without Orient. Of course, for one of us, there was something of a decision to be made...

Final Score

Leyton Orient	**0**	**1**	**Tranmere Rovers**
			Hemmings 37

League Two end of season table for 2021-22

Pos	Team	Pld	W	D	L	GF	GA	GD	Pts
1	Forest Green Rovers	46	23	15	8	75	44	31	84
2	Exeter City	46	23	15	8	65	41	24	84
3	Bristol Rovers	46	23	11	12	71	49	22	80
4	Northampton Town	46	23	11	12	60	38	22	80
5	Port Vale	46	22	12	12	67	46	21	78
6	Swindon Town	46	22	11	13	77	54	23	77
7	Mansfield Town	46	22	11	13	67	52	15	77
8	Sutton United	46	22	10	14	69	53	16	76
9	Tranmere Rovers	46	21	12	13	53	40	13	75
10	Salford City	46	19	13	14	60	46	14	70
11	Newport County	46	19	12	15	67	58	9	69
12	Crawley Town	46	17	10	19	56	66	-10	61
13	**Leyton**	**46**	**14**	**16**	**16**	**62**	**47**	**15**	**58**

Pos	Team	Pld	W	D	L	GF	GA	GD	Pts
	Orient								
14	Bradford City	46	14	16	16	53	55	-2	58
15	Colchester United	46	14	13	19	48	60	-12	55
16	Walsall	46	14	12	20	47	60	-13	54
17	Hartlepool United	46	14	12	20	44	64	-20	54
18	Rochdale	46	12	17	17	51	59	-8	53
19	Harrogate Town	46	14	11	21	64	75	-11	53
20	Carlisle United	46	14	11	21	39	62	-23	53
21	Stevenage	46	11	14	21	45	68	-23	47
22	Barrow	46	10	14	22	44	57	-13	44
23	Oldham Athletic	46	9	11	26	46	75	-29	38
24	Scunthorpe United	46	4	14	28	29	90	-61	26

Mrs Orient Nerd's (aka Kay's) Favourite/Most Memorable Awayday Food

In no specific order whatsoever, here are the missus' "food (and drink) highlights" from our Orient adventure:

1) Grecian pastie at Exeter – well we were in the West Country!

2) Scotch pie at Carlisle – not the tastiest but very appropriate, given we could almost see the border from there!

3) Pork scratchings at Walsall – an obvious choice from the West Midlands, but it gave her husband a chance to redeem himself for failing to bring any back from a trip to the Hawthorns a good few years back!

4) Bovril at Northampton – just about helped us to stave off hypothermia in the arctic conditions at Sixfields!

5) Burger van cheeseburger at Port Vale -- probably the moment when we realised we were beyond hope; plus it helped soak up all the beer!

6) McDonald's/Greggs sausage roll – perfect pitstop either to or from grounds that have either (or sometimes even both!) located en route!

7) Chips topped with a mouldy cheese slice at Sutton -- about as unappealing as it sounds, it doesn't score highly but is not something that is easy to forget!

8) Pies (steak-based, not the officially unlucky chicken balti options, of course!) -- too many good ones to mention individually, but particular standouts include Rochdale, Barrow, Scunthorpe and, of course, the standard home fayre at Brisbane Road!

9) Chips at Salford, although they definitely could have been more generous with the portion size!

10) Bacon buttie and a pint in any handy Wetherspoons (the go-to pub for any discerning travelling football fans) the morning after a Tuesday night awayday!

Pubs

Some of the best pubs that we had the pleasure of visiting over the course of our travels:

- ⇨ 'Spoons – as stated previously, this pub chain is the mainstay of the travelling football fan, with particular favourites for us being Harrogate, Exeter, Scunthorpe (yes, really, although that was as much to do with the old fellas arguing over who owed how much to whom for breakfast!), and from the 2022/23 campaign, the new one at Birmingham New Street station.

- ⇨ The Ratcliffe Arms at Rochdale's Spotland ground (could easily be confused with the Phoenix Club from Peter Kay's (in)famous TV series) – a "homely" ambiance with some interesting local characters as clientele; Kay is still devastated that we missed Limehouse Lizzy.

- ⇨ The Supporters Club ay Hartlepool – cracking little spot, which is literally just down there and through the car park!

- ⇨ The Signal Box at Euston, the Parcel Yard at Kings Cross, the Mad Bishop & Bear at Paddington -- all three provide the perfect place to while away your time while waiting for the train.

- ⇨ The Beer House at Leeds station – the ideal venue to pass time during a changeover between trains, assuming they are running on time, of course.

- ⇨ Titanic Bod Bar at Stoke station -- an improvement to the facilities that used to exist at this place, although be warned, the beer is noticeably strong.

⇨ The Old Post Office (x2) – the one at Port Vale, simply due to the upside-down clock to really confuse both local and visiting drinkers, and the one in Stevenage, simply because it is possibly the new town's only place to have a pint.

⇨ The Star Inn Salford -- where the whole adventure got underway, a community-owned pub with very cheap beer. What's not to like even if it is a little bit out of the way?

⇨ The Hungry Horse (x2) – the one in Scunthorpe because Kay won not one, but two prizes on the fairground grabber machine, and the one in Northampton because it helped us to recover from hypothermia.

⇨ The hotel bar at Walsall -- simply because it added a very surreal feeling to the pre-match preparations.

⇨ Slipping Jimmy's Bar & Grill in Newport -- great music, friendly staff and decent prices; we're still amazed we didn't decide to stay for the evening after the match.

⇨ The Beehive at Carlisle and the Prenton Park Hotel at Tranmere – they are both literally across the road from the respective grounds; why waste valuable drinking time?

⇨ Duke of Edinburgh at Barrow -- excellent beer and literally the first thing you see when you come out of the station.

⇨ The Railway at Crawley -- it is literally across the level crossing at the start of the 20-minute walk up the hill to the ground, and then at the top of the hill is the

New Moon -- perfect partnership working.

...and, of course, notable and honourable mentions to: Leyton Orient Supporters Club, the Coach & Horses, the wine bar and the Leyton Star -- we have probably spent more time in these fine establishments than we have in the ground!

The Grounds

Category A: Proper

⇨ Boundary Park – Oldham Athletic

⇨ Holker Street – Barrow

⇨ Brunton Park – Carlisle United

⇨ Vale Park – Port Vale

⇨ Prenton Park – Tranmere Rovers

⇨ Spotland – Rochdale

⇨ Bescot Stadium – Walsall

⇨ Victoria Park – Hartlepool United

⇨ Valley Parade – Bradford City

⇨ Rodney Parade – Newport County (even if it is actually a rugby ground!)

⇨ Field Mill – Mansfield Town

⇨ St James Park – Exeter City

Category B: Out of town and soulless

⇨ Sixfields – Northampton Town (plus it was proper brass monkeys weather, as we say oop north!)

⇨ Broadhall Way – Stevenage (the bad news, especially for Kay, is that we are due back there in 2023/24, as we will Northampton!)

⇨ Moor Lane – Salford City

⇨ Colchester Community Stadium – Colchester United

Category C: Decent enough, but no beer

⇨ Memorial Stadium – Bristol Rovers

⇨ Broadfield Stadium – Crawley Town

⇨ Wetherby Road – Harrogate Town

⇨ Gander Green Lane – Sutton United (although it does now have beer and is better now they have finished the building works!)

Chapter 14: The Decision

Arsenal wants me back...but I've been bitten by the Orient bug. Time to weigh my old club loyalties against my season-long adventures.

The email pinged into my Inbox in the third week of March confirming that my original Club Level seat at Emirates Stadium was still available for 2022/23, and that if I wanted to return after my season ticket holiday, all I had to do was follow the link and part with my hard-earned cash. With somewhat ironic timing, it was just a week after the traumatic incident at Forest Green and the visit I made to the Emirates to watch Arsenal lose, yet again, to Liverpool.

The details of the "generous offer" were that should I choose to return, the credit on my account from the games that I was unable to attend as a result of the Covid lockdown would be used to discount the price of the season ticket, but if Arsenal were to qualify for Europe, an additional fee would be required, depending on which of the three continental competitions they would be competing in.

Without giving too much away about the eye-watering price that I used to pay, if the Gunners were to achieve a return to European football's flagship competition/gravy train (please delete as appropriate!) that is the Champions League, then that would cost me more than the rebate I was due. What a deal! I remember wondering at the time how the potential increase in cost would affect other Gooners' feelings about the chase for European qualification, especially given the cost-of-living crisis that was starting to become oh so evident for everyone in the country.

Being brutally honest, all through the season and especially in the last few months, I really wasn't sure what I was going to do. On the one hand, the camaraderie of the Orient family, the ability to go to every single game home and away and the refreshing atmosphere of football in League Two, far removed from the commercially driven/money-mad world of the Premier League, was definitely pulling me towards Leyton Orient; however, as we all know, it is complete anathema to any self-respecting football fan to change teams.

From that fateful day back in 2017, Kay and I had committed ourselves to the Orient cause, but it was something that I could balance with my Arsenal-watching commitments. Now it felt like I had to make a choice one way or the other: if I decided to take up my seat in North London once again, that would necessitate drastically reducing the number of Orient matches we could go to each season and probably not renewing my season ticket at Brisbane Road. Deep down I knew that wasn't really an option, as the pair of us were way too far down the rabbit hole for that, but then it dawned on me...

... My estrangement from top-level football has never been just about Arsenal's declining performances and status. It was the continuing alienation of real fans from the game that was ours to start with but now seems much more focused on broadcasting and commercial revenue, with TV markets across the globe rating just as highly, if not more, with the Premier League's owners, than us, the humble paying live stadium audience.

As a result, my decision became a lot more straightforward -- if the owners and powers that be want to treat me as a customer, then I would exercise my right to behave like one. Instead of committing to being fleeced at every possible opportunity, I would choose how I followed Arsenal and the Premier League, so if the priority for the club is the global TV market, then I was already part of that with the multiple TV subscriptions required. I haven't actually researched how many Arsenal matches I watched live on TV in 2021/22, but suffice it to say, it was the significant majority of them, with those that weren't screened live available in highlight form on Match of the Day, etc.

Thus, I could realign my football supporting identity, and while I will always be an Arsenal fan, I now feel like I have become a fully-fledged follower and supporter of the humble club from E10 that has captured my soul. Kay often says that you don't pick your football club, it finds you, and in this case, it feels very much as if Leyton Orient has done just that to me. Just the other week I was in the barber's, and the guy cutting my hair asked me if I liked football and, if so, who did I support? It should surprise no one reading this that my immediate and emphatic response was "Leyton Orient!" One day, maybe the O's will draw Arsenal in a cup match as they did back in 2011. If that ever comes to pass and is at the Emirates, then the away section is the one part of the ground that I haven't been in yet!

Chapter 15: What Happened Next?

From the foundations laid last season, Leyton Orient go on an amazing title run for the ages...and Kay and I are right there to witness the scenes, the pandemonium and the trophy lift that gets us back into League One.

I think we all knew it was going to end up like this, didn't we? After we had dedicated an entire season to following our beloved O's around the country, there was no way in the world that Kay and I weren't going to carry on doing very much the same the following season. The one concession that we permitted ourselves was that we would actually take some non-Orient related holidays in the early months, something we really hadn't been able to do since March 2020 and the start of the Covid pandemic. It turned out to be quite some campaign for the Orient faithful.

July 2022

Orient kept most of the players that they wanted to keep ahead of the new season but bid farewell to those that hadn't made much of an impact, with perhaps the only real surprises being the departures of young midfielder Hector Kyprianou, who moved up a level to League One Peterborough, and Otis Khan, who had made something of an impact since his arrival in January.

In terms of incoming signings, Theo Archibald was signed on a permanent basis from his parent club Lincoln City, the experienced attacking midfielder George Moncur arrived from Hull City of the second tier, and Rob Hunt, a full-back capable of operating on either side of the pitch, came to E10 after having played for Richie Wellens previously at both Oldham Athletic and Swindon Town. Two loan signings, forward Charlie Kelman from QPR and midfielder Idris El Mizouni from Ipswich Town, quickly established themselves as first choice players.

After something of a patchy pre-season for Orient, the action proper got underway on 30th July (an early start due to the Qatar World Cup getting underway in November), with newly promoted Grimsby Town coming to Brisbane Road. The O's secured a 2-0 opening day victory, thanks to a successful penalty from George Moncur, our first successful conversion from the spot in a league match since Josh Wright back in early 2020, and a wonder strike from Tom James with his supposedly weaker left foot.

August 2022

Next up was a trip to Crawley, where we had ended our travels for 21/22 just a few months previously. Another late Tom James goal from distance, this time with his right foot, was enough to secure all three points.

The O's defeated a resolute Mansfield side, 1-0, in sweltering conditions in London, before dropping points for the first time in the campaign after being held to a draw at Swindon the following Tuesday evening, in a game that we probably could and should have won.

Kay and I were in my unofficial "home town" of Rotterdam celebrating her birthday, but rest assured, we watched the 3-1 win at Colchester on my iPad; we can only wonder what the other residents in the apartment block made of our chants of "We're Leyton Orient, we're top of the league!" emanating from our balcony after that one.

We were back in E10 to see us dismantle Hartlepool, 4-2, thanks to another Moncur successful penalty and goals from Kelman, Paul Smyth and Ruel Sotiriou.

September 2022

During August and September, Kay and I (ok, well, mainly me!) became absorbed in New York Yankees star slugger Aaron Judge's pursuit of the American League single season home run record, so we decided that a trip to New York was required to join in the fun. After watching us see off Tranmere Rovers, 2-0, at home, it was across The Pond we went. This decision did mean that we were going to miss the game away at Wimbledon in their new stadium, a venue I really wanted to visit, having been to the old Plough Lane many years previously. As we will all remember, however, the sad passing of Her Majesty Queen Elizabeth II meant that the game was eventually postponed. For the record (and in case anyone is in the slightest bit interested!) Judge didn't hit any home runs during our time in the Big Apple, much to Kay's chagrin, as she was already starting to plot how to spend the money she might reap from catching and then selling the record-breaking home run ball. He did, however, break the record right at the end of the season.

Upon our return, we watched the O's win, 1-0, at Rochdale through bleary, jet-lagged eyes in the company of Dulcet Dave and Matt Hiscock, having literally landed just that morning. The O's then saw off Walsall, 1-0, before heading to Barrow, a game that I opted to miss to watch St Helens win their fourth consecutive Super League Grand Final at Old Trafford, having missed the two previous ones -- once thanks to Covid and the other as a result of being on the way back from Barrow the previous season. The O's won, 2-0, to continue their hugely impressive start to the season, which had seen us win nine out of our opening ten matches, the draw at Swindon being the only dropped points. Of course, as naturally pessimistic Orient fans, no one was even considering, let alone talking about the "P" (promotion) word.

October 2022

With the O's having started the season so well, a bump in the road was always likely, and it came on the first day of October when Newport inflicted our first defeat, triumphing somewhat fortuitously, 2-1, at Brisbane Road. That result was followed by two draws: 1-1 away at Doncaster, a game that the national train strikes meant that we had to make our debut on the Supporters Club coach to get to, and then 0-0 at home to Northampton. The results provided something of a slight reality check for anyone getting too carried away with our start to the season.

It was at this point that I was very kindly invited onto the Orient Hour radio show on Phoenix FM. I must have come across as knowing a bit of what I was talking about despite being a relative newbie Orient supporter, and one with a northern accent to boot, as I then joined the four-weekly rota. As you may have gathered from this book, waffling on about football and Orient for an hour on a Wednesday evening is something that sits comfortably with me, and who knows, some people might even listen!

The O's snapped out of their funk with three consecutive victories in a week to see out the month, winning 3-2 at Carlisle, which we sadly had to rule out due to more train-based fun and games, then 2-0 over Gillingham, and 1-0 over our old friends Salford at home, in which Smyth scored a goal after being fouled and appealing for a penalty, only to then get up when none was forthcoming and beat a couple more defenders before rifling the ball home. It was one of a number of magical goals the diminutive Northern Irish magician scored over this period of the season.

November 2022

November started with a FA Cup First Round exit at Crewe, meaning the much desired (both by Chairman Nigel Travis and a large proportion of the Orient faithful) extended cup run would have to wait for (yet) another year.

A midweek trip to South London for the rearranged game against Wimbledon saw the O's go down, 2-0, and fall to their second defeat of the season. Orient fans reportedly received some terrible treatment from the stewards, which was so bad that The Don's Chief Executive Danny Macklin (yes, once of Orient) sacked the security company the very next day. For once, I was actually thankful that Kay and I hadn't bought tickets for the initial fixture as we were in the States at the time.

Kay finally got to watch a match in Harrogate next, and as I had confidently predicted, she thoroughly enjoyed the food available, and (somewhat unusually) we didn't even mind too much that there was no beer available. Our experience was made even more pleasant by the O's cruising to a comfortable 2-0 victory, thanks to a "towering" header by the 5-foot-4 Smyth and another Moncur penalty, both coming before half-time.

We watched the 2-1 victory at Stockport at home because as soon as it had finished, we were off to Heathrow ahead of a very early flight to Doha, Qatar, the following morning for our third World Cup adventure.

December 2022

After five matches in five days, many, many £9-a-pint beers and another thoroughly enjoyable World Cup experience, we were back at Brisbane Road for the visit of promotion-fancied Bradford City. The O's very much picked up where they had left off, easily sweeping past Mark Hughes' charges 3-0, thanks to first-half goals from Kelman and James and a late one from Sotiriou.

We had been planning to go to the Crewe game along with my cousin Ian (he who made me an Arsenal fan all those years ago) and his partner Liane, as they live fairly locally; however our plans had to be put on hold thanks to the first weather-based postponement of the season. It had echoes of the previous winter but thankfully less of an impact this time around, although the home game against Sutton the following week was played in freezing conditions, with snow cleared from the pitch piled up in front of the stands. A goal by Smyth just past the hour mark and an own goal 10 minutes from time were enough to secure another three points.

The visit of Stevenage in the "traditional" Boxing Day fixture was selected by Sky Sports to be shown live across the nation, although that did necessitate it being moved to the following day, which deprives the affected fans of the usual post-festivities fixture, and was given a lunchtime kick-off of 12:30 pm. This did, however, allow me to sneak in a Boxing Day evening trip to the Emirates to watch Arsenal take on West Ham, in place of Kay's dad, who was tied up on family duty. The two top-placed teams in the division played out a stalemate of a goalless draw.

Kay and I briefly contemplated a trip to South Wales ahead of the New Year's Eve celebrations, having enjoyed our trip to

Newport so much the season before; however, in the end, we concluded that as the weather was unlikely to be as hospitable as it had been in the early September sunshine, and since we were striving to maintain some kind of "normal people's" routine to our life (reluctantly, it has to be said), we decided to watch on the live stream. It ended up being another frustrating 0-0 draw, as the O's momentum started to stutter just a little bit.

January 2023

Having completely ruled out a return trip to Sixfields after the artic conditions and a poor performance by Orient in late November the previous campaign, Kay surprised both of us when she woke up the day after the Stevenage match and wondered why we weren't going to Northampton. Rather than churlishly point out to my beloved that it had been entirely her decision to skip it (and that obviously I wanted to go!), I did what every self-respecting football obsessive husband would do and fired up the laptop to order two tickets. This time, the weather was nowhere near as unpleasant as it had been on our first visit, but Orient's performance and subsequent 1-0 defeat were just as infuriating, if not more so. To cap off a miserable afternoon, we lost three centre backs in just the one match: Dan Happe and later on Shad Ogie to injury, and Omar Beckles thanks to an ill-disciplined red card in added time.

For the home game against Doncaster five days later, we had to cobble together a centre back partnership of young midfielder Jordan Brown and reserve full back Adam Thompson. In the end, the pair performed admirably well, and we secured all three points thanks to a Theo Archibald wonder strike that sparked the invasion of Brisbane Road by a flock of parakeets (yes, it really did happen, and no, I was not still feeling the effects of the festive period!).

We followed that up with another goalless draw at home to Barrow the following Saturday, which saw the arrival of Brighton youngster and Wales Under-21 skipper Ed Turns to shore up the back line, before we were off on the relatively short hop to Hertfordshire for the return fixture against Stevenage. This time, gaffer Richie Wellens opted to pair Turns with another new loanee: the experienced Jamie McCart, who had come in from Rotherham having made a name for himself in Scotland with St Johnstone. We simply couldn't cope with Stevenage's direct approach and were 2-0 down after just 10 minutes. To cap off a thoroughly depressing afternoon, El Mizouni, who had been so influential up to this point, was sent off just before half-time, and we conceded a third in added time.

Next was another return "home" for me for the trip to the Wirral. Of course, we met up with Ian and Liane for a Lunya tapas feed-up, and while Tranmere Rovers die-hard Paul couldn't make it down from the North East, Roger, another fellow Wirralonian from our Qatar World Cup squad, along with his partner Caroline were able to join us for pre and post-match drinks. Sadly for the O's, it ended in another defeat, 1-0 thanks to an own goal by the returning Beckles.

At that stage, Orient had won just one of their seven matches since beating Sutton in the middle of December, and it is fair to say that nerves were jangling amongst the faithful, mindful of the way things had gone drastically wrong 12 months previously. Granted, we still retained a relatively healthy lead of 14 points ahead of fourth place, so we were fairly confident that if we could start to put some more points on the board, our destiny in terms of potential promotion was very much in our own hands.

February 2023

After surviving that "wobble", the lads seemed to knuckle down and to start grinding out results again, starting with "revenge" over Wimbledon with a 1-0 win thanks to a George Moncur goal just past the hour mark from open play, something of a relative rarity up to that point despite his ongoing success from the penalty spot.

Next up was the rearranged trip to Crewe, which being scheduled for a Tuesday night meant that Kay and I once again watched via the live stream. It was a comfortable enough 2-0 win, thanks to a debut goal from Turns and a second half strike from Archibald.

It was back to Walsall next, but this time the hotel had been taken over by the local council/UK government to host refugees and asylum seekers while they didn't process their individual cases. Thankfully, through no pre-match organisation whatsoever, we had chosen to have a few pre-match pints in the newly opened Wetherspoons at New Street station. Orient managed to salvage a point after going behind early, thanks to Turns' second goal in a week and his second for the club.

We spent Valentine's evening at Brisbane Road (seriously, where else did you think we would be?), where goals in the first half hour from Sotiriou and El Mizouni were just about enough to see off a struggling at the bottom end of the table but resolute Rochdale side.

We built on the momentum of that victory with a hard-fought 1-0 victory over Crawley, thanks to another El Mizouni strike, the young Tunisian seemingly bouncing back from his enforced absence at Prenton Park with a renewed drive. Such had been his impact over the course of the campaign that the "We want you to stay...we want you to stay..." chant intended to convince him to join us permanently was growing in prevalence and volume with each impressive performance.

We finished off the month of February with a trip to the Cleethorpes seaside, for as any dedicated follower of English lower league football will know, Grimsby Town's Blundell Park is not actually in fact in Grimsby. We failed miserably to have the fish and chips that I had faithfully promised Kay we would sample, but in fairness, we were distracted by the two pubs that form part of the actual station building, as well as the excellent Swashbuckle Tavern, which is exactly what you would think it is: a pirate-themed bar which had pirate metal (yes, it really is a thing!) blaring out of the speakers when we arrived.

After taking an early lead through Kelman's first goal in ages, we then conspired to let our advantage slip with some uncharacteristic play at the start of the second half, conceding two goals in the opening seven minutes. Moncur, on as a substitute, equalized with just over 20 minutes remaining. There was to be more late drama, however, when Lawrence Vigouroux saved another penalty (his third of the season), and this time, he hadn't even given it away.

March 2023

We started March with two consecutive home draws: 1-1 against Swindon and 2-2 against Colchester, the latter being especially galling, as we were 2-0 up going into the final two minutes of the match.

It was then off to the North East coast again exactly four weeks after we had been up to Cleethorpes, this time to Hartlepool. On the way up there, Kay and I shared a table on the train with Ketan, the O's physio, who had been on duty at the training ground and unable to travel up with the team the previous day. It was fascinating to hear about the club and football in general from the "other side" so to speak, and the conversation helped the three-hour journey slip by very easily. Although, full credit to Ketan's professionalism, when I asked him if there was any truth that Turns was being pulled out of the Wales Under-21's squad to be available for this match, he gave absolutely nothing away.

This time, we did manage to have the fish and chips that I had promised Kay (again!) at the excellent Mary Lambert's. It was another frustrating performance and result from Orient, who took the lead through Smyth just after the break but then conceded an equalizer less than 10 minutes from time. That was our fifth draw in seven matches, and while the points cushion we had built up earlier in the season was sufficient to keep us top, we were starting to worry ever so slightly about being caught by the teams chasing us.

Any frustration the travelling faithful might have been feeling soon melted away at the station, as a spontaneous and truly heartfelt singsong broke out. It felt almost defiant, a recognition, if you will, that our beloved O's might have been doing it slightly tough at that particular moment but there was still every reason to keep the faith.

April 2023

Next up was a home game against one of the teams pushing for a top-three spot and automatic promotion in the form of Carlisle United. It was another hard-fought match, which was won thanks to an own goal by the visitors with just over quarter of an hour remaining, although Kelman was sent from the field for a second bookable offence moments later, meaning he would miss the Good Friday trip to Salford. After struggling to gain maximum points too often over the previous weeks, it felt very much like an important statement of a victory.

Sadly, yet more Avanti West Coast fun and games meant that Kay and I also had to rule out a trip to the Peninsula Stadium, where our whole adventure had got underway a year and a half previously. In the absence of Kelman and with Aaron Drinan, who had been struggling to regain his form and fitness of the previous season for the entirety of the campaign, once again not available, Sotiriou was given the nod to lead the line in the central striking position. The O's made light work of the team that had been promoted from the National League with them back in 2019. Sotiriou opened the scoring midway through the first half with a typical poacher's goal,: turning home a cross from the left from Kieran Sadlier, an important contributor in the second half of the season brought in on loan from Bolton in the January transfer window. The lads wrapped up all three points just past the half-hour mark with a sweeping team move that ended up with Moncur slotting it home.

On Easter Monday, a struggling Harrogate Town came to town, and once again we steamed into a 2-0 lead before half-time, both goals coming from a seemingly rejuvenated (reinvented?) Sotiriou. As his career has developed with the club, there has always seemed to be some confusion about what his most suited position is. He has often scored goals but has been deployed as a wide forward and even as a dribbling number 10, and as the season wore on, there was increasing evidence that he may provide an option as the main striker. Whether it was fatigue after playing two matches in two days or a drop in the intensity of our play, perhaps both, we conspired to let Harrogate back into it, conceding twice just after half-time and being held to a draw once again.

Next was the relatively short trip to Sutton, once again whether by design or default on Grand National Day. This time, Kay managed to win another £3 with her hedging her bets tactics, and the O's played their part, thanks to two early strikes: the first a free kick curled into the top corner by Sadlier, the second (yet another) drive from distance by James. Rather bizarrely after the final whistle, both Sky Sports News and the BBC website reported that we had secured promotion, while the travelling faithful all knew full well that we still needed another point to be absolutely sure.

The following Tuesday evening, we were off to Gillingham with the chance to secure our promotion to the third tier. I had been so nervous and excited throughout the "working" day that I had scarcely been able to concentrate on anything very much at all other than worrying about the match that evening. It was actually a relief to close down my laptop and make our way to Victoria Station for the relatively short trip to Kent. Amazingly for someone who is obsessed with football who had lived in Kent for a couple of years, I had never actually had the "pleasure" of visiting Priestfield. The football gods, however, deigned that my first visit was going to be one that I wouldn't ever forget, for very, very positive reasons.

All thoughts of a celebration were quickly put on hold after less than quarter of an hour when Beckles was shown a straight red card for allegedly denying a goalscoring opportunity. It was harsh, if not just a downright poor decision from the referee. When the resultant free kick found its way into the back of our net, all thoughts of a promotion party were pushed to the back of our minds. When the home side made it 2-0 late on, thanks to another generous decision-- this time a penalty for an alleged handball -- it seemed we would have to wait until Saturday's home game against Crewe to confirm our promotion.

Then it all disorientingly (pun very much intended!) went pitch black around the ground as the floodlights went out (what was that about typical Leyton Orient?).

As we stood in the darkness wondering whether the match would be able to continue, a crackle of excitement started to spread its way through the away end, as it turned out Swindon had scored against Bradford, meaning that as things stood, we would definitely be going up despite losing. When the match at the County Ground ended while we were still in our power outage delay, the pandemonium amongst the Orient faithful really got going. The scenes all around us were exactly what we had all been waiting for, for so very, very long. It was a feeling of pure emotion, as it started to dawn on all of us that after reaching our lowest ebb six years previously when we were relegated out of the Football League (Kay's and my first match on our Orient journey, of course), through all of the hardship, the sorrow, and the tough times, we were back where we all knew we belonged. Even writing this now, a tear has come to my eye thinking about the sheer relief that the entire Orient family were all sharing together. As you can well imagine, Kay and I carried the party on all the way home and well into the wee small hours.

With promotion secured, we knew that a victory over a midtable Crewe side would be enough to crown our promotion with the league title. The O's sealed the win in the second half through another successful Moncur penalty and a late second when Kelman pounced on an error by the Crewe keeper and rolled the ball home. At the final whistle, the stands emptied onto the pitch (permitted and facilitated by the stewards, it has to be said), as we got the party well and truly underway. I don't think Kay and I actually stopped until well into May!

The following Tuesday at Mansfield, despite all the celebrations and a much-rotated side, we managed to come back from going 1-0 down to an early goal, beating the Stags, 2-1, thanks to goals from Kelman and Sotiriou, although Ogie was shown a red card in the last half hour for a desperate tackle.

For the final home game against Stockport, it was announced before the match that the trophy presentation would take place afterwards, along with numerous appeals from the club to fans to stay off the pitch this time to allow it to take place, the most effective of which came from gaffer Richie Wellens, who quite frankly could have asked us to do anything at all and we would have complied, such has been his impact on our club. We went down, 3-0, in that one but all anybody really cared about was getting to the end of the match and the next stage of the celebrations, which carried on long into the evening.

May 2023

The final game of the season saw us head to Valley Parade to face Bradford (a first-time visit for Kay, of course!), which due to the coronation of King Charles had been moved to the Bank Holiday Monday with all League Two fixtures given a 12:30 kick-off. It was no real hardship for us, as we travelled up on the Sunday and came back after the match the following day. It was a surprisingly well contested 1-1 draw, played on the day that Bradford mark the tragic passing of the 56 supporters in the fire all those years ago. That and the fact that it was the end of the season made for a very emotional afternoon.

A couple of weeks later, Kay and I were given the absolute honour and pleasure of attending the Supporters Club's Star Man Awards, where the club gives awards to the best performing players of the season based on our voting as members throughout the campaign. It was great to be able to meet the players and chat to them properly, to be amongst the Orient family for one final time for a few months and to reflect on the journey we have been on. We didn't realise it at the time, but that fateful decision in the midst of the pandemic would change our football-supporting lives forever. Beyond that, though, we have been welcomed into a genuine family and a new way of life that neither of us could have ever anticipated.

As they say, you don't choose your football team, it finds you.

As I am sitting and writing these final few lines in late June 2023, the League One fixtures were released this morning, and I have spent the first couple of hours scanning the schedule and seeing where we will be and when.

We couldn't do it all again, could we...

Photos

Do you fancy seeing if we can go to every single Orient match in a season?

Moor Lane Salford – where the adventure got underway.

Welcome to Carlisle.

Essential Awayday supplies.

Your author and the Easy Lovers at the Signal Box Euston
post-Port Vale.

My garden shed is bigger than this! (the Away End -Holker
Street Barrow)

The unfinished stand at Ice Station Sixfields.

Oh what a night...up in Scunthorpe on a Tuesday night!
(Glanford Park- the first midweek away game)

An Awayday at "Home". (Prenton Park
home of Tranmere Rovers)

Does it count as an Awayday if the match is called off?
(Harrogate in the snow)

Your author meets his long-time nemesis:
former Premier League referee Mike Dean.

We are the Champions!!!

Printed in Great Britain
by Amazon

36922384R00175